CHARTWELL
BOOKS, INC.

THE JEWS AND EUROPE

2,000 YEARS OF HISTORY

ELENA ROMERO CASTELLÓ
URIEL MACÍAS KAPÓN

CHARTWELL
BOOKS, INC.

Frontispiece: Jewish Wedding in Frankfurt, *painting by Moritz Oppenheim, 1861 (Israel Museum, Jerusalem). In accordance with German Jewish custom, the wedding takes place in the synagogue courtyard, the bride and groom standing beneath a tallith that acts as the* huppah, *or canopy.*

Grace is on her head,
Beauty in her face,
Splendor in her body
And Glory in her train
—*Solomon ibn Gabirol, 12th century*

Published by
CHARTWELL BOOKS, INC.
A Division of **BOOK SALES, INC.**
114 Northfield Avenue
Edison, New Jersey 08837

Copyright © 1994 by Anaya Editoriale s.r.l./
Fenice 2000 s.r.l., Milan
All rights reserved.
First published in the United States in 1994
by Henry Holt and Company, Inc.
Published in Canada by Fitzhenry & Whiteside Ltd.,
195 Allstate Parkway, Markham, Ontario L3R 4T8.

Editorial creation by Anaya Grandes Obras

Library of Congress Cataloging-in-Publication Data
Castelló, Elena Romero.
[Los Judíos de Europa. English]
The Jews and Europe : 2000 years of History / Elena Romero Castelló,
Uriel Macías Kapón.
p.   cm.
Includes bibliographical references and index.
1. Jews—History—70-   2. Jews—Europe—History.   3. Judaism—History.
4. Jews—Civilization.   5. Europe—Ethnic relations.
I. Kapón, Uriel Macías. II. Title.
DS123.C3613   1994
940'.04924—dc20

94-16970
CIP

ISBN 0-7858-0954-6

First American Edition—1994

Typesetting by Jay Hyams and Christopher Hyams Hart

Printed in Italy
All first editions are printed on acid-free paper. ∞
10 9 8 7 6 5 4 3 2 1

Contents

6

Festival of the Joy of the Torah in the Synagogue of Leghorn, *oil painting by the English artist Solomon Hart, 1850 (Jewish Museum, New York, Oscar Gruss Collection). Jews openly display their religiosity in synagogues, places of worship that have always been the center of traditional community life. In the synagogue teachers pass on to their pupils the law, knowledge, and traditions whose safekeeping has meant the continuity of the Jews' very existence.*

To fulfill Thy words with the daybreak I awake
and banish my slumber to tell of Thy deeds;
with the dawn I rise praising Thy glory
and I foresee wakeful nights saying Thy sayings.
—*Abraham ibn Ezra, 12th century*

Introduction

Jews have been present in virtually all the countries of Europe for 2,000 years. This fact alone makes writing a book on the Jews and Europe a difficult undertaking; but in addition there is the fact that geographic delimitation itself is somewhat artificial in the case of the Jews. The close relations among Jewish communities scattered all over the world have had little to do with national borders or continents, and in truth the modern outlines of European geography have not always coincided with political realities. Nor should we forget the European colonies in the Americas, Africa, and Asia, linked until independence to their home countries. Here European Jews settled and founded communities where, at times, none had existed before. Conversely, Jews from the colonies were also linked, to a greater or lesser extent, to the European reality. We have been able to draw these branches of the European world only as sketchy outlines. Nor have we been able, except in passing, to deal with the world beyond Europe, a world by no means less important in the shaping and development of European Judaism. Such was the case in ancient times with the extremely prolific communities of Babylonia, for centuries Judaism's center of gravity and until the 9th century the torchbearer of Jewish thought and creativity. And such is the case in modern times with the European Jews who settled in the Americas and those who emigrated to the state of Israel.

This book is a work of synthesis, of necessity brief and written for the nonspecialist. Consequently, many subjects have barely been dealt with, for entering into a deeper discussion of one obliged us to leave untouched others that were nevertheless equally important to an understanding of the development of the Jewish people in Europe. It is in this obviously subjective work of synthesis where any originality in this book must be sought. We have concentrated on those aspects that, to our mind, best demonstrate the uniqueness of Judaism, with special emphasis on literature, for it is in this field that the Jews have always displayed their creativity most fully and where European Judaism's greatest legacy to mankind lies. Thus, in the text, captions, and boxes in this book, we have attempted to provide the reader with an overall view of the historical and creative development of the Jewish people in Europe from the time of the first settlements to the Nazi Holocaust, using material based on the works of authors and scholars who have written with wisdom and in depth. The Holocaust led to not only the physical disappearance of over half of the Jews of Europe but also to the end of an era; after a prolonged period in which the creativity of the Jewish people was basically to be found outside the Old Continent, European Jewry, particularly in countries like France, England, and Italy, has slowly begun what, without any doubt, is to be a new stage in its development. Only time will tell where it will lead.

A special debt of gratitude is owed all the writers referred to in this book and on whose work we have based our synthesis; to make reading easier, we have not always placed their ideas within quotation marks, but their names are included in the bibliography. We sincerely hope that this book will encourage many readers to consult these works.

The subjects dealt with in *The Jews and Europe* are divided into four sections. The first presents a brief summary, in necessarily broad strokes, of the history of the Jewish people dispersed in the various regions of the European continent. The second gives an overview of the laws and rites that govern Jewish life, for although certainly not particular to the Jews of Europe—they are part of the heritage of the entire Jewish community across all its generations worldwide—they are necessary to a fuller understanding of the basic reasonings and principles that inform the development of the Jewish people as well as Jewish artistic and literary activity. The third section is dedicated to the arts, which for the Jews in Europe has usually meant adapting the artistic forms of the surrounding environment to Jewish needs and interests. The fourth and final section concentrates on literature, for it is one of the fields in which the creative talent of the Jewish people has always been expressed with the greatest fullness, and it is here that one can most clearly perceive the contribution of European Judaism to the culture of all humanity. The book ends with a glossary, bibliography, and index.

We hope this book offers readers a new and deeper understanding of the history and significance of the Jewish people and Europe. For although a minority, Jews have constituted an integral part of the "fabric" of the peoples of Europe, contributing in a significant way to giving form to the rich and multi-colored reality, fruit of the blending of races and cultures, that is the Old Continent.

—ELENA ROMERO CASTELLÓ and URIEL MACÍAS KAPÓN

7

2,000 Years
of History

Till when our sunset without a dawn?
How long shall we walk as captives,
Shall beauty and glory flee from us like deer
And we be riders of clouds of exile?
—*Solomon Bonafed, 15th century*
Opposite: The Torah and the Jew, *by Marc Chagall
(private collection). Above: Menorah from the Jewish
catacombs of Villa Torlonia (Rome, 1st century A.D.).*

Greece and Rome

The Jews first came into contact with European civilization when the Greek Empire began expanding throughout the Near East. From the time of Alexander the Great's conquest of Asia Minor and the subsequent expansion of the empire through the East (332 B.C.) to the destruction of the Second Temple in Jerusalem by Titus in A.D. 70, the Jews of the small kingdom of Judaea lived under the political and cultural influence of the Hellenistic and Roman worlds. It was during this long period that the dispersion of the Jews through Europe, from the Iberian Peninsula to southern Russia, took place.

At the time of Alexander, the small territory of Judaea was like an appendix to its disproportionately large capital of Jerusalem. Its rulers had fashioned a totally homogeneous state whose main cultural characteristic was the acceptance of the Torah (the Mosaic Law) as a civil and religious constitution and a centralized cult.

When Alexander died, two of his generals, Ptolemy and Seleucus, took control of Egypt and Asia respectively. Palestine thus came under Ptolemaic rule for more than a century, with Jewish citizens, generally speaking, enjoying the protection of the kings. Given such favorable circumstances, the impact of the Hellenistic culture on the Jewish world was considerable, having its greatest effect on the Jewish upper classes, who grew accustomed to the Greek way of life (games, the gymnasium, theater, and so on), benefited from its culture, literature, and philosophy, adopted Greek architectural styles in the construction of their synagogues, and even took Greek names. Spoken at all levels of Jewish society, the language of the Greeks was to be a lingua franca among Jews until after the rise of the Roman Empire and made a deep impression on Hebrew, the traditional tongue of the Jewish people, and on Aramaic, the language spoken by the Jews in exile in Babylonia. With the passage of time, the distance grew ever wider between the strongly Hellenized upper levels of Jewish society, increasingly alienated from their own cultural and religious traditions, and the mass of the people, who continued to observe traditional Jewish ways.

This benevolent attitude toward the Jews of Ptolemaic Egypt gave rise to a work of extreme importance, the translation into Greek of the Bible. Upon the request of Ptolemy II (reigned 285-264 B.C.), the high priest of Jerusalem sent seventy elders to the city of Alexandria to translate the first five books of

10

Funeral monuments showing clear Greek and Egyptian influence in the Kidron Valley, which begins at the foot of the eastern wall of the Temple of Jerusalem: in the middle is the reputed tomb of Zechariah, cut from living rock; to the left in the background is that of the children of Hezir, which bears an inscription with the names of the family members buried there. During the latter period of the Hasmonean kingdom, the influence of Greco-Roman culture made it customary in Israel to build this type of monument for the burial of members of aristocratic families. Many eminent rabbis condemned such customs as ostentatious and alien to Jewish tradition.

the Old Testament, which are known as the *Pentateuch* (Greek for "five books") and which constitute the Law of Moses—the Torah. This translation, known as the *Septuagint* (from the Latin word for "seventy"), was to be the version of the Bible used by Jews all over Europe when, as time passed, Hebrew became a language known only to the minority.

This gentle penetration of Hellenism into Jewish culture might well have brought the traditional Jewish world to an end, fated to be buried beneath the stones under which so many of the nations of antiquity now lie, but the course of events changed when Palestine fell into Seleucid hands and the process of Hellenization accelerated brutally. After a long war with Egypt, Antiochus III occupied Jerusalem in 198 B.C. The attempts made by his successors and certain sectors of the Hellenized Jews to "modernize" the Jewish religion brought an end to any chance of a state of peaceful coexistence between the two cultures. In 168 B.C. Antiochus IV ordered an altar to Zeus to be raised in the Temple of Jerusalem and forbade the Jews to practice their most fundamental observances. This action sparked off a revolt (168-165 B.C.) led by Mattathias the Hasmonean and his five sons, among them Judas, known as the Maccabee. Judas defeated superior Syrian forces and on entering Jerusalem purified the profaned temple, which was reconsecrated in December 165 B.C. (the event celebrated by the feast of Hanukkah). The wars of the Hasmoneans and Syrians continued almost until the reign of Judas Aristobulus (104-103 B.C.), the first of his line to adopt the title of king: king of a territory whose population had converted to Judaism and was by now considerably larger thanks to the conquests of his ancestors.

Rome, which at first had encouraged the rebellion of the Maccabees against Syria, looked on suspiciously as the little kingdom of Judaea expanded—it grew even larger under the second king of the dynasty, Alexander Jannaeus—and seized the opportunity offered by the civil war between Jannaeus' successors to enter the unsettled kingdom. Pompey occupied Jerusalem in 63 B.C. and declared the territory a Roman province. For the next seven centuries, Palestine was subject to Roman rule.

Alas the synagogues, which turned to ruins,
And hawks and vultures nested there
When the children of Israel departed!
—*From an anonymous elegy*
Ruins of a synagogue in the ancient city of Gerasa (in present-day Jordan, 4th-5th centuries); it was built in the new style that appeared in the 5th century with buildings on a basilica ground plan with an apse, in this case square, to house the ark of the Torah, an entrance with three doors, and an interior divided up by two rows of columns. The exterior—austere, for it dates from Byzantine times, when the construction of new synagogues was forbidden and only old ones could be repaired—contrasts with the lavish interior. Inside are highly decorated marble capitals, a candelabrum, other sacred objects, and lovely floor mosaics with Greek inscriptions depicting the animals entering Noah's ark.

Judaea Captive

The monarchy was restored with Rome's blessing in the figure of Herod the Great (reigned 37 B.C.-A.D. 4), who annexed territories to his kingdom and ordered the construction of castles, among these Masada, and founded towns, such as Caesarea. Most important of all, Herod rebuilt the Temple of Jerusalem. Upon his death, Rome abolished the monarchy, and Judaea came under the control of Roman procurators who on various occasions did much to injure Jewish religious sensitivity. The oppressive, arbitrary rule of these procurators, whose harshness increased during the second half of the 1st century, was soon to cause general discontent among the Jewish masses, arousing nationalistic feeling and reviving the idea of liberation through religion. This situation led to the great revolt of A.D. 66, referred to by the Jewish historian Flavius Josephus, an active participant in the events (his betrayal of his own people facilitated the victories of the Roman general Vespasian). Following Nero's death and the brief reigns of Galba, Otho, and Vitellius, Vespasian became emperor, and his son Titus

took charge of the war, occupying Jerusalem and destroying the Temple in A.D. 70. Resistance continued for a further three years at Masada until the death of Eleazar ben Jair and his men, who preferred to commit suicide rather than surrender to the enemy. Two years before this, Vespasian and Titus had celebrated their triumph in Rome, parading the sacred objects taken from the temple through the streets. The Arch of Titus, commemorating Titus' conquest of Jerusalem, was later erected by Domitian next to the Forum. During the decades that followed, Rome increased its pressure on Judaea and the Jews of the Diaspora—those living outside the Holy Land—replacing the annual half-shekel contribution made by all Jews to the temple with the *Fiscus Judaicos*, a tax paid to the Temple of Jupiter Capitolinus in Rome. In 115, during the reign of the emperor Trajan, the Jewish communities rose up in Egypt, Cyrenaica, and Cyprus. Even more serious was the revolt in Judaea (132-35, during the reign of Hadrian) that occurred in response to decrees prohibiting circumcision and ordering the

Two views of a scale model of the city of Jerusalem and the temple at the time of Herod (Hotel International, Jerusalem). Although Ezra and Nehemiah (445 B.C.) began reconstruction of the city, which was destroyed by the Babylonians in 586 B.C., the greatest transformation was brought about by Herod, during whose reign the royal palace and the Tower of Antonia were built, the temple esplanade was extended, and the hill was surrounded by

gigantic walls, of which only part of the western sector, known as the Wailing Wall, now remains. The temple itself was completely rebuilt (top, in the background; above, in the background at left), the exterior being of white stone adorned with rich ornamentation of silver and gold. Work continued for forty-six years. The finishing touches were still being given when the temple was again destroyed—this time forever—by Titus.

reconstruction of Jerusalem as a Roman city with a shrine dedicated to Jupiter Capitolinus to be erected among the ruins of the temple. The revolt was led by Simon bar Kokhba, who succeeded in liberating Jerusalem but was defeated by the Romans after a heroic stand at the fortress of Bether. The bitter end of the Bar Kokhba rebellion was also the end of Judaism in Palestine; the ancient kingdom was devastated, towns and villages were razed, thousands of Jews were sold into slavery, and all Jews were forbidden to enter Jerusalem, now rebuilt and renamed Aelia Capitolina. The only remaining focal points of Jewish wisdom and religious instruction in Palestine were the academies in Galilee and Jamnia. The latter, founded during the reign of Vespasian, housed the reconstructed Sanhedrin (rabbinic court) and was a center for the most distinguished scholars of the times. Its *nasi*, or president of the Sanhedrin, was acknowledged as the official representative of the Jewish people and bore the title of patriarch, an institution that existed until 425, when it was abolished by the Byzantine emperor Theodosius II.

Silver tetradrachm minted during the second year of the war between Simon Bar Kokhba and the Romans, 133-134 (Israel Museum, Jerusalem). The obverse depicts the temple facade with the ark in the center and the Hebrew word Shime'on, *while on the verso, seen here, are the* lulav *and the* etrog, *fragrant plants typical of the Sukkot festival, and the legend "Second Year of the Liberation of Israel" in Hebrew.*

To scale a castle fate has forced him,
To remain on its peak alone and isolated.
No other voices reach him than the wailing of jackals
And the cawing of birds.
—*Moses ibn Ezra, 12th century*
Silos at the fortress of Masada near the Dead Sea, where the last warriors in the great revolt of Judaea against the Roman Empire in 66 B.C. entrenched themselves and died.

The European Diaspora

The Hellenistic and Roman periods saw the beginning of the great scattering of Jews throughout the European territories of the two vast empires; written testimony in Hebrew, Greek, and Latin refers to the large numbers of Jews involved and to their importance in the societies and economies of the areas in which they settled. This Diaspora (from a Greek word meaning "dispersion") was advanced not only by the many voluntary emigrants, but above all by the large masses of Jews sold into slavery or transferred by Pompey, Titus, and Hadrian to other areas. These Jews were soon freed by their masters or their freedom was bought by their coreligionists. The scattering of the Jews through Greek and Roman Europe also took place for commercial and economic reasons and due to the high incidence of proselytism during certain periods, above all in the final years of the Second Temple, when the number of converts to Judaism was particularly large in Palestine, Alexandria, Antioch, and Rome. This process continued until Christianity became the dominant religion in the Roman Empire, and conversion to Judaism was forbidden. In the time of Augustus, the Greek historian and geographer

14

Detail of a bas-relief on the inner face of the Arch of Titus. The arch was erected in Rome by Domitian, Titus's brother and successor, to celebrate the conquest of Jerusalem. Seen here are temple objects, including a seven-branched menorah, being carried in a triumphal procession by the victors.

The Destruction of the Temple of Jerusalem, *by Francesco Hayez, 19th century (Galleria d'Arte Moderna, Venice). The Jews rose up against the Romans in the autumn of the year 60 and freed Jerusalem of Roman domination for the next three years. In the spring of 70, Titus marched with four legions to subdue the rebels and besiege the city. On the ninth day of the month of Av, the Roman forces reached the temple and set fire to it. The higher part*

Strabo wrote that virtually nowhere in the known world was without its Jewish settlement.

Within the areas of influence of the Greek and Roman civilizations, there is evidence of the existence (apart from the extremely large community in Alexandria) of important communities of Jews in Asia Minor (Ephesus, Pergamum, Miletus, Priene, Sardis), which was also a place of transit for the Jews who settled on the shores of the Black Sea. There were also communities in a large number of towns on the Greek mainland and islands (Cyprus, Crete, and so on) and in Macedonia. In the territory of modern-day Italy, there were Jewish communities on the islands of Sicily and Sardinia and on the peninsula itself, in the principal towns both north and south. The majority of Italian Jews, however, lived in Rome, where Jews had begun to settle in the 2nd century B.C. Although the estimate may be rather high, Jews may have numbered 50,000 in the whole of Italy by the end of the 1st century A.D. Indeed, in Rome itself, there were at least twelve synagogues, although they were not contemporary with one another. Some of the most important evidence of the Jewish presence in the city and nearby areas during the classical period

of the city resisted for a further month, and the majority of the survivors were then executed or sold into slavery and deported. The city lay in ruins until 130, when Hadrian established the Roman colony of Aelia Capitolina there. Scattered all over the world, the Jews passed on the memory of the lost city from parent to child.

Detail from a bas-relief of the Arch of Titus with the conquerors carrying objects pillaged from the temple—the table and various trumpets and censers. In the Middle Ages, Jews were forbidden to pass under the arch and could cross to the other side only by passing through a nearby house where they were obliged to pay a sum of money.

15

farmers, artisans, shopkeepers, traders, administrators, bankers, shipbuilders, actors, poets, painters, doctors, and even politicians, particularly in towns with large Jewish communities. There was also a large mass of poor Jews, who in Rome were the butt of satirical works written by Juvenal and Martial.

Wherever the Jews settled, they set up close-knit communities whose members were grouped together in the same neighborhood, thus making it easier to center their traditional religious way of life on the synagogue. After the destruction of the temple, the synagogue became the focal point of Jewish religious and liturgical life as well as a study center and place of assembly. Though there was no central organization for all the Jews in the empire, the communities nevertheless felt a bond with the leaders and high priests in Jerusalem, and, after A.D. 70, to

is in the catacombs of Rome and Ostia, some of which contain frescoes. The surviving inscriptions on the walls, though mainly in Greek and Latin, include phrases in Hebrew.

Jews also lived in Gaul during the time of the Roman republic, particularly in the Mediterranean coastal towns, from where they spread inland. There is evidence, too, of Jewish settlements dating from the beginning of the 1st century in what is now Germany; these probably sprang up with the Roman legions that occupied the west of the region in the 1st century. Furthermore, an edict dictated by the Roman emperor Constantine the Great (reigned 306-37) in Cologne in 321 defined the rights and obligations of the Jewish people who lived in communities organized and officially recognized by the state in the Rhineland and elsewhere.

The arrival and settlement of the Jews in the Iberian Peninsula is shrouded in legend, with dates going back as far as the reign of Solomon. There is no doubt, however, that there were Jewish settlements around the 1st century, which does not automatically rule out the possibility that some groups may have reached the Phoenician and Greek trading colonies on the Mediterranean coast at an earlier time.

Jews engaged in all kinds of occupational activities in the Greco-Roman world; they were

Details of frescoes from the synagogue of Dura-Europos in Syria, 244-245 (Museum of Damascus). This ancient city on the banks of the Euphrates was discovered by chance by a British patrol during World War I. The synagogue's astonishing frescoes are the oldest known pictorial example of Jewish art. When they were painted (being completed only five years before the destruction of the city) Dura-Europos was controlled by Rome and remained under its

jurisdiction until 256, when it was conquered by the Sassanids. The frescoes are composed primarily of scenes from the Bible and display the work of at least two artists, one influenced by Greek art, the other by Persian art. Top: Detail from the northern wall that illustrates various episodes from Ezekiel's vision of the resurrection of the dead (Ezek. 37:1-14), with the hand of God bringing up the bodies while the souls, endowed with butterfly wings, flutter.

Above left: Detail from the frescoes on the northern wall: the Israelites are defeated by the Philistines (1 Sam. 4:1-6). The great battle is centered on two knights attacking each other with spears, while (above and below) other warriors fight fiercely. The champions, black and white, are on horseback. It is thought that the scene is based on the battle of Ebenezer, in which the ark was captured, but it also reflects the struggle between light and darkness.

Detail from the Dura-Europos frescoes depicting the duties of the priesthood and symbols related to it. Inside a porticoed temple surrounded by walls with three gates is the ark of the covenant with the menorah and an altar next to it. Accompanied by two figures in Persian clothing, Aaron, whose name is written in Greek letters, overlooks the scene. The frescoes in this synagogue led experts to change many theories on supposed Jewish iconophobia.

the *nasis* in Jamnia and Galilee, so that there were indeed strong ties and close contacts among the Diaspora communities.

When Rome became master of the Mediterranean world, its Jewish policy was based on the general principle of noninterference in the religious practices of its subjects. The basis of this attitude was established by Julius Caesar and Augustus, who acknowledged the Jews' right to maintain their own organizations, thus exempting them from the general ban on such associations (the ban was intended to prevent political subversion or labor unrest). The Jews were also granted administrative and judicial autonomy and were exempted from compulsory participation in pagan rites, such as worshiping the emperor, and from other obligations that would have clashed with the canons of Judaism. Except for a few isolated periods, this situation remained stable for several centuries, until finally, in 212, the Jews were included in Caracalla's edict whereby Roman citizenship was granted to all free people in the empire.

The situation changed radically when Christianity became the official religion of the empire. The Middle Ages can be said to have begun for the Jewish people when Constantine the Great, the first emperor to pass laws restricting the Jews' rights as Roman citizens, came to power. Although the church did not seek to do away with Judaism completely, as it needed the physical presence of Jews as testimony of its law, it did attempt to humiliate them and subject them both socially and economically, putting constant pressure on the emperors to deprive Jews of their civil rights. Thus, from the earliest times of institutionalized Christianity, preachers publicly incited the common people to attack the Jews, their districts, and their synagogues.

When Rome fell to the Vandals in 455, the Western Roman Empire came to its political end, and the papacy, whose moral authority was acknowledged by all western Christendom, became the dominant force in the old capital of the empire. From then on, over a period of 1,400 years, the history of the Jews of Christian Europe was a reflection of papal policy.

Frontal of a 4th-century sarcophagus discovered in the Jewish catacomb of Vigna Randanini (Vatican Museum, Rome). This is one of the few existing sarcophagi whose decoration combines Jewish symbols and classical motifs—a menorah surrounded by putti in the purest pagan style who bear birds, animals, and baskets of fruit. It is a magnificent example of cultural symbiosis within the empire.

17

Byzantium

With the definitive separation in 395 of the Eastern Roman Empire (Byzantium) from the Western, a large number of Jewish communities in the Balkans, present-day Greece, Asia Minor, and Constantinople (where there had been a Jewish community since the city's foundation in 330) came under the authority of Constantinople. There were also communities in Syria, Palestine, and Egypt, but the Byzantine Empire eventually lost these to other eastern nations in expansion. Italy, on the other hand, formed part of Byzantium after it was recovered (535-54) from the Ostrogoths by Justinian I, and, though later confined to southern Italy, the Byzantine occupation continued until the 11th century.

The ancient status of Judaism as a *religio licita* did not change dramatically, but after the conversion of Constantine to Christianity the emperors gradually reduced the rights of the Jews. Moreover, the brief exception to this situation, during the reign of Julian the Apostate—who sought unsuccessfully to restore paganism—led only to stronger Christian resentment against the Jews, which was to exist from the time of Julian's death until the fall of Constantinople in 1453.

Hunting down heretics with the emperor's blessing, the church now began to use a progressively more violent form of language when referring to Jews. This led in the 4th century to a virulent kind of polemical literature whose fiercest exponent was John Chrysostom. In eight sermons delivered from the pulpit in Antioch, Chrysostom attributed all manner of perversions to the Jews, even comparing them to the Devil.

His preachings were to pave the way for the anti-Semitism of the Middle Ages. Violent actions, such as the burning of synagogues and banishment, serve to underline the fact that in Byzantium the supremacy of the church's views on the regulation of Jewish affairs was accepted both in theory and in practice. The Jews were then gradually stripped of their civil rights, excluded from their professions, and transferred to other areas of residence.

The Theodosian Code, issued in 438 by Theodosius II, included bans on the building of new synagogues and the public celebration of certain holidays. Nor did the Jews fare better under Justinian I, under whom persecution and humiliation became law, and the policy of stripping Jews of all their rights, first brought to bear by the emperor's predecessors, was intensified.

Mosaic from the synagogue in the historic city of Bet Shean (Israel, c. 4th century), in its time an important center of communications and an affluent focal point for trade. The building, whose ruins are located to the north of the Byzantine wall, testifies to the presence of Jews in the city from the 4th century on and was in use for approximately 200 years. It stands on a basilica ground plan, its floor being composed of this clearly Byzantine-influenced mosaic framed by geometric and floral forms. The mosaic contains a fine representation of the ark of the covenant flanked by two candelabra, shofroth, or ritual horns, censers, and three inscriptions in Greek. The synagogue was apparently destroyed by fire in 624.

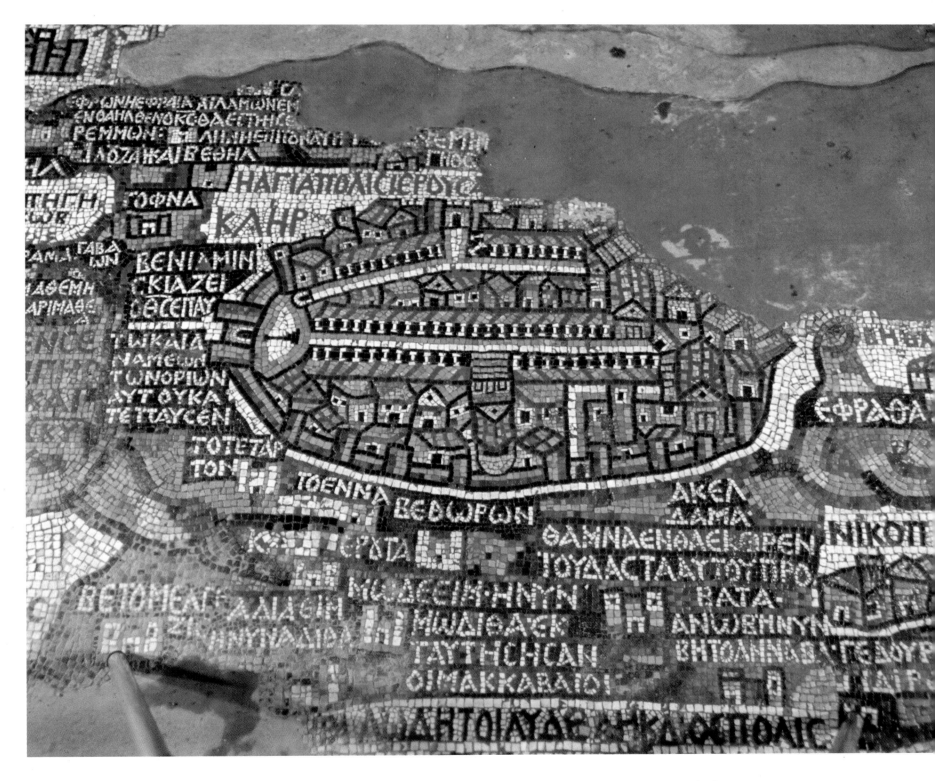

Mosaic map from a church in Medeba in central Jordan (560-565). Based on a Roman road map, it includes vignettes representing the major cities of the biblical Holy Land and neighboring regions, including the oldest known representation of Jerusalem. Such was the city in the time of Justinian. The city was surrounded by walls with six gates and twelve towers. The main street began inside the wall at a square with a column (center left) and, together with another, narrower parallel street, ran across the city. At the end of the easternmost street (center right) stood the Wailing Wall (of which this is also the oldest known representation). With the exception of certain periods, Jerusalem was controlled by Byzantium until it was conquered by the Muslims in 637 (they made the city their chief shrine after Mecca).

hundred and fifty years prior to the Fourth Crusade, their lives and property were protected by law, and they were not forced to convert to Christianity.

The economic structure of the Jewish communities nevertheless remained virtually intact during this period, as was confirmed by the Hispano-Jewish traveler Benjamin of Tudela (12th century), who wrote of Jewish communities in the Balkans, Greece, and the main islands whose members were doctors, farmers, silk dealers, and dyers.

The Fourth Crusade (1202-4) left the Jewish communities in the Eastern Empire under the control of the various administrations established by the western countries that took part in the crusade. The power of these "Latin States" continued until 1261. For the Jews the fall of Constantinople in 1453 brought a change for the better, and a few years later, in 1492, the communities in the eastern Mediterranean and the Balkans benefited from the cultural and economic growth that came with the arrival of the Jews expelled from Spain.

Through his edicts Justinian achieved what none before him had dared to do: interfere with the religious functions of the synagogue. Thus he prohibited the interpretation of the Scriptures—an act directed not only against the sermons delivered in the synagogues but also against the study of the Talmud in schools—and also ordered the wording of certain prayers to be modified. His legislative work, the *Corpus Juris Civilis*, and his *Novels*, or *Novellae* (compilations of later legislation), included all previous anti-Jewish legislation and served as the model for all the ordinances passed in the Middle Ages in relation to the Jews.

Subsequent Byzantine emperors were no more benevolent in their attitude toward the Jews, and pressure of all kinds was brought to bear, including the violent reappearance of anti-Jewish disturbances after the iconoclastic period (c. 720-843) and the numerous forced conversions ordered by emperors from 608 until 943. Furthermore, during the 11th and 12th centuries, the Jews of Byzantium lived under the most absolute oppression, although during the two

Obverse (top) and verso (above) of a Byzantine gold coin minted in the reign (610-641) of the emperor Heraclius (Israel Museum, Jerusalem). Heraclius cruelly oppressed the Jews in punishment for their collaboration with the Persians, who had conquered and occupied Jerusalem (614-629). After recovering the city, Heraclius endorsed the indiscriminate slaughter of Jews and the subsequent expulsion of the survivors. Shortly after, the Arabs conquered Syria,

Palestine, and Egypt. Convinced of Jewish sympathy for Islam, in 631 Heraclius decreed the conversion of Jews to Christianity throughout the empire (although this was enforced only in Carthage) and applied Justinian's Novella 146, which affected the synagogal liturgy.

Gold medallion (Jewish Museum, London) with an enigmatic inscription in Greek ("According to the vow of Jacob, leader of the synagogue, pearl merchant") and Jewish symbols—the menorah, at its base, a shofar (left) and a lulav *(right). Possibly an ornamental plaque of the* Sefer Torah, *it has also been interpreted as an 8th-century Byzantine medallion and even dated as 2nd or 3rd century, in which case it would be the oldest example of its kind.*

The Europe of the Barbarians

The barbarian peoples—the Vandals, Franks, Goths, Burgundians, Lombards, Angles, Saxons, and Huns—who invaded the Roman Empire between the 4th and 6th centuries were at first pagans, but as Romanization set in, they began to embrace Catholicism (with the exception of the those who adhered to Arianism).

For the duration of the invasions, the Jews were caught up in the turmoil of the fierce battles, faring no better or worse than the rest of the population. Furthermore, it is true to say that after the process of settlement, they were, in general, treated well by the barbarians—for as long as the latter remained pagans and Arians. When the young barbarian states embraced Catholicism in the late 6th century, however, the situation quickly worsened. From then on, the resolutions of the councils, once approved by the kings, became law, the Jews lost their ancient rights, and the persecutions began.

In Italy, the position improved considerably for the Jewish communities with the beginning of Ostrogothic rule; in 493 Theodoric the Great (c. 454-526) restored their ancient rights, granted them administrative autonomy, and defended them from the attacks of the Catholic clergy and the violence of the common people. As the result of the Goths' tolerant attitude, new Jewish communities sprang up in the north of Italy (Milan, Verona, Genoa, and other cities), in addition to the existing old Roman settlements and those in the south (Naples, Sicily). This period of peace and prosperity came to an end when Justinian I took control of the Gothic kingdom (535) and his repressive code, which was to remain in force throughout the Middle Ages, was promulgated in Italy.

The situation was similar in the rest of western Europe, from the Rhineland to Gaul and the Iberian Peninsula, where the Visigoths, Burgundians, and Franks had established their kingdoms. At the outset, Jews were treated as Roman citizens rather than as a lower class. Indeed, in the Frankish and Burgundian kingdoms Jews continued to be engaged in trade and industry, to occupy public positions, and to work as farmers, doctors, lawyers, and even as mercenaries.

The situation began to change in the kingdom of the Franks with the conversion of the

The Ashburnham Pentateuch, *from Tours, 6th-7th century (Bibliothèque Nationale, Paris). The illustration tells the story from Exod. 24: God (top left) gives the Tables of the Law to Moses, who is accompanied by Aaron, Nadab, Abihu, and (below them) the elders of the tribe of Israel. Before an altar (right) Moses gives the law to the Israelites. The figures in a semicircle may be the souls of the Jews yet to be born who, according to rabbinic tradition,* *were present on Sinai. Below are the Tabernacle, Joshua, Moses (left) and Aaron, Nadab, and Abihu (right). A large number of illustrations from this Christian Pentateuch clearly support the rabbinic tradition, which has led many to believe in the existence of some kind of Jewish prototype of Pentateuch illumination—now lost—that served as inspiration to later Christians and Jews.*

Merovingian king Clovis to Christianity in 496. In the course of the 6th century, seven councils dealt with the question of the Jews, issuing decrees approved by the monarchs and aimed at reducing the Jews to the status of second-class citizens. The same harsh policy was put into practice in Burgundy, in the Middle Rhine, and in the kingdom of the Lombards in northern Italy. But the fate of the Jewish communities south of the Pyrenees was even worse.

When the Visigoths seized the Iberian Peninsula they found a long-established Jewish population whose numbers were much greater than in Gaul. The first immigrants to arrive in Roman times had been joined by fugitives from North Africa and Carthage who had settled first in the ports of Cadiz and Cartagena and later in Andalusia, from where they entered the hinterland. By the 4th century, Toledo, Mérida, Granada, Córdoba, Tarragona, and the Balearic Islands had large Jewish populations, most of whom worked on the land, though some

23

St. Ildefonsus debating with a Jew, from the De virginitate Sanctae Mariae, *Castile, 10th century (Biblioteca Medicea-Laurenziana, Florence). Ildefonsus (c. 610-667), made archbishop of Toledo in 653, attended the Ninth Council of Toledo, during which the bishops were ordered to watch closely over the many Jews converted to Christianity as a result of King Recared's harsh legislation.*

Detail from a floor mosaic in the synagogue of Elche, 4th-6th century (Museo de la Alcudia, Elche). It displays interlacing stars surrounded by a border and various inscriptions in Greek containing the words proseuche *(the usual term for "synagogue"),* presbyteroi *("elders"), and* archontes *("in charge of community affairs"). These words are commonly found in Jewish inscriptions in synagogues in Rome, Campania, Syria, Egypt, and Cyrenaica.*

worked as administrators of private estates.

Even before Christianity became the official state religion, the church had dealt with the subject of the Jews. At the Council of Elvira (c. 306) the first anti-Jewish decrees were drawn up to separate the Jewish and Christian populations and restrict the former's actions. However, under the Arian Visigoths the Hispanic Jews were left in peace to enjoy equal civil and political rights. This continued for over a century, but ended in 589, a short time after the Visigothic king Recared converted to Roman Catholicism (c. 587-589), which, after the suppression of a number of Arian revolts and conspiracies, meant the conversion of the Visigoths. A harsh policy was then implemented against the Jews, with the decisions of the councils becoming the law of the state.

One of the worst periods of oppression for the Hispanic Jews took place under King Sisebut, who in 613 decreed that all Jews should be baptized as Christians or face banishment (many crossed the straits to North Africa). Except for a few brief periods, the situation continued in this manner until the fall of the

Tree of kinship from the Fuero Juzgo, *a 14th-century manuscript (Biblioteca Nacional, Madrid). The* Fuero Juzgo *is the romance version of the* Liber Iudicorum, *the Visigothic code promulgated by Recceswinth in 654 and drawn up with the aid of the members of the Eighth Council of Toledo (653). Among its prohibitions was marriage between non-Christians to the sixth degree of consanguinity.*

The Conversion of Recared, *by Muñoz Degrain, 19th century (Palacio del Senado, Madrid). Recared abjured Arianism at the Third Council of Toledo (c. 587-589) and was the first Visigothic king to dictate anti-Jewish laws since the promulgation of the Breviary of Alaric (also known as the* Lex Romana Visigothorum) *in 506. The ensuing deterioration of the situation for the Jews was comparable to that of three hundred years earlier in the Roman Empire*

Adam and Eve blessed by God in the Fuero Juzgo *manuscript. The anti-Jewish regulations contained in the code include the separation of small children from their parents so that they could be brought up in the Catholic faith; the annulment of marriages in which either spouse was Catholic; the prohibition on Jews to bear witness, to hold public office, or to own Christian slaves. New regulations, including forced conversion, were dictated by Erwig at the end of the 7th century.*

Visigothic kingdom, the culmination of anti-Jewish legislation appearing in Recceswinth's *Liber Iudiciorum* (654). Yet the Hispanic Jews were to suffer times of even greater oppression, for in 681 King Erwig ordered all Jews to be baptized as Christians within the space of one year, which led a large number of Jews—who were later to collaborate with the Muslims preparing to invade the peninsula—to flee to North Africa. A few years later, in 694, King Egica reduced all the Jews to slavery, confiscating their goods and forbidding them to practice their religion. Furthermore, Jewish children over the age of seven were taken from their parents and brought up in Christian households.

The Visigoth reign of terror and despotism ended in July 711, when the army of Roderick, the last Gothic king in Spain, was defeated by the Arab and Berber troops under Tarik, who had invaded the peninsula. When the Moors arrived in Spain, there were no communities of openly practicing Jews, but their arrival was to mark the beginning of a new age for the Hispanic Jews in what came to be known as Al-Andalus (Muslim Spain).

25

when Constantine was converted and Christianity triumphed over paganism. Partially preserved in the Lex Visigothorum, *Recared's laws refer to the prohibition on the ownership of Christian slaves—extremely detrimental in a society in which the land was worked solely by serfs—exclusion from public office, forced baptism of the offspring of mixed marriages, etc. Certain evidence demonstrates that Recared was more tolerant at heart than his laws*

suggest, however. For example, he did not confirm the harsh canons of the Council of Narbonne, which met shortly after the Council of Toledo, nor did he respond to the pope's call to exclude Jews from slave trading.

Al-Andalus

From the very beginning, the Jews stood by the invaders, who in the 8th and 9th centuries reinforced the Jewish colonies in towns such as Córdoba, Granada, Seville, and Toledo with Jews from North Africa. Ninth-century Lucena became a Jewish town, and the Arabic geographers of the 10th to 12th centuries were to use this same term when describing Granada and Saragossa.

The attitude of the Arabs toward the Jews was one of tolerance. They called them the "people of the book," meaning of the Bible, and the Jews became efficient assistants in trade and administration in the service of their new masters. The most glorious period for Judaism in all of Europe and indeed of all times began with the reign of Abd ar-Rahman III (reigned 912-961) and continued until the 12th century. One Jew, Hisdai ibn Shaprut (c. 915-970), held a prominent position at Abd ar-Rahman's court as royal physician. He was also a diplomat, representing the caliphate in negotiations with the peninsular Christian kings and with the emissaries sent by the German emperor Otto I in 953 and by the emperor of Byzantium. Of particular interest is Ibn Shaprut's letter to Joseph, last king of the Khazars. This eminent courtier was also a patron of other Jews. As well as endorsing the translation of scientific works from Greek to Arabic, he furthered the cause of Hebrew poetry and grammar. The development of Hebrew literature in the Iberian Peninsula and the renascence of Hebrew as a literary language can also be directly attributed to him. Rabbinic studies also received his decisive support, with academies created in Córdoba and Lucena. Indeed, Al-Andalus was finally to usurp Babylonia's position of preeminence in this field and become a spiritual center for Jews everywhere.

With the fall of the Cordovan caliphate at the beginning of the 11th century and its fragmentation into the so-called *taifa* kingdoms, Hebrew culture did not—contrary to all expectations—decline, but reached even greater heights, particularly in the Jewish communities of Granada and Saragossa. The greatest Jewish figure in the kingdom of Granada was Samuel ibn Nagrela (993-1055), known as ha-Nagid, vizier

26

Reception of Abd ar-Rahman III at the palace of Medina Azahara in a detail from a painting by Domingo Baixeras, 1885 (University of Barcelona). Famous all over Europe, the Cordovan caliphal court became a center for sages and artists and vied with the most illustrious Arab cities in the East. The most important Jewish community in the Iberian Peninsula flourished in this opulent city. Its greatest Hispanic Jew, Hisdai ibn Shaprut, exercised all of the most important Jewish professions of the peninsula in the Middle Ages; a physician, he also translated scientific works and was responsible for the finances of the realm and the control of commodities. Thanks to Hisdai's medical skills, King Sancho I of Léon, known as Sancho the Fat and removed from power due to his corpulence, regained his throne. Hisdai received ten fortresses as his reward.

Bronze statue of Maimonides, by Amadeo Ruiz Olmo, 1964 (Plaza de Tiberíades, Jewish Quarter, Córdoba). The great rabbi, philosopher, and physician was obliged to leave Córdoba's Jewish quarter when the southern part of the peninsula was conquered by the Almohads in 1148. The Almohads, a fanatical Muslim sect, brought an end to the centuries-old coexistence among the Muslims, Jews, and Christians.

Viziers and Poets

Opposite: Interior of the synagogue of Córdoba (1315), built by Isaac Mohep ben Ephraim, showing the entrance and, above it, the women's gallery. Almost square in shape, it was built in the Mudéjar style and is adorned with fine floral-motif decoration and Hebrew inscriptions. After the expulsion it was converted into a hospital and in 1688 was given to the cobbler's guild. In 1884, it was declared a national monument.

to King Badis and a skillful politician who for many years made all the major political decisions in the realm. He was also a general, an extraordinary poet, and an erudite rabbi. Upon his death, he was succeeded by his son Joseph, who also appointed Jews to high administrative positions. Joseph's pride and ambition angered certain Muslims, however, and he was assassinated in 1066. His assassination sparked off a massacre of Jews in Granada, the first persecution of Jews in Muslim Spain.

Jews also held high positions at court in the kingdom of Saragossa, their patronage doing much to further the works of such poets as Solomon ibn Gabirol and moralists like Bahya ibn Paquda.

The type of Andalusian Jew portrayed in the Hebrew poetry of the age was that of the cultured, refined courtier, who, though a lover of life's pleasures, the arts, and sciences, attempted to reconcile all with the traditional Jewish sense of religion. In addition to the Talmud, the young men of Al-Andalus studied such subjects as poetry, philosophy, medicine, and astronomy.

When the *taifa* kingdoms disintegrated as the result of the ever-advancing conquests of the Christian kingdoms of the north, they were replaced by the Almoravid Empire. From North Africa, the Almoravids were much more intransigent in matters of religion than their Andalusian coreligionists, and a large number of Jews fled their hometowns to the Christian kingdoms. However, peace soon returned, and at this point the rabbinic academy at Lucena saw its moment of greatest splendor. The death blow to the brilliant Jewish culture of Al-Andalus was dealt by the Almohads, religious fanatics from North Africa who, having come to the peninsula to help their Almoravid brothers in the struggle against the Christian kings, demanded that all subjects in the realm should convert to Islam. The vast majority of the Jews of Al-Andalus fled from their traditional places of settlement. Some escaped to Muslim countries; others went to Provence, taking with them their knowledge and thus making a decisive contribution to the intellectual development of the communities already there. However, most of the Jews of Al-Andalus settled in Castile and Aragon.

28

Among the many Jewish quarters of Spain that still retain their medieval urban structure are those of Córdoba (above left; the cathedral can be seen in the background) and Seville (above right). Córdoba was the most important Jewish center in the Al-Andalus of the caliphate; Seville was the most important of the Jewish quarters in 13th-century Castile; today the area forms part of the Santa Cruz district. In both quarters are places where time seems to stand still.

The Carolingian Empire

Detail from the Catalan Atlas (see caption bottom right). In his chronicle, Charlemagne's biographer Einhard wrote of the return of a certain Jew named Isaac to the palace of Aachen in July 802. Five years earlier, Isaac had been sent with two other ambassadors (who died on the journey) to visit Harun ar-Rashid, king of the Persians. He returned with rich gifts from Harun, including an elephant.

The period from the 8th to the late 11th century was one of peace and prosperity for the Jewish communities of the West and continued so until the Crusades. The foundation for this change was laid by Charlemagne (reigned 768-814), his son and successor, Louis the Pious (reigned 814-840), and their successors, under whom the Jews reaped the benefits of a period of tolerance considered unique in the history of central Europe.

Charlemagne took the Jews under his wing, guaranteeing them the wherewithal to live, the ownership of property, independent courts, and complete freedom of trade and religion. Educated and enterprising, the Jewish population was a boon to Charlemagne's empire, doing much to further the development of industry and above all of trade. During this period the Jews were the only people capable of trading with the countries of the East; countries inaccessible to a Christian world within a Europe encircled by Islam and enclosed within an area extending from the eastern and southern shores of the Mediterranean in an arc from the Atlantic to the Caucasus. The Jews of Europe, however, were able to move about freely in the Muslim world, being welcomed and taken in by the numerous communities scattered all over the Arab empire. In Jewish hands lay the slave, fur, and brocade trades from the Near East and the spice trade from China. Within Europe itself, the Jews controlled the great trade routes that from Marseilles to Nijmegen linked the Mediterranean with the North Sea and the Baltic and stretched as far as the British Isles. The Jews moved freely through Europe blessed by the bonds of solidarity that existed among the many communities. Free to engage in any occupation, they were to be found in all walks of life, as ambassadors, artisans—glassmakers, dyers, jewelers, goldsmiths, and silk dealers—as physicians (even at court), as farmers and landowners, and as merchants and shipbuilders.

During his reign, Louis the Pious took the Jews directly under his protection, extending their privileges and even appointing them as tax inspectors. Such favorable circumstances led to a significant flowering of Jewish intellectual life, particularly important in the talmudic schools in the north of France and in the Rhineland, which gave birth to such famous rabbis as Gershom ben Judah (born Metz, 960), also called *Meor ha-Golah* "Light of the Exile"), who taught at Mainz, and Solomon ben Isaac, known as Rashi (Troyes, 1040-1105).

From the south of France (Narbonne, Nîmes, Montpellier, Marseilles, Toulouse, etc.) the Jewish population gradually spread north and eastward along the Rouen trade fair area, and to the Lorraine, Champagne, Lyons, and Limoges regions. Around 1066, French Jews also settled in England. The eastward migration continued along the banks of the Rhine, encountering the same benevolent attitude under the emperors of the Saxon and Salian realms as under the Carolingians. At this point Jewish communities sprang up in towns such as Magdeburg, Merseburg, Mainz, Speyer, and Worms, and in others, such as Cologne, Regensburg, Metz, and Trier, which had had Jewish populations five centuries before. Jews also reached Moravia, Austria, and Bohemia, the main center of settlement being the city of Prague.

Above and above right: Two pages from the Birds'-Head Haggadah, *southern Germany, c. 1300 (Israel Museum, Jerusalem): making the matzoth (above) and the bitter herbs (right). The reason the faces are distorted into birds' heads appears to be connected to the Christian iconophobic practices of the times, which were reinforced in the case of Judaism by the influence of the ascetic ideas of the 12th-century Ashkenazic Hasidic movement.*

Opposite: Caravan of merchants on the route to China, from the Catalan Atlas (Bibliothèque Nationale, Paris) made by the Majorcans Abraham Cresques and his son Jafuda, who worked in the service of Peter IV of Aragon. With Charlemagne's support, Jewish merchants, known by Arab writers as Radanites, exchanged goods from western Europe with merchants from Constantinople, Baghdad, Damascus, India, and China.

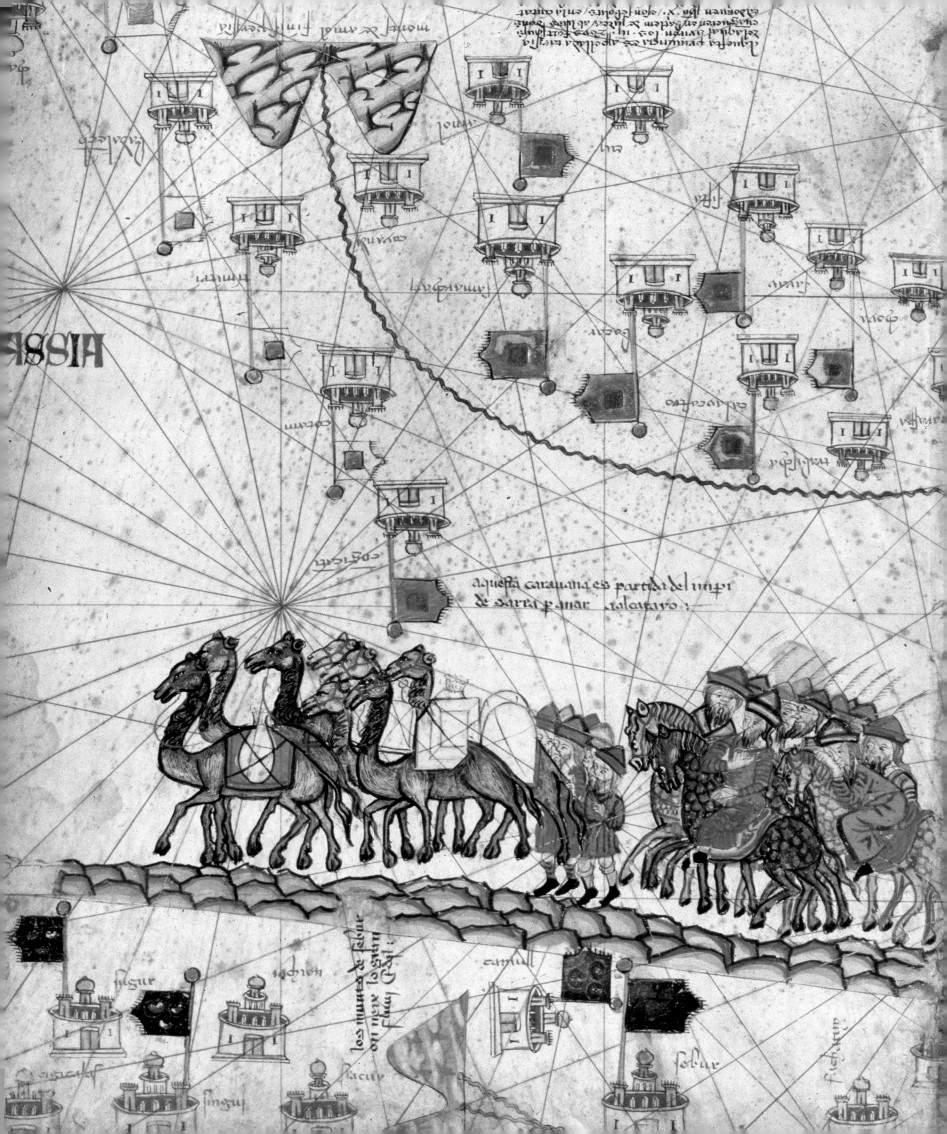

The Crusades and Their Aftermath

The favorable times in central Europe ended with the Crusades. A turning-point in the history of the Jewish people, the Crusades severely affected relations between Christians and Jews virtually until modern times.

Proclaimed by Pope Urban II to free Jerusalem from Muslim control, the First Crusade was launched in 1096. When the crusaders began to realize how many "heathens" lived among them, as a preliminary exercise to facing the powerful Muslim armies, they killed, virtually without opposition, all Jews (the vast majority) who refused to be baptized into the Christian faith. The first Jewish community to fall was that of Rouen, in Normandy, and from then on the crusaders left death and devastation in their wake as they advanced along the Rhine. In spite of the emperor Henry IV's attempts to prevent such slaughter, whole communities were annihilated, with an estimated 12,000 people killed within three months. For the first time a

bloody wound was opened between Christians and Jews, and attacks on Jewish communities became a commonplace occurrence.

The Second (1146-1147) and Third (1189-1193) Crusades were no less devastating. Despite the efforts of Bernard of Clairvaux and other princes of the church, such as the emperor Conrad III, to curb the cruelty of the crusaders, many French and German Jews perished during the Second Crusade. The Third Crusade had repercussions of its own in England. In 1190 anti-Jewish rioting began in London and spread to the outlying communities of Norwich, Stanford, and King's Lynn. In York, the members of the Jewish community managed to hold off the attackers for several days and then, rather than fall prey to the enraged mob, committed mass suicide, burning themselves to death inside their own houses. The massacre in York, as elsewhere, was motivated in large part by greed: the rioters hoped to seize Jewish property and avoid

32

Top: Peter the Hermit preaching the First Crusade, from the Egerton Manuscript, *France, 1500 (British Museum, London). Above: The taking of Jerusalem by the Crusaders in the* Storie degli Imperatori *(Arsenal Library, Paris). On learning that the Muslims had desecrated the Holy Sepulcher, Pope Urban II proclaimed the First Crusade at the Council of Clermont (1095). The knights were joined by a host of thieves and vagabonds lured by the prospect of*

plunder and incensed by the preaching of Peter the Hermit and others. After a three-year journey and leaving a trail of blood behind it throughout the Jewish communities of central Europe, the army reached the Holy Land. After a six-week siege, the Franks under Godfrey of Bouillon took Jerusalem on July 15, 1099, putting to death all non-Christians.

repayment of debts owed the Jews. As one chronicler, William of Newburgh, wrote, the rioters were led not by righteousness but by "the business of their own greed."

Relations between Jews and Christians in Europe underwent a drastic change with the Crusades, and the foundation of the irrational hatred of Jews typical of the Middle Ages was laid. Such hatred is often to be found in the imagery and paintings of Christian churches and cathedrals, with the Jew depicted as the symbol of evil and the synagogue as a decrepit old woman wearing a lopsided crown, her eyes blindfolded, her scepter cracked, bearing broken Tables of the Law, sitting astride a pig, and portrayed with other equally denigrating features. The Jew was also mocked and derided in the Christian mystery plays and attributed with the most heinous and abominable vices. With the advent of the printing press Jews became the subject of offensive engravings, which appear to have originated in Germany. Such portrayals obviously made a deep impression on the common people, who, with their minds poisoned by the lower clergy and the mendicant Dominican and Franciscan orders, began to fabricate wild stories about the Jews. The consequences of such tales were appalling. Notorious among these was the accusation of ritual murder, in which it was said that the Jews sacrificed Christian children during the Passover in a travesty of the Passion of Christ and used the blood in their rituals. This fantastic accusation was first made in Norwich in 1144 and, in spite of the denials of kings, emperors, and popes, spread across all of continental Europe.

Of all the false accusations made against the Jews, that of poisoning wells and rivers was to have the most terrible consequences. The first instance of this occurred in France in 1321. Later, in the period from 1348 to 1350, when the Black Death swept Europe, the accusation was made again, and the Jews, who were dying of plague just like their Christian neighbors, were held responsible. In spite of the various orders issued by Pope Clement VI to ensure the safety of the Jews, hundreds of communities from Aragon to eastern Europe were destroyed, and tens of thousands of Jews slaughtered.

Jerusalem besieged by the Franks, from the Book of the Crusades, *15th century (National Library, Vienna). During the First Crusade, the members of the Jewish community died in the flames of the synagogue, where they withstood attack for three days. The surviving Jews of the kingdom of Jerusalem (Judaea, Galilee, and the coast from Jaffa to Tyre) fled to Egypt, Syria, and Mesopotamia. With the threat of attack by the Muslims of Syria, the Second Crusade was proclaimed in 1146, Pope Eugenius III issuing a bull in which Crusaders were released from any obligation to repay debts to Jews. Saladin finally occupied Jerusalem on October 2, 1187, and the city was repopulated with Jews. On the initiative of Saladin's brother, sultan Aladil, in 1211 three hundred rabbis from France and England emigrated to Palestine, where the Jewish culture was restored in the city.*

Particularly bloody was the persecution of Jews in Germany, where over 350 communities came under attack.

So it was that from the 12th century on and for what remained of the Middle Ages, the Jews of Europe learned that the edicts issued from time to time for their protection by their Christian overlords were, in fact, no more than a mere stopgap. They realized that they would have to go on living exposed to the destructive force of Christian rage, which could be provoked by any change in social or political circumstances, and even more so in times of religious agitation. Examples of this are the Albigensian Crusade in France between 1204 and 1229; the hysterical mass movement known as the Pastoureaux, for the shepherds who started it, which brought turmoil to France in 1320; the marauding so-called Jew exterminators of Bavaria in 1336; the wars waged against the Hussite heretics of Bohemia in the 15th century;

34

Profanation of the Host (1465-69), series of six tempera panels by Paolo Uccello (National Gallery of the Marches, Urbino) originally intended for the predella with the altarpiece of the Communion of the Apostles *by Justus of Ghent in the Corpus Domini Church, Urbino. In Uccello's panels, a woman (top) sells a consecrated host to a Jewish merchant; the members of the local council hear of the matter (above) and sentence her to be hanged, while an angel appears to expose the Jew. In the presence of his family, the Jew (opposite top) burns the host, from which blood begins to flow, while the local people break down the door of his house; the whole family is led to the stake (opposite bottom). This is yet another example of the insidious accusations against Jews that led to bloodshed. After the doctrine of transubstantiation—according to which the host was transformed into the body of Christ—was established*

and the inflammatory sermons of the Capuchin monk John of Capestrano, the pope's legate in Germany, to enforce the anti-Jewish rulings of the Council of Basel (1431-49).

Public disputations between Jews and Christians were staged during the Middle Ages, and during the 13th century these took on the character of great political debates. These debates differed from those of previous times in that rather than being actual open debates, they were more a form of compulsory indoctrination of the Jewish community leaders (who were allowed little opportunity to reply), and the Jewish speakers suffered all kinds of indignities and were threatened, among other things, with banishment. Converted Jews, the only ones truly capable of launching scathing attacks on their former coreligionists, played an important part in these debates. In one such debate held in Paris in 1240 an attack was made, for the first time ever in Jewish history, on the Talmud itself; Nicolas

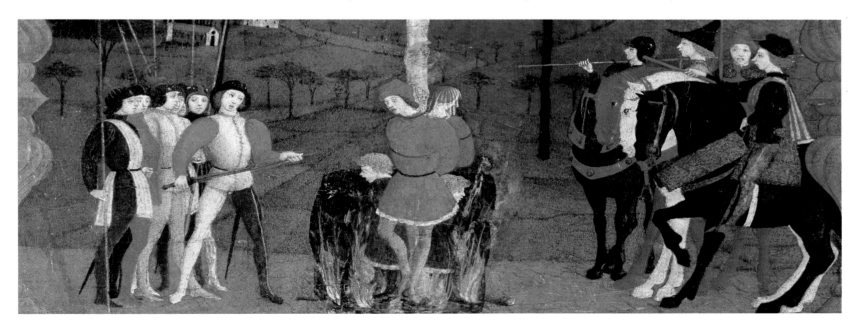

35

at the Fourth Lateran Council (1215), rumors began to circulate that Jews were defiling consecrated wafers. The first such case occurred in Beelitz, near Berlin, in 1243, where the entire Jewish population was burned at the stake for this offense. By the end of the 13th century, Jews everywhere were being accused of such crimes, and the accusations continued for centuries to come. Particularly devastating were the actions of the petty German nobleman Rindfleisch of

Rottingen in 1298, who with a band of followers marauded through Bavaria and Austria, pillaging and destroying one hundred and fifty Jewish communities and slaughtering over 100,000 Jews. The last Jewish victims of such calumny were massacred in 1631, but isolated cases were recorded even after this, such as in Rumania in 1836.

Donin, a convert, took it upon himself to prove that this essential book in Jewish worship slandered and insulted the Christian faith and succeeded in having it declared pernicious and sacrilegious. As a result, in 1242 twenty-four cartloads of copies of the work were burned in a public square in Paris.

In the wake of the Crusades and as the Middle Ages wore on, European Jews were forced out of the majority of their traditional trades and professions, hastening their financial decline. First, the guilds linked to the religious life of the towns were barred to Jews, and, later, the breach made in the Islamic front by the Crusades enabled the Christians to recover the trade routes with the East, which were soon monopolized by the rich Genoese and Venetian merchants, thus virtually excluding Jews from international trade. As an example of the measures taken by the Venetian lords to rid themselves of undesirable competitors, Jewish merchants were forbidden to live in Venice or to transport their own merchandise. Overland trade was also severely affected, as, in view of the

general atmosphere of hostility, any Jew who traveled risked his life. The risk increased after the Fourth Lateran Council (1215), summoned by Pope Innocent III, where it was decreed that Jews should wear a badge on their clothing to set them apart from Christians. At the same council they were also forbidden to hold public office or engage in "Christian" professional activities, which virtually closed off all channels to Jews. Finally, the feudal system itself was to alienate Jews from the land, as they could be neither lords nor vassals. They were also forbidden to employ Christian labor, but this law, although serious, came to make little difference, since Jews were soon forbidden to own land. Consequently, Jewish populations drifted from the country to the towns and villages, where they became scattered in small communities usually numbering no more than a hundred and rarely reaching a thousand. It was during the mid 13th century that the legend of the "Wandering Jew"—a Jew who mocked Jesus while he was on his way to the cross and was condemned to a life of wandering until

36

Top: Jewish bankers in the Digesta seu Pandectae, *northern Italy, 14th century (British Museum, London). Above: The Black Death in Florence from Boccaccio's* Decameron *(Bibliothèque Nationale, Paris). In France in 1321 it was given out that in order to destroy Christendom the Jews and lepers had formed an alliance with the Devil and the Muslims of the Iberian Peninsula and had poured poison made of blood, urine, herbs, the "body of Christ," vipers'*

heads, frogs' legs, women's hair, and other abominations into wells. Spread by the minstrels and chroniclers, the rumor became a common theme in European folklore and was revived with a vengeance during the years of the Black Death, which struck Florence in 1348 and then went on to sweep Europe. Between one half and two thirds of Europe's population died.

Judgment Day—was first applied by Christians to the Jewish people in general.

Jewish activity, particularly in central Europe, was then limited to moneylending, forbidden to Christians since the Third Lateran Council (1179). From the 12th century on this was to become the main source of income for Jews in France, England, and northern Italy. The same situation arose in Germany, Poland, and Bohemia in the 13th century. Similar to the modern-day banks, the small- and large-scale moneylenders were indispensable during this period, when a desperate need for money arose as the result of the transition from an exchange-based economy to a more capitalist system. Furthermore, it was particularly profitable for monarchies to have Jews engaged in moneylending, as this meant that it was the Jews who paid the high taxation imposed on the activity, along with the other taxes, which, both ordinarily and extraordinarily, they were already obliged to pay into the public coffers. In this way wealthy Jews became indispensable to monarchs and church leaders, financing wars and great works of construction. This practice had its heyday in the 13th century, and the financial ruin of the Jewish communities later brought a sharp decline in the economic influence of Jews.

Moneylending, particularly in small amounts and from pawn shops where the customer made personal contact with the lender, led people to hate Jews for reasons other than those of religion, to the extent that outbreaks of violence were often caused intentionally by those who wished to avoid repayment of debts or to rid themselves of trade or craft rivals. In southern Europe, where moneylending was less common, the Jews still worked in many of their traditional trades as textile merchants, silk manufacturers, dyers, tanners, and physicians. After the First Crusade, the extremely harsh living conditions of Jews north of the Pyrenees led to the impoverishment of the once thriving rabbinic schools of the Carolingian period. Yet eminent men of learning were still active, among them Rabbenu Tam, Rashi's grandson and a leader of the Tosafists (from a Hebrew word meaning "to add"), who added explanations to the Talmud.

Assault on the Jewish Quarter of Venice, *oil painting by Robert Fleaux, 1851 (Augustine Museum, Toulouse). Jews were hated not only for their religion but also for their functions within society, particularly as moneylenders. From the 12th to the 15th century, violence against Jews could break out in European towns at any time. The struggle between the church and the empire during the pontificate of Gregory VII led to a particular form of preaching to the masses by* the monks and lower clergy. The Franciscans' *traditional abhorrence of the Jews as expressed by St. Bernardine of Siena was taken up by Bernardine's companion and disciple John of Capestrano, known as the "Scourge of the Jews," who in 1417 launched a campaign against Jews in Italy, Austria, Germany, and Poland that led to anti-Jewish riots and expulsions.*

The Expulsions

Because of the general atmosphere of hostility, constant pressure from the church, and impoverishment of the Jews as a whole, the Jewish communities in medieval Europe stopped playing a significant or beneficial part in the life of the countries in which they lived. Their very weakness was often used against them, serving as the excuse for their expulsion, usually accompanied by the confiscation of their remaining property. In England, the communities were impoverished by the brutally high taxes imposed on them by King John, his son Henry III, and Edward I. When Edward I finally banished the Jews in 1290, most emigrated to France and Germany and were not to set foot on English soil again until 1657. In France, where the situation had worsened under the rule of Louis IX (reigned 1226-70), there were several temporary periods of banishment until 1394, when the Jews were expelled by Charles VI; they settled in Provence—only to be expelled again a century later—in northern Italy, Germany, and in the

papal possessions of Avignon and Comtat Venaissin. Jews were not to live in France again until the 16th century. In the old Holy Roman Empire, the Jews were never expelled as a group, but there were many expulsions of small numbers from specific regions or towns, sometimes only temporarily, the kings and princes being forced to readmit them when the need arose to reactivate the economy. In Germany, the first of these expulsions took place in Mainz in 1012, but they did not become common there until after the Black Death. In Austria, part of the Jewish community was expelled in 1420; those who remained were burned at the stake the next year. Some were allowed to reenter Vienna a century later. Jews were expelled from Cologne in 1426, from Saxony in 1430, from Brandenburg in 1446, from Bavaria in 1450, and from Regensburg in 1519. As a result of the bitterly anti-Jewish climate, of one expulsion after another, of the forced converts' deep longing to return to the religion of their fathers, and of the massacres during the period of the Black Death, the Jewish population of central Europe gradually drifted west, east, and southeast to Hungary and Poland.

38

Above: Representations of the church and the synagogue from a missal in the abbey of Saint Pierre, Ghent, 13th century (Bylocke Museum, France). In the 11th century, one type of anti-Jewish propaganda spread by the church took the form of representations in which the church appears as a crowned and haughty maiden bearing a standard and chalice in her hands. The synagogue, in contrast, was depicted as a disheveled old woman with a distorted face and body, *a lopsided crown, eyes closed or blindfolded to symbolize "Jewish blindness," and holding the Tables of the Law in one hand and a broken scepter or the head of some animal (in this case a goat, symbol of the Devil) in the other. Common all over Europe, such images were found in the sculptures, paintings, and stained-glass windows of churches and cathedrals and in the decorations and bindings of Bibles and prayer books.*

The "Satanization" of the Jew

Opposite top: Satan blindfolding a Jew in the *Breviari d'Amor*, a late 14th-century manuscript by Ermengaut of Béziers (Biblioteca Laurentina, San Lorenzo de El Escorial). The text is the biblical story (Num.) of Korah's rebellion and Aaron's rod, a story seen as a prefiguration of the True Church by Christians but "misinterpreted" by Jews because they have been blindfolded by the Devil. Right: The legend of Theophilus in the *Lambeth Apocalypse*, c. 1260 (Lambeth Palace Library, London).

In the eyes of most medieval Europeans, Jews were perverse creatures of the Devil, allied with him against truth. For the medieval Christian, Satan, the very essence of evil, was a real figure, ubiquitous, constantly able to tempt the believer and eager to destroy mankind, which Jesus, the essence of good, had come to save. The struggle between Jesus and Satan became an ever-present axiom in the minds of medieval church leaders, and in its zeal to destroy Satan, Christianity fell upon his creatures—the Jews. That the Jews can be identified with the Devil is an ancient belief (John 8:44 and Rev. 2:9 and 3:9), and it appeared in church literature from the 4th century onward, becoming deeply rooted in Christian thought and leaving an indelible mark on the minds of the masses. Time and time again, the theme of the Devil inciting the Jews appeared in art, in the medieval Passion plays, and in the mysteries of the miracles of the lives of the saints.

Such was the case of the legend of Theophilus, which became popular all over Europe, with versions appearing in all the European languages and the legend told in a variety of literary forms. According to the legend, which was later to influence the story of Faust, the Devil and Jews had common interests: a Jew acted as go-between for the Devil and the Archdeacon Theophilus, who was prepared to sell his soul to recover his lost prestige. In some versions the Jew even appears as the Devil's lord and master. The synagogal ritual was also depicted as satanic, with the Devil himself often portrayed wearing the Jewish distinguishing mark and as a member of the Jewish community. Jewish practices were seen as sinister; the Jews prayed for the destruction of Christendom, their ceremonies required Christian blood, etc. It is therefore not surprising that in the Middle Ages the masses, manipulated by their spiritual and intellectual mentors, believed any accusation made against the Jews to be absolutely true and repeatedly rose up in rage and violence against Jews.

The Christian Kingdoms in Sepharad

I have sought Thee, my Lord, in the night,
In the depths of my soul amid darkness;
I have remembered Thee at nightfall
And the glory of Thy name shone for me
As the light of the resplendent sun.
—Bahya ibn Paquda, 12th century
*View of Toledo: as was common during the Middle
Ages, the city is dominated by its cathedral; the Jewish
quarter is located to the left.*

The name Sepharad comes from a place-name mentioned in the Bible (Obadiah 20), which early biblical commentators identified with the Iberian Peninsula. For the Jews in the medieval Christian kingdoms in Sepharad life was very different from that in the countries north of the Pyrenees. In the rest of Europe, the beginning of the end of coexistence between Jews and Christians was marked by the First Crusade in the late 11th century, but in the Iberian Peninsula there were no great expulsions until the end of the 15th century. During this long period, Jews could be found at all levels of society, from the great courtiers and financiers to the humble folk, small craftsmen, and traders.

By the end of the 10th century, a large number of Jews had settled in Catalonia, and the Barcelona community became particularly important in the 11th century. Inland, Jewish commercial centers dotted the route to Santiago, the Léon community being of particular importance. In the period from the second half of the 11th century to the early 12th century, the Christians pushed back the Arab lines considerably, thus taking in large numbers of Jews. When Alfonso VI took Toledo in 1085, he designated the Tagus River as the border between his kingdom and that of the Muslims. Some years later, Alfonso I of Aragon occupied the Ebro Valley, and the count of Barcelona took Tortosa and Lérida. As the Christian front was pushed forward, the kings granted codes of laws and privileges to the recently occupied or newly founded towns. These codes usually took Jews into consideration, assigning them a plot of land to live on and a place in the commercial areas to set up their businesses. This established a balance among Jews, Moors, and Christians, whose different communities formed separate groups with equal rights.

During the period in which the Christian kingdoms were at war with the Muslims, the Jewish community was indispensable in the repopulation of the conquered areas and in the organization of trade and administration. In this way, Jews held public office in Castile, Aragon, and Catalonia. Their presence at court was aided by their knowledge of Arabic, which made them particularly useful in matters of diplomacy as

40

Detail of the ornamentation of the east wall (right of the ark) of the El Tránsito Synagogue in Toledo, a masterpiece of Mudéjar art built around 1357 on the orders of Samuel Abulafia, treasurer to Peter I. The interior consists of one hall whose coffered ceiling runs the whole length of the building. Above the south wall runs the women's gallery. Of great interest are the Hebrew inscriptions, particularly the historical references that flank the area in the east wall where the ark was situated. In these inscriptions, under the lions and castles that are the emblems of Léon and Castile, the sanctuary is poetically described. After the expulsion, the synagogue became the priory of St. Benedict belonging to the Order of Calatrava. Later it became a hermitage dedicated to the Passing of the Virgin, and during the Napoleonic Wars it was used as a barracks. In 1877 it was declared a national monument.

Opposite: The Golden Haggadah, *perhaps from Barcelona, c. 1320 (British Library, London). One of the oldest and most sumptuous of the existing illuminated Hispano-Hebrew Haggadoth, it consists of fourteen full-page miniatures illustrating festival rituals and episodes from the Bible. Northern French Gothic in style, it dates from the time of the Catalan school during the reign of James II. Shown here are the enslaved Israelites building pharaoh's cities (above); and the first plague, in which the waters of the Nile turned to blood, and the staffs of Moses and Aaron turning into serpents (below).*

country estates and urban properties, which they received in payment for their services. They could not be tried by the normal Christian courts of law and were exempt from certain taxes. Their position within their own communities was also special, in that they were not subject to the Jewish courts and ordinances and were exempt from the payment of all taxes.

Of course, these leading businessmen, along with the great sages and rabbis, were no more than a small minority, the position of the mass of the Jewish population being altogether different. During the 11th and 12th centuries, the Jews were most actively engaged in agriculture, though they were also to be found as small traders and in urban areas as cobblers, tailors, leather dealers, silversmiths, spice merchants, potters, dyers, and so on. Indeed, these continued to be their usual occupations throughout the Middle Ages. Jews were also physicians, some Jewish doctors ministering to entire towns and receiving remuneration directly from the municipality, and from the 12th century on, a small number of Jews began to lend money on a small

well as medicine and other sciences. One such Jew was Joseph ha-Nasi Ferrizuel (Cidellus), doctor and counselor to Alfonso VI. The most influential Jew of the age, he was the prototype of the great businessmen who were to appear in all of the Christian kingdoms until just before the expulsion. In the 13th century, eminent Jews served as counselors, doctors, diplomats, and financiers at the courts of such kings as Alfonso X and Sancho IV of Castile and James I and Peter III of Aragon.

The 12th century saw the development of a class-based Jewish society at the highest level of which stood a veritable courtier oligarchy of wealthy families often vying with one another for the king's favor and for power within their communities. From these families came the great financiers, landlords, and tax collectors who were able to advance their monarchs the large sums of money needed for the wars against the Muslims. They were also army provisioners and crown administrators, comparable in the eyes of the law to the upper nobility. As high functionaries they signed state documents and owned large

42

scale, this activity becoming exclusive to Jews in the 13th century, when a church law forbidding usury to Christians came into force.

The Jewish communities were governed by their own laws, which had to receive approval of the crown and varied from one community to another. Internal power lay with the members of the *aljama* (equivalent to the town council of the Christians), an oligarchy that appointed the holders of internal posts, the most important being that of the "governor," who was a kind of community executive. The *aljama* also appointed judges, treasurers, tax collectors, and those who managed the community's charitable institutions. The law courts, or *Bet Din,* dealt with both civil and penal cases and could even pass the death sentence.

From the legal point of view, until the expulsion Jews were crown property, their rights being established according to privileges granted by the monarch to each community. For example, a fine was imposed on towns as a whole whenever a Jew was found dead in the vicinity and the murderer was not apprehended. The atti-

Three pages from the Rylands Haggadah, *Spain, mid 14th century (John Rylands Library, Manchester). This Haggadah contains not only illustrated texts but also several complete pages illuminated with scenes from Exodus. Top left: Preparations for Passover: in the upper register the lamb is ritually slaughtered and cooked in the oven; the lower register shows the Passover supper and blessing of the wine. Above: The angel calls Moses from the burning bush, Moses takes off his shoes so as not to tread on holy ground, and Moses and Aaron turn their staffs into serpents. Top right: Moses, his wife, Zipporah, and their two children return to Egypt to meet Aaron. Aside from their beauty, these miniatures are of enormous interest because they depict the clothing, furniture, and utensils used by the Jews of the period.*

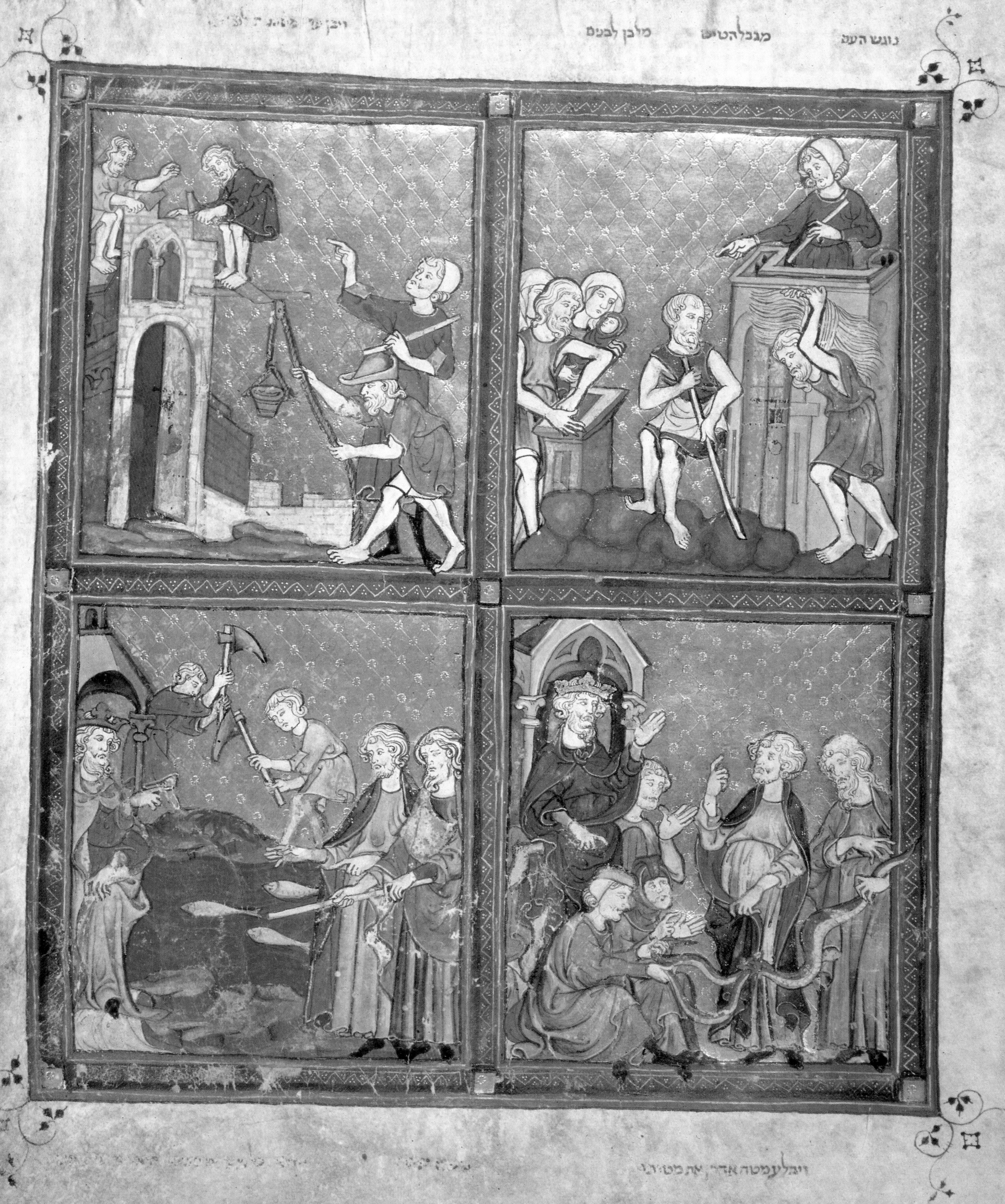

נוגש העם
מגבלהטיש
מלבן לבנים
ויבלע מטה אהרן את מטותם

Cantiga 108 *from Alfonso X's* Cantigas de Santa María, *Castile, 13th century (Biblioteca Laurentina, San Lorenzo de El Escorial). Merlin debates with a Jewish scholar. Despite the wise king's sympathy for the Jews, this work contains all the Christian world's anti-Jewish prejudices, portraying Jews as the enemies of Christianity, disciples of the Devil, and the epitome of avarice and treachery. The Jewish dress of the age is also depicted in these miniatures—the* pointed hat, sometimes adorned with scale shapes, and the closed cape with a tunic beneath it in the manner of a skirt.

tude of the kings toward the Jews was, in general, favorable, but the same could not be said of the rest of Christian society, which was particularly irritated by the privileged position of the Jews at court. Furthermore, the pressure brought to bear by the church after the Fourth Lateran Council and the anti-Jewish feeling prevalent in Europe began to take effect, particularly in Catalonia. In the kingdom of Aragon, too, more and more Christians were assigned to administrative posts, and although Jews were not completely ousted from positions of importance, they were no longer indispensable.

The 13th century, particularly during the reigns of Alfonso X and James I, was perhaps the time of greatest well-being for the Jews of Castile and Aragon. Nevertheless, even the legislation of that age, as for example Alfonso X's great code of laws, the *Siete Partidas* ("The Seven Divisions of Law"), began to reflect the influence of the laws of the church vis-à-vis the Jews. In 1263, due to increasing pressure from the Franciscans and Dominicans, James I authorized a public disputation led by the convert

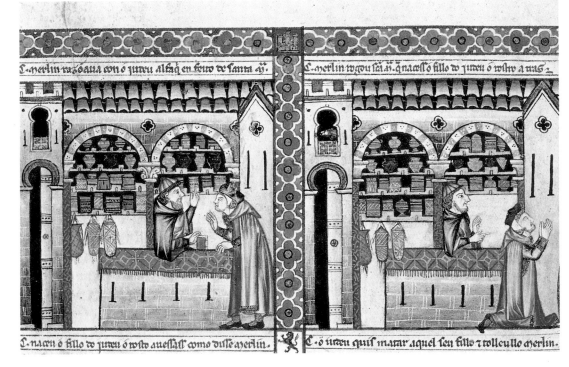

Pablo Christiani in which the famous rabbi from Gerona, Moses ben Nahman (Nahmanides), a close friend of the king, took part, having been granted absolute freedom of speech. Two years later, however, Nahmanides was accused of blasphemy by the Dominicans and, in spite of the king's protection, he eventually chose to leave the peninsula for Palestine.

The pressure brought to bear by the church eventually bore fruit, first in Aragon and then in Castile, leading to the decline of Hispanic Judaism. Hatred of the Jews seems to have increased in the 14th century, and three levels of society—the church, the nobility, and the municipalities—joined a common cause in parliament to put pressure on the kings against Jewish "power" and moneylending. Around 1320 accusations that Jews were poisoning water and defiling the host began to circulate in the Hispanic kingdoms, their frequency increasing considerably during the years when the Black Death swept Europe (1348-50).

In Castile, the beginning of the end of the peaceful coexistence between Jews and

Cantiga 25 *from the* Cantigas de Santa María, *in which the Jew is depicted as the symbol of avarice and thoroughly dishonest in trade. A Christian who asks a Jew for a loan pledges repayment to Jesus and the Virgin. Being in a far-off land and unable to repay his debt on time, the Christian places the money in a small chest and throws it into the water, beseeching the Virgin to ensure that the money reaches the moneylender. The Jew finds the chest and hides it* under his bed. When the Christian returns, the Jew denies receiving the money and demands payment, but the Virgin bears testimony on behalf of the Christian, and the Jew converts to Christianity.

Christians was marked by the civil war between Peter I and his stepbrother Henry of Trastámara (who defeated and killed Peter in 1369) and by the anti-Jewish propaganda of Henry's followers. Disaster struck the communities of the Hispanic kingdoms in 1391 as the result of the inflammatory sermons delivered in the diocese of Seville by Ferrant Martínez, archdeacon of Écija. A mob attacked the Jewish quarter of Seville, the violence spreading like wildfire to other Andalusian cities and even as far as Toledo and towns in the north of Castile. Jews were massacred in Valencia, the Balearic Islands, and in Barcelona, from where the attacks spread across all of Catalonia. The riots left in their wake not only a trail of blood but also large numbers of Jews forced to convert to Christianity in order to avoid death. The displaced Jewish population sought refuge outside Spain or else scattered across the whole country far from the large towns. Some of the greatest Hispanic communities, such as those in Barcelona and Valencia, were completely destroyed forever, while others with a glorious past, such as Toledo, were left wretched and diminished, never to return to their former grandeur.

Harsh new regulations were drawn up against the Jews early in the 15th century. Though later abolished in Castile and Aragon, they totally crushed the communities. During this period (1413), a public disputation in Tortosa, conducted by the convert Jerónimo de Santa Fe in the presence of Pope Benedict XIII, ended with a large number of conversions. During the 1430s the Jewish communities of Castile and Aragon began to recover, but the great families had disappeared, and Jews now lived from small-scale businesses and their traditional trades. In 1432, representatives of the *aljamas* of Castile met in Valladolid to draw up *takkanot*, general ordinances of internal control within the communities. These remained in force until the expulsion of the Jews from Spain and subsequently governed life in many Sephardic communities.

The question of coexistence now became a matter for a new social group belonging to communities under constant pressure and attack.

Book of Chess, Dice, and Tables (*Biblioteca Laurentina, San Lorenzo de El Escorial). Compiled at the court of Alfonso X, this is without doubt the most important medieval work of its kind. Dating from 1283, it features one hundred and fifty miniatures illustrating various games and the woodworkers' shops where the boards for them were made. Among the games mentioned are checkers, chess, dice, and what is now known in the West as backgammon. The* players form a veritable gallery of characters: ladies, knights, clergymen, commoners, musicians, soldiers, Moors, and Jews. The miniatures are Oriental in style and very much in keeping with literary sources. In this scene two groups of people play dice. Judging from their headgear, those on the right are Jews.

The Inquisition

St. Helena's Discovery of the True Cross, 14th-century fresco in the Santa Lucia Chapel, retrochoir of Tarragona Cathedral. To the right, two Jews look on. As was common in medieval paintings and mysteries, they are dressed not in the clothing of biblical times but in contemporary garments, in this case including the rodela, *the distinguishing sign that Jews were forced to wear after the Fourth Lateran Council (1215).*

These were the converts, or "New Christians," who had accepted baptism while, in numbers impossible to estimate, continuing to practice Judaism in secret (known by the Spanish epithet of *Marrano*, meaning "swine"). The vast majority of these converts continued to work in their previous trades, but some were tax collectors and went on to hold senior posts in state administration or occupied the highest positions in their municipalities, such as treasurer and clerk. Their privileged position often led to animosity on the part of the "Old Christians," occasionally turning to all-out war.

All of Spain except for the Moorish kingdom of Granada was united in 1469 when Ferdinand II of Aragon married Isabella I of Castile. The royal couple were known as the Catholic kings, and the beginning of their reign brought a period of peace whose tragic end could not possibly have been predicted. Once again Jews held important positions at court,

examples being Abraham Senior and Isaac Arabanel, both of whom served the rulers in matters of finance. The Catholic kings took it upon themselves to protect the communities, ensuring that Jewish commercial activities and the Jewish way of life were in no way threatened. Yet little by little they gave in to the demands of the clergy, who insisted that all converts be kept under surveillance and be set apart from their former coreligionists, so as to avoid any possibility of their continuing to practice Judaism. To discover and punish converted Jews who were insincere, the Spanish Inquisition was established in 1478. It was controlled by the Spanish kings, the pope's only hold over it being the naming of the inquisitor general. One of the first and most notorious heads was Tomás de Torquemada. In 1483 the Jews were expelled from Andalusia, many moving to the region of Extremadura. This small expulsion was merely a "dress rehearsal" for something far larger, however, and pressure on the monarchs to find a final solution increased.

On January 2, 1492, Granada, the last Muslim stronghold, fell to the army of the Catholic kings: for the first time since the Muslim conquest of 711 the Iberian Peninsula

46

Details from the St. Stephen altarpiece by Jaime Serra, Catalonia, 14th century (Museo de Arte de Cataluña, Barcelona), in which Jews in the synagogue listen to the saint preaching. In Christian pictorial art, the figure of the Jew is intentionally distorted, so that it is the clothing and facial features that define the character. It was in the Serra workshop—until then neutral in the matter—that Catalan paintings first began to feature some of these

examples of Jewish perfidy, the expression on the face being malevolent to represent the diabolical nature of the Jew.

was entirely Christian. Ferdinand and Isabella then turned to the Jews. On March 31, they signed a decree whereby all Jews who refused to accept baptism into the Christian faith had to leave the country. According to the edict of expulsion, the monarchs were convinced that the only way to protect the converts once and for all from the pernicious influence of the Jews was to banish the latter forever. The royal counselors Abraham Senior and Isaac Arabanel led a delegation to plea for mercy but were rejected. The Jews were told they must leave Spain by August 2, 1492 (the day before Christopher Columbus set sail from Palos).

Many Jews went to Portugal, where there was an ancient, numerous, and well-organized community whose history was similar to that of Spain's community. In Portugal itself, over the ages the clergy and a certain sector of the aristocracy had spoken out in favor of restricting the rights of the Jews. Although their demands had borne fruit, the 15th century proved to be a particularly peaceful time for the Jews of Portugal, thanks to the protection of John I, who had taken in those fleeing persecution in the Hispanic kingdoms and had even allowed the converts to return to Judaism. During this period, some Jews reached high positions at court, as in the case of certain members of the Abrabanel family. The Jews expelled from Spain in 1492 were admitted by John II, but only for a period of eight months and upon payment of substantial tribute to the king. The hostility their arrival aroused in the common people, however, led to them being given short notice to leave the country, and all those who were not able to do so in time were declared slaves of the king. Furthermore, over 2,000 children under the age of seven were taken to the island of Sao Tomé to be brought up in the Christian faith. In 1496, King Manuel I, who at first had freed the enslaved exiles, dictated an expulsion edict in which all Jews were ordered to leave the country by the end of October 1497. This edict was followed by a campaign of forced conversion applied to virtually the whole of Portuguese Jewry. The outcome of this was that the secret practice of Judaism reached much higher proportions in Portugal than in Spain, and not even the Inquisition could put an end to it.

The Expulsion of the Jews, *by Emilio Sala Francés, 1889 (Museo de Bellas Artes, Granada). On March 31, 1492, in Granada the Catholic kings signed the expulsion edict, stating that damage by Jews to converts and Christians could thus be avoided and, in view of the futility of previous measures, also ordering the isolation of Jews in special districts, the establishment of the Inquisition, and the expulsion of Jews from Andalusia. According to the edict:*

"We order all Jews, both male and female, of all ages ... to leave ... our realms and territories with their children ... servants ... and Jewish relatives both close and distant ... by the end of the month of July ... and may they not dare to return hither or remain in such places ... neither to live nor pass through ... on pain of ... death and confiscation of all their goods," confiscation of goods being extended to all Christians who dared to hide Jews in their houses. The Jews were guaranteed the freedom to sell their possessions or to take them with them *"by land or by sea, provided that they do not take gold or silver nor minted coins nor the other things forbidden by the laws of our realm, save in merchandise that be not in the form of forbidden things or exchanged things."* Thus, at a stroke, fifteen centuries of Jewish life in the Hispanic kingdoms came to an end.

The Sephardim in the Ottoman Empire

The Jews who left Spain after the expulsion edict took effect and the converts who in later periods left Spain and Portugal are known as Sephardim, natives of Sepharad. In the hope that the expulsion was not to last long and that the Catholic kings would reverse their terrible decision, a large number of Sephardim sought a new place of settlement close to Spain, many choosing Portugal (with the results we have seen). They also settled in North Africa, northern Italy, and the Ottoman Empire, where successive waves of Jews arrived to write yet another important chapter in the history of European Judaism of Hispanic origin.

By the 16th century, the Ottoman sultans had conquered large areas of Europe (particularly in the Balkans and the Slavonic countries) and parts of Asia and North Africa. This vast territory contained a diverse population of ethnic, national, and religious groups. When Constantinople fell in 1453, bringing a thousand years of Byzantine history to an end, it was renamed Istanbul and became the capital of the Ottoman Empire. To repopulate the city, the Turks transferred large numbers of people from Turkey and the Balkans, among them many Romanita Jews, a name given to Jews born in the old Byzantine Empire whose mother tongue was Greek.

The Jews expelled from Spain took with them the splendid cultural, social, and economic heritage they had acquired in the Iberian Peninsula and were warmly welcomed by sultan Beyazid II (reigned 1481-1512), who opened the gates of the empire to them. The first places of settlement in Europe were Istanbul, Salonica—a city whose population from the 16th century on was mostly Jewish—and Edirne. They also set-tled in Safed in Palestine. By the 17th century the number of exiled Spanish Jews was clearly higher than that of the Romanita community, who had adopted the former's ways in law and religion as well as their customs and tongue. Now spoken outside Spain, this tongue developed into a different language—Judeo-Spanish.

With the legal status of "protégés," the Jews were generally treated with tolerance, as the "Sublime Porte"—the central office of the Ottoman goverment under the sultans—never attempted to limit the economic activities of minorities within its frontiers, and the Ottoman Jews were never prevented from engaging in any kind of profession or activity. Like other "infidels" within the Ottomon Empire, they were forced to pay a heavy poll tax, but they were left in peace and were free to openly practice their faith.

48

View of Istanbul and its mosques in an anonymous 17th-century painting (Museo Civico Correr, Venice). Among the Jews who held high positions at the Ottoman court in the 16th century were the Mendes, a family of Hispano-Portuguese Jews, most particularly Doña Gracia and her son-in-law and nephew Joseph Nasi. Forced to convert to Christianity in Portugal, they fled, traveled throughout Europe, and eventually settled in Istanbul in 1552, where they openly returned to Judaism and engaged in trading, competing with the Venetian merchants for control of the Levant trade. A Spanish traveler, possibly Cristóbal de Villalón, described Doña Gracia's arrival in the city (Viaje de Turquía, ed. de Salinero): "She entered Constantinople with forty horses and four triumphal carriages full of Spanish ladies and maids. She brought with her no fewer possessions than a duke of Spain, and she could do so for she is very rich; she has had influence with the Great Turk since she was in Venice, and did not wish him to grant her any other thing in his land than that all her servants should not have to wear headgear like that of the other Jews, but rather caps and clothing in the Venetian style. This he granted her and would have granted more had she so desired for the sake of having such a tributary as she."

The greatest period of well-being for the Sephardim was the 16th century, the age that also saw the height of the Ottoman Empire's political, economic, and military power, particularly during the rule of Sulayman the Magnificent (reigned 1520-66). At war with Christendom, the sultans preferred to place their trust in those who practiced other religions, so the Jews were in a better position than the Christian minorities. Examples of the high status achieved by some Jews in Ottoman society are Joseph Nasi and his aunt Doña Gracia Mendes, who served as tax collectors and counselors in the sultan's service in the mid 16th century. Originally from Spain, the wealthy Nasis had been forcibly converted to Christianity in Portugal and, after much wandering in the Low Countries, France, and Italy, finally settled in Istanbul in 1552, where they returned openly to Judaism. During Selim II's reign, Joseph Nasi controlled the foreign policy of the "Sublime Porte" and was made duke of Naxos.

In the 16th century, the communities were organized with legal bases, economic activity flourished, and there was a period of intense cultural activity. Many Jews occupied important posts related to the economy and politics, serving as ministers and senior functionaries in the imperial administration, as diplomats and translators, as tax collectors, as counselors and physicians to the sultans, and as army provisioners (an activity in which they were engaged until the 18th century). Among the Jews expelled from Spain, moreover, there was no lack of experts in international trade or of skilled workers in such fields as the textile and arms industries. Indeed, the empire developed a modern arms industry of its own. The Sephardim also settled in cities with ports on the Mediterranean, such as Salonica and Smyrna, and in important centers of communication, such as Edirne, where they created a trade network linked to other communities in Europe. This led to an extremely important exchange of goods with Amsterdam and certain Italian cities, such as Venice and Leghorn. For example, the Ottoman Empire imported silk from Venice in exchange for lead, woolen cloth, linen, cotton, furs, wax, spices, pearls from the Far East. The towns of Safed (Palestine) and Salonica (Macedonia) were important centers of the textile industry during the 16th century.

The common people engaged in a wide variety of activities on a smaller scale as button makers, musicians, actors, jewelers, goldsmiths, metal forgers (who were familiar with the processes of the gunsmith's shops of Toledo and Saragossa), pharmacists, perfumers, innkeepers,

49

View of Istanbul with the Galata Tower, 17th century (private collection, Florence). The Frenchman Nicolas de Nicolay, who traveled to Turkey in 1551 (Les quatres premiers livres de navigations et pérégrinations orientales faicts en Turquie, Lyons, 1568), described the situation of the Jews: "What particularly attracts the attention is the great number of Jews who live in Turkey and in Greece, and especially in Constantinople. Their numbers continue to swell, and this is due to the fact that they trade throughout the entire country ... as the most diverse products arrive here by land and by sea from all over the world. To them belong the commercial companies of greatest importance in Constantinople and also the shops, which are full of the most diverse merchandise. Also, there are skillful artisans, teachers, and foremen among them ... in particular among the Marranos expelled from Spain and Portugal. The Jews are also outstanding in their knowledge of languages ... so that they are sought as interpreters."

dyers, and, in port towns, even as stevedores. Sephardic Jews also founded the first printing press in the empire, producing books in Istanbul two years after the expulsion. Other presses in Salonica, Smyrna, and Edirne printed hundreds of books in Hebrew and Judeo-Spanish. The first Hebrew printing press was established in Safed in 1563, and its books were soon in demand worldwide.

Guided by rabbis and leading men of the community, the communities were strictly organized in accordance with the *takkanot,* or ordinances. The leaders were usually members of the powerful oligarchy who appointed their own functionaries—administrators, tax collectors, those in charge of relations with the authorities, etc. The Ottoman Tanzimat reforms of the 19th century, designed to strengthen the ailing empire by granting rights to its many minorities, saw the appearance of the chief rabbi, under whose religious control all the communities lay.

The economic and political decline of the empire began in the 17th century with a process that culminated in the 19th century. One indirect but important reason for this decline was the expansion of Atlantic trade to the detriment of Mediterranean trade. The situation affected all minorities in general and the Jewish community in particular, leading to general stagnation and decline accompanied by isolated instances of economic and cultural growth out of keeping with the general tendency. The crisis in the empire coincided with economic recovery and industrial development in western and central Europe, in the late 16th century favoring the appearance of European economic establishments in the empire's commercial towns and ports. These were the French, English, and Dutch Levant companies, and the Sephardim collaborated actively with them as agents and suppliers. Through these companies, Europe was able to gain a foothold in the empire and gradually increase its influence.

In the 17th century a commissions system was established by which political, legal, economic, and religious privileges were granted to Europeans who settled in the empire. This system had two far-reaching effects. First, it encouraged European Jews, mainly of Italian and

Jew, *etching from a painting by Jean-Baptiste Vanmour in M. de Ferriol,* Recueil de cent estampes représentant différentes nations du Levant, Paris, 1714 *(Museum of the Jewish Diaspora, Tel Aviv). The Ottoman sultans held the Jewish contribution to medicine—and to many other fields—in high esteem. Outstanding among these Jews in the 16th century were the members of the Hamon family of Granada, particularly Joseph and his son Moses.*

Jewish cloth-seller in Istanbul, watercolor by Amedeo Preziosi, 1855-57, in Constantinople customes album *(Gennadius Library, Athens). The textile industry, one of the most important of those developed by the Sephardim in Turkey, provided thousands of Jews with jobs. Its center was Salonica, where clothes, textiles, and equipment for the Janissaries were made. Textiles made by the Jews of Salonica were occasionally used to pay the community's taxes.*

Portuguese origin (who were the driving force in the modernization of the Ottoman Sephardic world), to settle in the commercial towns and ports. Second, this process strengthened the position of the Christians in the empire, thanks to the support they began receiving from the European powers. Indeed, from the end of the 18th century, these nations came to play a decisive part in the consolidation of nationalistic movements in the Balkans, particularly among the Greek and Armenian populations. This same position of strength also enabled Christians to gradually replace Jews working in important positions related to the economy, such as those involved in international trade and banking, and also to politics. Rivalry between Jews and Christians grew, at times accompanied by accusations and persecution, particularly in areas where central authority had become weak and the communities were subject to the arbitrary actions of virtually independent local governors. This happened in Egypt (where even the Jews of Cairo were expelled for a time in the 18th century), Palestine, and a number of other places.

With the empire suffering an economic crisis, the empire's textile industry began to decline. The death blow was dealt by the Industrial Revolution in Europe and the subsequent technological development that made it unnecessary for the European powers to import manufactured textiles. At the end of the 16th century, the Safed textile center collapsed, leading to the virtual disappearance of a previously rich and vigorous community. To a lesser extent this crisis also affected Salonica, which managed to survive until the beginning of the 19th century by supplying the domestic market.

Differences existed between the Sephardic Jewish communities of the Ottoman Empire and those within the Christian environment of the rest of Europe, known as Ashkenazim, a term applied to the Jews in German lands (from *ashkenaz*, a Hebrew word for "Germany"). These differences were due in part to differing religious and legal developments, as, for example, in the codification of religious and legal disputes in the *Shulhan Arukh*, by Joseph Caro (who had left Spain as a child when the Jews were expelled and settled in Safed). Many cen-

51

turies before, a rift had appeared between the rationalistic ideas of certain eminent Hispanic rabbis and the concepts of the German pietists and Ashkenazic mystical movements. The discrepancy between these two branches of European Judaism was reflected not only in the way of thinking but also in everyday practice. Furthermore, the Sephardim of the Ottoman Empire had, to a large extent, become detached from European Jewry and now found themselves far removed from the great ideological movements that were to bring agitation to the Jewish world in the rest of Europe from the 16th to the 18th century. For example, they had had no part in the undercurrents of skepticism of the secret Jews who had returned to the open practice of Judaism in Amsterdam in the 16th and 17th centuries, and the echoes of the Haskalah (Enlightenment), which developed in central Europe in the 18th century, reached them only faintly, and then not until the second half of the 19th century. Nor were they touched by the changes brought by Polish Hasidism, which affected Judaism in eastern Europe, or by the polemics of its opponents.

One terrible storm that rocked European Jewry, however, originated in the Ottoman Empire, in the very bosom of the Sephardic community. This was the movement of the pseudo-messiah Shabbetai Zevi (1626-76). Born in Smyrna, he was deeply influenced by the teachings of the cabalist Isaac ben Solomon Luria (1534-72), called Ari ("Lion"), who had a large following in Safed. According to the Lurianic cabala, the situation of the Jews—scattered in exile and facing humiliation and persecution— was soon to change. Indeed, the entire universe was soon to be restored to its proper order by the Jewish people themselves, bringing forth the Messiah as the consummate act of earthly redemption. Luria's vision was made particularly appealing by its proclamation that this process of restoration was nearly completed and that the final redemption of the Jews was soon to take place. In 1648 Zevi proclaimed himself the messiah and named the year 1666 as the millennium. His appearance seemed to confirm Luria's vision, and Zevi drew wild masses and won over a large following that included eminent rabbis

Hakham *(rabbi) and a widow in the Pera cemetery, color lithograph by Amedeo Preziosi, Constantinople, 1857, printed in* Stamboul souvenir d'Orient, *Paris, 1865 (Museum of the Jewish Diaspora, Tel Aviv). Today only four Jewish cemeteries with graves dating from before the beginning of this century remain in Istanbul—Kuzguncuk, Hasköy, Ortaköy, and the Italian cemetery. The tombstones, which date from the 17th and 18th centuries, often belong to the type seen*

in this picture—a marble block reminiscent of a coffin that in many cases rests on a rectangular base; the sides are carved with floral motifs and funeral inscriptions in Hebrew, although these were also written in Judeo-Spanish beginning in the 17th century.

and scholars from all the Jewish communities from Aleppo to Amsterdam and London and from Hamburg and Lvov to Egypt and North Africa. Many sold all their possessions and made ready to set out for the Holy Land. Great miracles were expected.

Zevi announced he was going to Constantinople, where, he said, the sultan would surrender his throne and he would become the king of kings. In 1666 he attempted to land in Constantinople, was captured, and under pressure from Mehmet IV converted to Islam, as did many of his followers, leading to the formation of the Donmeh sect within the Muslim religion, with its center of worship at Salonica (this center existed until this century). Zevi's apostasy caused a profound shock, and many Jews refused to believe it, seeing it as a mystery that would lead to some new revelation. For many years afterward the spirit of Shabbeteanism lived on in communities all over Europe, communities agitated by the propaganda of those who continued to believe in their apostate messiah.

In 1832 most of Greece won its independence from the Ottoman Empire, and only Macedonia and Salonica remained within the empire (Greece conquered Salonica in 1912). Within the empire, tension between Jews and Greek and Armenian Christians increased as a result of questions of trade and religion. This tension appeared with the accusations of ritual murder so often heard in the 19th century. Furthermore, in the heart of the communities, the differences between the rich families and the rabbis and the great mass of poor (increasing because of the economic crisis) grew more and more acute. These differences were finally to shake the very foundation of the—until then—stable community organization. The largest Jewish populations continued to be those of Istanbul, Smyrna, and, above all, Salonica, where there were over 75,000 Jews in the mid-19th century. Thanks to its busy port, the growth of the tobacco industry, and an increase in tobacco imports to Macedonia, the city managed to recover from the devastating blow suffered by the textile industry when the elite Janissaries, which had always ordered the bulk of Salonica's cloth production, were disbanded in 1826.

53

Interior of an Istanbul synagogue, color lithograph from Syria, the Holy Land and Asia Minor Illustrated, *by J. Carne, London, 1840 (National and University Library, Jerusalem). When the Jews expelled from Sepharad reached the Ottoman Empire they adopted the same form of congregational (*kehalim, *singular* kahal*) organization as the resident Jewish communities, which were separate and independent and grouped according to their places of origin. Each* kahal *had its own synagogue, which served as a religious and social center. The congregations of the main cities, such as Istanbul and Salonica, were extremely large. The thirty-nine that existed in Istanbul at the end of the 17th century included the Portugal, Catalonia, and Córdoba congregations, while those in Salonica included the Evora, Otranto, Italy, Aragon, Lisbon, Castile, and Catalonia congregations.*

The reforms set in motion to modernize the Ottoman Empire together with the growing European influence had repercussions in the Jewish world, bringing changes to the Jewish system of education and indeed to the habits of everyday life. In education, the creation of the modern European Christian schools in the early 19th century spurred the Jewish community to follow the example, the process culminating with the introduction of the Alliance Israélite Universelle group of schools. These belonged to an organization founded in France in 1860 whose aim was to provide Jews with the necessary means that would allow them to be integrated into the modern world. One product of this educational process was a new cultural elite of laymen, a large number of whom became community leaders.

The long economic crisis afflicting the foundering empire led many Sephardim to emigrate to countries in Europe (particularly France), to Palestine, and to the Americas. New waves of migrations followed the Balkan Wars, when Salonica became a Greek possession, and World War I. These migrations were spurred by the deteriorating legal situation, the anti-Jewish laws passed in the 1920s (which culminated in the pogrom of 1931), and the economic and social relegation of Jews due to the waves of Greek immigrants who entered the country in population exchanges between Greece and Turkey. The Jews who remained in the city paid dearly for their loyalty, for during World War II virtually the whole of the Salonica community as well as the communities of many other Greek towns were deported and later exterminated in the gas chambers. In Turkey, on the other hand—by then a national state with the same boundaries as those of today—Jews were granted the same civil rights as the rest of the population. Zionism, a cause which took root in many sectors of the Turkish community, attracted a large number of followers, although the Zionists met with opposition, particularly in Salonica, in the form of the strong and very well consolidated socialist Jewish workers' movement.

Above: Woolen wall carpet with silk embroidery from the Ottoman Empire, 17th century (Wolfson Museum, Hechal Shlomo, Jerusalem). Opposite: Shivviti, by Moses Ganbash, Istanbul, 1838-39 (Jewish Museum, New York). Shivviti ("I have set") votive panels for adorning the synagogue or home came into use during the 18th century. Their name comes from the first words of Psalm 16:8 ("I have set the Lord always before me"), which appear in their ornamentation.

Many were decorated profusely, the most common motifs being the candelabrum and buildings representing sacred places in the Holy Land. This paper shivviti decorated with paint, ink, and strips of paper—a technique typical of Turkish illuminated manuscripts—presents a map of the Holy Land featuring a Turkish ship (bottom) serving Turkey and Palestine and the port of Yafo (right), with Mount Carmel and the city of Acre next to it; in the middle,

Jerusalem and the temple area (right), followed (left) by the Mount of Olives and the city of Shechem; top, the villages of Galilee (right), the Lake of Gennesaret, and the town of Tiberias (center) with the tombs of the sages (Maimonides, Rabbi Johanan ben Zakkai, and others) and the mountain and city of Hebron; above this, the Jordan and (top right) the Dead Sea.

The Jerusalem of Holland

Below: The city of Amsterdam, engraving by Georg Braun and Frans Hogenberg, Civitates Orbis Terrarum, Cologne, 1572 (Salamanca University Library). Opposite top: View of the Overtoom (left) near Amsterdam in an 18th-century engraving (Bibliothèque Nationale, Paris). The Jews of Amsterdam were not legally recognized until November 8, 1616, the authorities of the Dutch provinces having first to consult two legal experts.

In his report, the famous theologist and jurist Hugo Grotius (1583-1645) wrote with extreme pragmatism: "It is obvious that God wishes the Jews to live somewhere, and if such is the case then why not here? What is of great importance is that the Christian religion should receive some advantage from the Jews. Their scholars can help us to study Hebrew. The way in which the Jews have remained true to their religion can serve as an example to us

When the Jews of the Hispanic kingdoms were forced by the Catholic kings to choose between conversion or expulsion, most opted for the second alternative, and many of those who chose to convert continued to practice Judaism in secret. To these must be added all those Jews who settled in Portugal in 1492 and were obliged to embrace Christianity five years later. Over both groups loomed the Inquisition, ever ready to lead them to the stake should they be found guilty of backsliding. This situation led to a long and arduous historical process from the beginning of the 16th century until the first quarter of the 18th century: the development of the so-called Portuguese Nation, those converts who, having lived for many generations as Christians in the Iberian Peninsula, left their countries so as to be able to return openly to the faith of their fathers.

These new Jews had lived far removed from the open practice of Judaism (itself not possible for several generations), and the little knowledge of Judaism they had was based on the already meager experience their forefathers

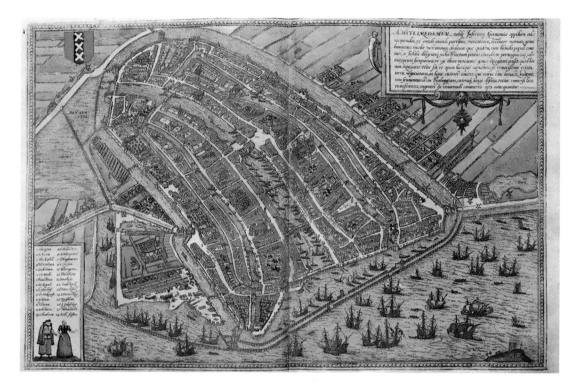

had been able to pass on to them. As they had no exact information on subjects relating to Judaism, they had to start again virtually from nothing and make up for lost time by rushing through a thicket of questions to which they did not always find answers.

The encounter with official Judaism, with the *halakah*, or religious law, with its numerous precepts and dictates cannot have been easy for many of these people who had grown up in a world with a very different culture and indeed a very different mentality. This explains why some underwent an identity crisis that left them alienated yet again from the synagogue. Intellectual activity was, then, typical of the Western Sephardim, who until well after the turn of the 18th century continued to question rabbinic authority, the validity of at least part of the talmudic heritage, the exclusive nature of Judaism, and the status of the Jews as the chosen people of Israel. Yet in spite of the difficulties experienced by many of those who returned to Judaism, the phrase used by Solomon ibn Verga in his *Shevet Yehudah* ("The Staff of Judah")

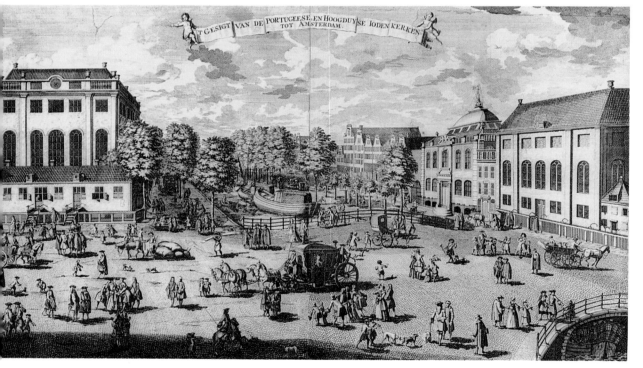

View of Amsterdam showing the Portuguese synagogue (left) and two Ashkenazic synagogues (right), engraving by Adolf van der Laan (1684-1755), c. 1710 (Joods Historisch Museum, Amsterdam). The first Ashkenazic Jews who settled in Amsterdam, c. 1620, were socially and financially dependent on the Sephardic community, working mainly as pedlars and secondhand dealers. In 1636, they began organizing their own religious services under Rabbi Moses Weile

of Prague, and their numbers grew considerably, particularly after the arrival of Polish Jews fleeing from Chmielnicki's massacres (1648-49) and the Swedish invaders (1655). In 1671, the Ashkenazim built a lavish synagogue close to the Sephardic one on the other side of the canal. Another, adjacent synagogue was raised in 1686, followed by two more (1700 and 1730) in the same area.

... However, assuming that the Jews are allowed to settle in the country and that they are granted freedom of worship, we must give special consideration to the conditions in which such settlement is to take place ... Two factors must be taken into account: the good of the Christian religion and the good of the state. Anything connected with these aims should be permitted to Jews and Christians alike."

A large number of Portuguese New Christians settled in southeast France and in towns such as Bordeaux and Bayonne, living until 1730 under the guise of Catholics and, except for certain exceptional cases, left alone by the Inquisition. Others set out on a new wave of migrations to the Low Countries, settling first in Antwerp and later in Amsterdam, which became the main center of Sephardic mercantile trade at the end of the 16th century. Although the Portuguese and Spanish converts who swelled the ranks of the Amsterdam community practiced Judaism in private and were never troubled by the authorities, they did not gain official recognition as Jews until 1616, by which time they had become a decisive factor in the economic and commercial development not only of the city but also of the republic.

By the middle of the 17th century, the Amsterdam community had become the most famous and prosperous in Europe. It reached its greatest heights in the first quarter of the 18th century and remained an important Jewish center for almost three hundred years more. From

might well be applied: "And what good will it do our king and master to sprinkle holy water over the Jews? Know you, sir, that Judaism is one of our incurable ills."

Like the Jews before them who had left Spain in 1492, some converts chose to take refuge in those parts of Italy that did not belong to Spain. These new immigrants soon became part of the complex commercial web that stretched from the Ottoman Empire to the Low Countries, their business experience proving particularly attractive to the Italian lords and princes, and indeed even to the popes. Thus, the people of the "Nation" enjoyed special privileges in the Papal States, as in the port of Ancona, where they were able to practice Judaism openly and live in peace. This situation continued until the persecutions unleashed in 1555 by Pope Paul IV. Other settlements of converts were in Florence and Ferrara, but from the end of the 16th century, the most important Sephardic center in Italy was Venice, its splendor inherited in subsequent centuries by centers in Pisa and Leghorn in the duchy of Tuscany.

57

Above: The Sephardic cemetery at Ouderkerk, Amsterdam, in an engraving by the Dutch artist Romeyn de Hooghe (1645-1708), c. 1680 (Joods Historisch Museum, Amsterdam). Located along the Amstel River a few miles from Amsterdam, the cemetery was established in 1614. Its spectacular mausoleums contrast with the usual soberness of Jewish cemeteries, while the symbols on the gravestones (worked on by famous Dutch sculptors) *reflect strong Catholic influence. The cemetery contains the graves of a number of eminent figures from the Amsterdam Sephardic Jewish community, among them Manasseh ben Israel, Joseph Athias, Elijah Montalto (died 1616, physician to the grand duke of Tuscany and later to the queen of France Marie de' Medici), and two men associated with Baruch Spinoza—his father, Michael (died 1654), and Orobio de Castro, one of his fiercest opponents.*

the very beginning, it was one of the best organized communities in Europe, its numerous institutions being the focal point of the religious, social, and cultural life of its members. The community's educational system was particularly outstanding, as it was very different in concept from the traditional Jewish schools of central and eastern Europe. Its extensive community library, which belonged to the Etz Hayyim rabbinic academy, may be considered the first Jewish public library. In Amsterdam, furthermore, hundreds of publications were printed in Hebrew, Spanish, Portuguese, and even Yiddish.

Spanish involvement in the Thirty Years War, as well as wars with the Netherlands and France and other territorial disputes, brought the country to a financial crisis. Some of this was

Two engravings by Bernard Picart from Cérémonies et coutumes réligieuses de tous les peuples du Monde, *1725 (Biblioteca Nacional, Madrid). Top: Putting on phylacteries. Above: The Hoshana Rabba festival in the Portuguese synagogue of Amsterdam. In their reencounter with Judaism, the Portuguese and Spanish new Jews underwent a period of mental turmoil. Their situation was exactly the opposite of that experienced by the Haskalah Jews—the Jews of*

the Jewish Enlightenment in central Europe—who came out of their physical and mental ghettos to draw closer to modern European culture. The new Jews left behind their European environment to follow the narrow path of the minority; a minority with laws and customs very different from those of the Christian environment to which these crypto-Jews belonged at least intellectually. The path chosen by some was to estrange them from the synagogue and

cause them to lose their unique identity in the mainstream. Such was the case of Baruch Spinoza, Uriel da Costa, and many others.

59

Interior of the Portuguese Synagogue of Amsterdam,
oil painting on canvas by Emanuel de Witte, c. 1680
(Israel Museum, Jerusalem). Around 1670, when the
old Sephardic synagogue of Amsterdam had become
too small for its congregation, work began on
another. The new synagogue was inaugurated in 1675
in a ceremony with a choir and orchestra, followed by
six days of celebrations. In its day it was the largest
synagogue in the world.

Aristocrats and Intellectuals

By the end of the 16th century Hamburg had become an important commercial center. In 1595 the first families of Portuguese New Christians settled there and when the Bank of Hamburg was founded in 1609, its shareholders included more than forty merchants belonging to the "Nation," most of them financiers, shipowners, sugar, coffee, and tobacco importers, and textile merchants. By the time the Jews of Hamburg were given permission to celebrate their religious ceremonies publicly in 1650, the community had grown to some seven hundred members, one being Diego Teixeira de Sampayo (Abraham Senior), formerly a Catholic who had lived in Antwerp until 1646 as a supplier to Philip IV and whose conversion

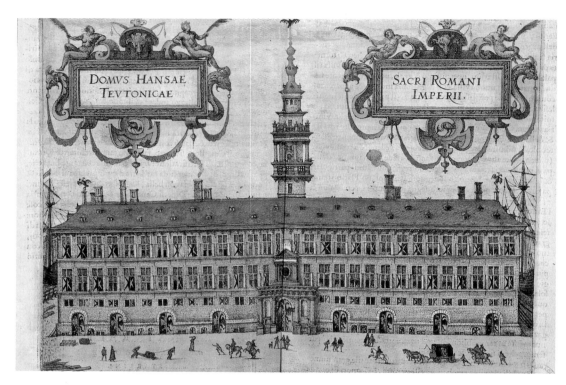

DOMVS HANSAE TEVTONICAE

SACRI ROMANI IMPERII.

The first rabbis in the Amsterdam community came from the Ottoman Empire, Italy, and the Ashkenazic world, but with the passage of time, rabbis who had studied at the city's rabbinic academy, such as Manasseh ben Israel, swelled their ranks. Fearful that they might fail in ensuring that the new Jews readapt to the Jewish environment, these rabbis, together with Jewish community leaders, severely suppressed the least sign of freethinking or departure from the strictest of orthodoxy. The members of the "Nation" themselves—having finally obtained the right to practice Judaism openly—tended to be strict observers of tradition; but because they had been deprived of a deep understanding of the traditions of Jewish life, some inevitably found themselves dissatisied with the Judaism and questioned aspects of the religion. This led to various famous instances of excommunication: Uriel da Costa, a convert born in Oporto, who questioned the validity of certain observances and wrote criticism of the Talmud; Juan Prado, who studied medicine and theology at Alcalá

blamed on Philip IV's chief minister, the conde de Olivares, and after his downfall in 1643 a new wave of Spanish converts reached Holland, fleeing both the financial crisis and the Inquisition, which by the middle of the 17th century had begun to intensify its attacks on the Portuguese Nation. Among those who fled to Amsterdam were rich merchants, important figures from the world of finance, intellectuals, literati (some famous in the peninsular literary academies), doctors, and scientists. In Holland, the great businessmen of the Sephardic community were typical examples of the baroque world, indistinguishable in their appearance, attire, and habits from the members of the aristocracy throughout Europe. Maintaining close ties with the Iberian language and culture, they became the patrons of writers, artists, and such literary academies as the Floridos and the Sitibundos, founded at this time in Amsterdam in the style of the Spanish academies of the golden age. As the result of these migrations and of others from Germany, Poland, and Lithuania, the Amsterdam community consisted of 5,000 Jews by 1657.

to Judaism caused an international uproar. In 1654 Queen Christina of Sweden stayed at his home and subsequently named him her diplomatic agent in Hamburg. The diplomatic representatives of Poland and Portugal were also Sephardim. Among other illustrious Jews who belonged to this community were the writer and physician Rodrigo de Castro (1550-1627) and the lexicographer and physician Benjamin Musafia (1609-72).

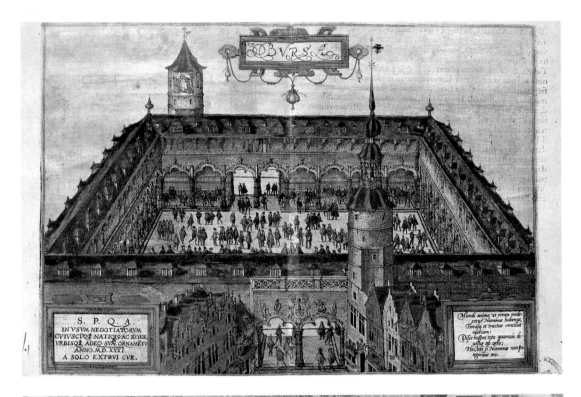

de Henares University in Spain and became an outspoken critic of the Jewish oral law; and above all the philosopher Baruch Spinoza, born in Amsterdam, who despite an impeccable religious education was influenced by the Cartesian school of thought and adopted an attitude highly critical of Judaism.

Closely linked to the Amsterdam community was the community in Hamburg, a major northern European port that traded mainly in sugar, spices, and other products from the colonies. There various families of Portuguese New Christians settled in 1595 and formed the basis of the future opulent Sephardic community, which in 1612 was formally recognized by the city's assembly. The glory of the Hamburg community lived on until the end of the 17th century.

In 1655, Amsterdam's Rabbi Manasseh ben Israel made contact with Oliver Cromwell, then leader of the English Protectorate, in an attempt to obtain permission for Jews to enter England. The jealousy of English merchants, fearful of competition, defeated the rabbi's proposal, but from then on members of the Portuguese Nation already in England were tacitly allowed to practice Judaism and even to build a synagogue. Furthermore, in 1660, after the restoration of the monarchy, Charles II officially recognized the Sephardic community. The community grew, although with the passage of time it was surpassed in number, if not in prestige, by the Ashkenazic community that settled in London in 1690. Sephardic Jews from western Europe also found communities in the New World.

Political and social change in the mid 18th century took their toll on the "Nation's" glory, alienating its members from their main source of wealth—international trade—and resulting in the demographic, social, and cultural decline of the western Sephardic communities. However, because of its special idiosyncrasies, its links with the Gentile world, and its deep knowledge of the Christian culture of Europe (in which the majority of its number had grown up), western Sephardic Jewry can be taken as the great precursor in the modernization of European Jewry, a modernization that was not to take place until much later.

61

important part in this field, as did the Jews who settled in London after the middle of the 17th century, when the British East India Company, which held the monopoly on British trade with India, allowed them to import precious stones. The stones were sent to Amsterdam for cutting, a speciality controlled in the 17th and 18th centuries by Sephardic Jews. The greatest demand for diamonds came from the courts of Europe, whose suppliers were the so-called

courtier Jews. The diamond workers, whose numbers had trebled with the Jewish migrations from eastern Europe, formed an important pressure group in Holland and Belgium, where in 1893 they led a strike for a minimum wage. After World War II Jewish refugees from Europe founded diamond-cutting centers in Palestine, Cuba, Brazil, Mexico, and the United States.

Italy and Humanism

At the end of the 15th century, Europe emerged from the Middle Ages to enter modern history. The transition is marked by the Renaissance and by humanism, which from its cradle in Italy spread across Germany and western Europe. The new ideas brought with them the restoration of culture, the development of national sentiment, and freedom of worship. They were also destined to cause a rift within the Catholic Church, which from Rome controlled the destinies of the Christian kingdoms.

In the previous centuries, Jews living in Italy had enjoyed a period of relative calm. The popes had not proved to be intransigent and, in fact, nowhere were the decrees of the Lateran Councils applied with less severity than in the Papal States. As in the German Empire, the fragmentation of the country into city states and independent duchies meant that Jews could always find somewhere to take them in. If one state expelled them, they would be welcomed in another. During the Middle Ages, most of the Jewish population of Italy lived in the south, in the Kingdom of the Two Sicilies. Here they were

engaged in major medical and scientific studies and the transmission of classical knowledge. The talmudic academies that thrived most were those of Bari and Otranto.

This peace was not affected by the Norman conquest of the 11th century, and, indeed, at the end of the 12th century the situation actually improved when southern Italy changed hands to become a possession of the German Empire. This was particularly so in the reign of Frederick II (1212-50), who took the Jews directly under his protection and granted them monopolies in the silk and dyeing industries and foreign trade. The situation changed, however, when Sicily fell into the hands of the Angevins and a period of persecution and forced conversion began. When Sicily became a possession of Aragon in 1282, the fate of its Jewish population was similar to that of the communities in the Iberian kingdom; in 1492 the Catholic kings' expulsion order was enforced against the Jews of both Sicily and Sardinia, obliging them to leave the islands. They were never to return. Furthermore, when the kingdom of Naples

dancers, and musicians. They were also doctors, some as physicians to the Italian courts, even to the papal court.

became a Spanish possession (1503), its Jews were forced to leave (1541).

The Jewish communities in Venice, Padua, Mantua, and Florence were among the most important in northern Italy, the greater or lesser degree of freedom they enjoyed depending on local laws and the attitude of the rulers. Especially favorable was the treatment received under the Medicis in Florence, the Gonzagas in Mantua, and the Estes in Ferrara (who upheld the religious rights of the Jews until Ferrara was incorporated into the Papal States in 1598). Despite this general state of well-being, the Jews were not unaffected by the waves of anti-Semitism provoked by the sermons of the Franciscans and Dominicans; sermons that culminated in accusations of ritual murder in Trent in 1475.

The Jews of Italy have always been closely associated with the ideas of the Renaissance, having made an outstanding contribution to its development. Perhaps the most important part was played by those who taught the Christian scholars who came to study Hebrew wisdom and

Above: A Jew touching a mezuzah *from the* Rothschild Miscellany, *northern Italy, c. 1470 (Israel Museum, Jerusalem). Including 300 illustrations in gold and beautiful colors, the* Rothschild Miscellany *is made up of over fifty works, both religious—from Psalms, Proverbs, Job, and a prayer book for daily use and at festivals—and secular—historical books, chronicles, and works on philosophy and morality. Above right: Jewish widow from the* Rothschild

Miscellany. *Renaissance ways were reflected in the everyday life of the wealthier Jews, particularly those of northern Italy who had made their fortunes in banking and moneylending. There, Jews adopted the customs and clothing typical of the enveloping culture. Jews from the aristocratic families commissioned the most eminent artists of the times to paint their portraits, paid for manuscripts to be illuminated (sparing no expense), while their*

household furnishings reflected a refined sensitivity. The Miscellany *is a fine example of the many Hebrew illuminated manuscripts of the 15th and 16th centuries.*

literature, an interest which, in the case of Germany, was to lead to the Reformation. Though such interest was perhaps not accompanied by an overfondness for Jews themselves, certain theologians and intellectuals were now speaking out against the use of violence against the Jewish people. Imbued with the spirit of the Renaissance, Jewish thinkers acted as guides to the Christian humanists and theologians drawn to the cabala, in which they saw allusions to Christian dogma. Pope Sixtus IV (1471-84) had cabalistic works translated into Latin, and the *Zohar*, an essential book in Jewish mystical doctrine, was translated by Baruch of Benevento upon the request of Egidio da Viterbo, who had invited Elijah Levita (1468-1549), the eminent grammarian and biblical scholar from Germany, to become his teacher of Hebrew. Levita was offered the post of professor of Hebrew at the University of Paris and was the key figure linking Jewish grammarians with the Christian Hebraists of the Reformation. Such a predilection for philosophy and the sciences on the part of these eminent rabbis led to a certain amount

of friction within the communities, particularly with the rabbis of German origin who had fled from their own countries to settle in Italy and were much more deeply attached to mystical pietism (for these rabbis, the Italians were anathema). One such eminent rabbi was Elijah Delmedigo (1460-97), originally from Crete, a rationalist philosopher who attained the privileged position of lecturer at the University of Padua and was a trusted counselor and familiar figure at the court of Lorenzo the Magnificent in Florence, where he associated with the Christian scholar Pico della Mirandola. In the 16th and 17th centuries, hundreds of Jews studied and graduated at the Italian universities, particularly in Padua, in the 17th century the greatest center of medical studies.

For the Jews of Italy the prosperity of the 15th and 16th centuries did not continue beyond the 1550s. During the Renaissance, the situation in the Papal States was in general favorable, particularly under the popes of the house of Medici, such as Leo X (1513-21) and Clement VII (1523-34), who even gave credence to the offer

A physician visits a patient in Avicenna's Canon of Medicine. *This illustration opens the fourth book of the* Canon, *which deals with different types of fever. At top left, the patient, in bed, is attended by the doctor, whose horse is held by a servant outside; at right, the doctor leaves the sickroom; bottom, a notary reads the patient's will.*

of a certain Arabian Jewish adventurer named David Reubeni to raise an army of Jews from the East to fight against the Turks. However, from the middle of the 16th century, the situation deteriorated, with the shadow of the Reformation looming large and the church holding the Jews responsible for the new heresy. With the Counter Reformation and the measures adopted by the church at the Council of Trent (1545-63), which were to remain in force for a further two and a half centuries, the long period of papal tolerance came to an abrupt end. In the face of ever-increasing Protestantism and in an attempt to protect Catholics from exposure to such heresy, the church acted with particular fury against the Jews. The bad omens were confirmed when, in 1553, the Talmud was burnt yet again in Rome and in many other Italian cities. When Pope Paul IV (1555-59) strictly enforced the church canons, Jewish economic activity in the Papal States ceased, and Jews were virtually reduced to the level of outcasts, forced to live apart in districts of their own and to wear a special cap. They were also deprived of the right to own

63

Cremona, the Talmud once again being seized and burnt. Expulsion from the duchy itself came in 1597. The situation was no better in Venice, the first Italian state to require all Jews to live in one area within the city (1516), in this case, in an old cannon foundry on an island (the Venetian word for foundry, *gheto*, gives us *ghetto*). Despite this, temporary expulsions still took place. By the end of the 16th century, the ghetto had become a common feature in Italian towns from Rome to the Alps and was to remain so until the 19th century. There were noteworthy differences between ghettos, however, from the wretched, overpopulated Trastevere ghetto in Rome, to that of Leghorn, a ghetto in name only whose Jews, under the protection of the house of Lorraine, had complete liberty to engage in trade and so make a decisive contribution to the city's development.

Despite general economic decline in Italy in the 17th century, the Italian ghettos seem to have remained relatively unaffected, and literature, art, and rabbinic studies continued to thrive within them.

property of any kind and were allowed to work only as secondhand dealers. In an attempt to convert Jews to Christianity, the church obliged them to attend sermons (a practice that continued in Rome until 1870), and the papal police often abducted Jewish children, who were later baptized into the Christian faith against their parents' will. Under Paul IV, the Jews of Ancona, a large port whose busy traffic was controlled mainly by Portuguese New Christians and Jews expelled from Naples, saw their ancient privileges abolished and were cruelly persecuted. When sultan Sulayman II intervened at the request of Joseph Nasi and demanded that the pope free all Jews of Turkish nationality, some were saved from the stake. Finally, in 1569, Pius V expelled the Jews from the Italian Papal States, allowing them to live only in Rome and Ancona. While some sought refuge in Ferrara, Mantua, Milan, and Tuscany, a large number fled to the Ottoman Empire.

In 1553, the duchy of Milan became a Spanish possession, and in 1559 Jews were expelled from the cities of Pavia, Lodi, and

Top: A rabbinic school from Maimonides' Mishne Torah, *Italy, c. 1450 (Vatican Library). Above: A rabbinic court in session from Jacob ben Asher's* Arba'ah Turim, *Mantua, 1435 (Vatican Library). The establishment of the ghetto in Italy in the late 16th century placed considerable restrictions on Jewish academic life, to the extent that enlightened Jews were no longer able to devote themselves to secular studies and lost their posts at the academic*

institutions. Life inside the ghettos was, however, extremely active. Several ghettos, such as those of Venice, Padua, Pesaro, and the Piedmont communities, had at least one synagogue, some boasting luxurious architecture. Religious and moral observance was strict but not oppressive, and the ghettos' social services covered all the people's needs, the organization of the Venice and Rome communities being particularly outstanding in this

respect. Isolation brought changes in literary production, and the number of books written on the cabala, ethics, and talmudic studies increased. Important works were also written by poets and playwrights, such as Moses Hayyim Luzzatto.

Medieval Judeo-Spanish Science

Astronomers Observing the Stars from
Maimonides' *Mishne Torah*, Italy, c. 1450
(Vatican Library). European Jews first made a
contribution to the science of their age in Sepharad,
although they were not to do so again until the age
of emancipation, well after the beginning of the
19th century. Their extremely important scientific
work was based not only on their own research but
also on that of classical Greece, which reached
them via the Arabs. Of the large number of
important 12th-century Jewish scientists, one was
Moses Sephardi of Huesca (Pedro Alfonso), who
specialized in the fields of medicine and
astronomy, first in Aragon and later in England,
where he was physician to Henry I and taught
Walcher of Lorraine, prior of Malvern. His Latin

translation of Aljuarismi's astronomical tables was
used by Adelard of Bath. Another Jew, Abraham bar
Hiyya, who worked in Barcelona, wrote several
works on geometry and astronomy. With the aid of
Plato of Tivoli, he also translated a dozen scientific
works into Latin, one of the most important being the
Sefer ha-Ibbur, which he himself either wrote or at
least compiled and thanks to which geometry and
trigonometry were brought to Christian Europe.
However, 12th-century Sepharad's most outstanding
Jewish scientist was Abraham ibn Ezra of Tudela
(c.1098-c.1164), who visited a large number of cities
in Italy, France, and England. Ibn Ezra's outstanding
contribution to astronomy includes the *Tabulae
pisanae*, a work widely diffused throughout Europe
and referred to by the Christian scholars Roger
Bacon (13th century) and Nicholas of Cusa (14th
century). Jews also played an active part in the great

cultural project begun in the 12th century by the
archbishop of Toledo Don Raimundo, through
whom that city became one of the most prominent
in Europe thanks to the Latin translations of the
scientific and philosophical works of Islam and
classical Greece by Christian, Jewish, and Muslim
scholars. This work continued during the reign of
Alfonso VIII and particularly under Alfonso X
(when translation into Castilian and original
scientific works reached their zenith). In this way
not only the philosophical works of Plato and
Aristotle, but also Greek, Arabic, and Jewish
knowledge of medicine, astronomy, and other
sciences reached all Europe. Among the most
important scientists during the reign of Alfonso X
were Isaac ben Sid and Judah ben Moses Cohen,
one of whose greatest works was the Alfonsine
tables, unsurpassed until the appearance of Kepler's
Rudolphine tables in 1627. Together with other
Jews, these collaborated on the *Libros del Saber de
Astronomía*, written under the patronage of Alfonso
X. Maimonides, for his part, made a particularly
outstanding contribution to the field of medicinal
science. His works, which were written in Arabic
and were soon translated into Hebrew and Latin,
dealt with specific subjects (asthma, sexual
intercourse, hemorrhoids, etc.), general themes
(the names of drugs, poisons and their antidotes,
etc.), and questions of doctrine (commentaries on
the aphorisms of Hippocrates and the works of
Galen and a collection of medical aphorisms).
Maimonides' most far-reaching medical work was
the *Guide to Good Health*, which circulated in
Christian circles under the title *De regimine
sanitatis*. Another Jew, Hasdai Crescas (Barcelona,
died c. 1412), whose work influenced both Pico
della Mirandola and Spinoza, wrote a criticism
of Aristotelian physics. In the reign of Peter IV
of Aragon, certain Majorcan Jews, among them
Abraham Cresques and his son Jafuda,
distinguished themselves both in the making
of precision instruments and the drawing of
sea charts and world maps. Of great importance in
the late 15th century was Abraham Zacuto of
Salamanca, whose *Ha-Hibbur ha-Gadol* was
circulated in Castilian in Juan de Salaya's version
and subsequently in Latin in Joseph Vizinho's
abbreviated *Almanach Perpetuum*. Both
Christopher Columbus and Vasco da Gama knew of
Zacuto's work, and some historians believe that it
was Zacuto who adapted the astrolabe to navigation
and applied cardan suspension to the compass.

Germanic Europe: the Haskalah

As in Italy, certain Christian circles in Renaissance Germany began to take an interest in the Bible and the Hebrew language and literature. The most important figure of the first generation of German Hebraists was the distinguished humanist Johann Reuchlin (1455-1522), author of the first Hebrew grammar written by a Christian. Deeply influenced by the enthusiasm of Pico della Mirandola, Reuchlin began his Hebraic studies under Jacob ben Jehiel Loans, court physician to Frederick III, continuing in Rome under the exegete and talmudist Obadiah Sforno, an outstanding humanist whose work was made possible by the fact that Hebrew had risen to the rank of a scientific subject, thus neutralizing the age-old prejudice against rabbinic literature. In 1505, when the Moravian Jewish apostate Johann Joseph Pfefferkorn and his Dominican supporters advocated the destruction of all Hebrew books, Emperor Maximilian I asked Reuchlin for his opinion in the matter, and Reuchlin spoke out in favor of the Talmud and the Jews. A violent controversy ensued, with members of the clergy and Inquisition leaders supporting Pfefferkorn and leading humanists supporting Reuchlin. Many of the outstanding men of the age stood by Reuchlin, including Erasmus, Egidio da Viterbo, and Ulrich von Hutten. The Lateran Council examined the issue in the presence of Leo X and ruled in favor of Reuchlin, with the result that, on this occasion at least, the Talmud escaped the flames. The matter did not end there, however, for the pope himself persuaded Daniel Bomberg, a Christian publisher from Venice, to print the Talmud, the result being the first ever uncensored and unmutilated version.

The supporters of the Protestant Reformation, which can be said to have truly begun in 1517 with Martin Luther's ninety-five theses, showed considerable interest in Hebraic studies; Luther himself was aware of errors in St. Jerome's Vulgate translation and translated the Bible from Hebrew into German. At the beginning of the Reformation, Luther attempted to draw Jews to Christianity, in some of his writings actually condemning the attitude of the Catholic Church toward them, but when he saw that they paid him little heed, he became a bitter

Passover seder in a German Haggadah, c. 1400 (Israel Museum, Jerusalem). In his unfinished novel Rabbi of Bacherach, *the Jewish convert to Christianity Heinrich Heine wrote of the Passover ceremony: "This nocturnal festival is melancholically gay in character, gravely playful, and mysterious as a fairy tale. And the traditional singsong in which the Haggadah is read by the head of the house, and now and then repeated by the listeners in chorus, sounds at the same time so awesomely intense, maternally gentle, and suddenly awakening, that even those Jews who have long forsaken the faith of their fathers and pursued foreign joys and honors are moved to the depths of their hearts when the old, familiar sounds of the Passover happen to strike their ears." (Translation by E. B. Ashton.)*

enemy of Judaism, venting his deep hatred in numerous writings that ultimately helped to establish anti-Semitism in Germany and further poisoned the Protestant world against Jews. The disastrous result was that Germany, a staunch supporter of the Reformation, became as intolerant toward Judaism as the Catholic Church, and the Jews, trapped between the struggle for Reformation and Counter Reformation, were persecuted by all and sundry.

The outstanding Jewish figure of the first half of the 16th century was Joseph of Rosheim (1480-1554), an Alsatian Jew who around 1510 began representing the Alsatian communities before the emperor and the German princes. Rosheim used his influence in the service of his people, averting outbreaks of violence and expulsions, such as the banishment of all Jews from Germany proposed by Emperor Maximilian I in 1516.

Despite the religious wars that raged in Germany until 1648, there were no large-scale anti-Jewish disturbances, although, like a chronic illness, there were further accusations of ritual murder followed by expulsions in both Catholic and Protestant Germany during the 16th and 17th centuries. When one door was closed to them, the evicted Jews went from town to town in search of an open one. They had to wait until well after the turn of the 18th century before there was a certain change of attitude within the European countries. An example of this change occurred when Maria Theresa ordered the expulsion of the Jews of Prague in 1745. The decree caused a wave of indignation that swept the whole of Europe, and thanks to diplomatic pressure she was forced to allow them to return.

From the time of the Thirty Years War (1618-48), the courtier Jew, who until then had appeared only in the medieval Arabic and Christian Hispanic kingdoms, became a common figure in central Europe. This development dated to the 16th century and continued until the Napoleonic Wars in the 19th century. After 1648, the central power of the Holy Roman Empire in Germany began disintegrating, and the country divided into small kingdoms instilled with the baroque ideal of the absolute state with its own court. At these courts,

67

Reading the Haggadah during the Passover night celebration from the Erna Michael Haggadah, *Germany, c. 1400 (Israel Museum, Jerusalem). In his* Rabbi of Bacherach—*which he intended as "an eternal lamp in God's cathedral, not a sputtering stage light"—Heine describes the fond memories evoked in the minds of Jews by the Haggadah, in this case a woman's thoughts: "But every now and then she also glanced at the quaint parchment book of the* Haggadah *which lay before her, bound in gold and velvet: an old heirloom with wine stains of many years on it, which had come down from her grandfather's time and in which were many bold and brightly colored pictures that even as a little girl she had so loved to look at on Passover evenings. They represented all kinds of biblical stories, such as Abraham smashing his father's idols with a hammer . . . Also she saw how Pharaoh drowned, thank god! and how the children of* Israel went cautiously through the Red Sea . . . and finally how Jerusalem, with the towers and battlements of its Temple, shone in the glory of the sun." (Translation by E. B. Ashton.)

The Enlightenment

Opposite: Lavater and Lessing Visiting Moses Mendelssohn, *oil painting by Moritz Daniel Oppenheim, 1856 (Judah L. Magnes Museum, Berkeley, California). Gotthold Ephraim Lessing (standing) looks on as Johann Kasper Lavater (right) and Moses Mendelssohn (left) discuss religion. Although the meeting never took place, Oppenheim must have drawn the inspiration for his picture from Lavater's written challenge to Mendelssohn in 1769 to publicly defend the superiority of Judaism over Christianity, or, should he not do so, to accept the consequences and convert to Christianity.*

whether Protestant or Catholic, the courtier Jew became indispensable among those in high positions entrusted with state government. Thus, Jews were to be found not only in the principalities of Germany but also in those of Poland and Denmark. In recognition of their services courtier Jews were exempted from the legal restrictions that limited the lives of their more humble coreligionists and had permission to travel and settle wherever they liked. Their positions in society were varied, and they held posts as financiers, bankers, diplomats, administrators, and tax collectors. Always in close contact with the powerful commercial companies that belonged to the Sephardim in Holland and the Ottoman Empire, they became fully authorized agents for the supply of provisions to the army (food, weapons, and uniforms) and of consumer goods and luxury items (such as jewels). With their enterprising spirit, they laid the foundation

of a new mercantile and banking economy, contributed to the process of industrialization, and were efficient instruments in the birth of the modern absolute states. The members of this powerful oligarchy often lived in luxury in magnificent mansions, integrated as much as was possible in the social manners of the environment in which they lived. At times they even had their own synagogues, adorned like their mansions by the goldsmiths, artists, and engravers they patronized. Jewish communities sometimes grew up around these distinguished figures in places where none had existed before. The most famous Jewish courtier during the Thirty Years War was Jacob Bassevi of Treuenberg (1570-1634) from Prague. Others included members of the Oppenheimer and Wertheimer families, who served at the imperial court in Vienna and in courts elsewhere, and the five generations of the Gomperz family, who

served at the courts of the Hohenzollerns. Of the long list of Jewish courtiers in Denmark, Sweden, Poland, and in the German principalities, more than a few were of Spanish and Portuguese origin.

The Jews who belonged to the powerful oligarchies during the 16th and 17th centuries were a minority; the vast majority of their coreligionists were small tradesmen and secondhand dealers living constantly on the poverty line.

After the expulsion of the Jews of Vienna in 1670, a few families emigrated to Prussia, where they were taken in by the Elector Frederick William (1620-88). There they were readmitted into Brandenburg and founded the Berlin community, which was to become one of the most important centers of German Jewry. Moses Mendelssohn (1729-86), founder of the Haskalah (Enlightenment) movement that was to revolutionize European Judaism, also settled in Berlin (1743). One of the greatest philosophers and intellectuals of 18th-century Berlin, Mendelssohn strove to bring an end to the physical and intellectual isolation of the Jews so that they would be able to embrace the culture of the Western world. So began a process of change that was to lead to the modernization of the Jewish educational system. With Naphtali Herz Wessely, Mendelssohn proposed that the Jews learn German and study the natural sciences, geography, and history. Furthermore, when the first free Jewish school, designed by David Friedländer, was founded in Berlin in 1778, classes were given not in Yiddish but in German. In 1783, Mendelssohn's disciples published *Ha-Me'assef* ("The Gatherer"), a Hebrew magazine that attracted a number of intellectuals who took it upon themselves to give lessons to their coreligionists. With this, European Judaism began the long uphill struggle to obtain its rights.

The Haskalah, which reverberated throughout the Jewish world of the times and was opposed by Orthodox Judaism, played an important part in the appearance of a new kind of Jew. At the same time, however, it also paved the way for the many who, wishing to be fully accepted into Christian society, converted to Christianity or were assimilated by it.

Jewish Wedding, *anonymous oil painting from Bohemia-Moravia, c. 1750 (Israel Museum, Jerusalem). The Patent of Tolerance dictated by the Holy Roman emperor Joseph II in 1781 affected all the Jews in the empire. Though an important step toward emancipation, the edict was also a threat to Jewish culture and religion, as Germanization was also the first step toward conversion to Christianity. The edict abolished all economic restrictions on*

Jews and allowed the foundation of Jewish schools in which teaching was given in German—a language indispensable in matters of trade. Jews were admitted to schools and universities and were also obliged to perform military service. Though such measures were warmly welcomed by the Haskalah in Prague, they met with fierce opposition from strictly religious Jews under rabbis such as Ezekiel Landau. The legal situation of the Jews of Bohemia was

described in the Judensystempatent *of 1797, rabbis being ordered to study philosophy at the imperial universities and only Jews who had completed German primary school education being able to obtain a marriage licence or be admitted into traditional talmudic schools.*

Slavonic Europe: Hasidism

The most interesting story of the Jews of eastern Europe in ancient times is that of the kingdom of the Khazars. From the 6th century A.D. this kingdom occupied a territory between Europe and Asia lying between the Caucasus, the Volga, and the Don. Its capital, Itil, was a crossroads for the trade of a number of countries. Around 740, the king Bulan and a large number of his subjects converted to Judaism, and from then on only Jews were allowed to succeed to the throne. The Khazar Empire fell in 965.

From the time of the Crusades, eastern Europe was an habitual destination in the migrations of German Jews. Here they found refuge from persecution and expulsion and were offered freedom by backward countries like Hungary, Bohemia, and Moravia that needed hardworking pioneers to help develop trade and the economy. However, from the end of the 14th century until the mid 15th century, these countries, particularly Poland, were no longer safe for Jews, despite the fact that small groups had lived there for many centuries.

In those days, Poland's borders extended as far as the Black Sea and from 1569 included the duchy of Lithuania. Poland began to take in Jews during the 12th century, the number of immigrants growing in subsequent centuries, as the process always received the support of the local princes and, after the reunification of Poland in the 14th century, of the Polish kings. A statute guaranteeing the Jews protection was issued in 1264 by Boleslav IV and was confirmed by Casimir III in 1334. Among other things, it protected their lives and property and allowed them to move freely about the country. With successive waves of immigrants, the number of German Jews grew larger than that of the indigenous Jews, and the German Jewish—or Yiddish—dialect became the common tongue of all the Jews in the land. Their communities were scattered throughout a large number of villages, from Breslau and Danzig in the west to Kiev in the east. Their activities were not limited to money-lending and the humblest of trades, as had been the case in western Europe; rather, the Jews of Poland engaged in a wide variety of occupations, with the Christian settlers making up a sort of urban lower-middle class unheard of until then in

Carved wooden doors of a Polish synagogue heikhal, 18th century (Wolfson Museum, Hechal Shlomo, Jerusalem). For many years the Jewish community of Kraków was one of the most important in Europe, its first members arriving from Germany in 1257. In 1335 the Jewish community of the recently founded town of Kazimierz, close to Kraków's southern area, was established. The community grew at the beginning of the 16th century with the arrival of Jews *from Bohemia, Moravia, Germany, Italy, Spain, and Portugal. From this time and until the middle of the 17th century was a period of great cultural development. By 1644 Kraków boasted seven major synagogues, among them the Alte Schul (late 14th century), the oldest preserved synagogue in Poland. When several rabbinic schools were opened a few years later, the city became one of the most important Jewish centers in Europe. In the middle of the 17th* *century the community began to decline as the result of political instability within the region—the Swedish invasion, subsequent Polish reprisals, constant power shifts in the area, and internal dissent caused by the growing influence from 1780 on of the Hasidic movement (whose members were excommunicated by the rabbinic authorities in 1785 and 1797). The community did not begin to recover until emancipation in 1867 thanks to the Haskalah.*

Poland. The great mass of the Jewish population worked as craftsmen (goldsmiths, weavers, blacksmiths) and also as small traders. A smaller number worked the land, while others were innkeepers. The more powerful Jews took an active part in industry, tax collection, the administration of lands belonging to the aristocracy and the crown, the working of salt mines, and the export of timber, cattle, and agricultural produce. However, not even in Poland could the Jews escape the enmity of the church or the ill-will of their Christian competitors in trade and the crafts, and on occasion the kings were forced to dictate measures restricting Jewish commercial activity. Moreover, the kings were not always able to prevent anti-Jewish legislation being approved by local magistrates.

Particularly important in Poland were the Jewish schools of study, which developed as the educational system was perfected, and the financial aid granted to students in the form of collective grants. In this way, the *yeshivot,* or rabbinic seminaries and colleges, proliferated, above all in Kraków and Lublin. To these came students from Germany, Italy, Moravia, and Silesia, and under this system even the most backward students acquired at least a minimum of Jewish education. Indeed, not one household in the country was without members engaged in religious study. As a result, from the beginning of the 16th century Poland became the greatest center of traditional Jewish learning in the world, producing such great rabbis as Solomon Luria (1510-73) and Moses Isserles (1530-72).

The number of Lithuanian Polish Jews increased during this period, from 50,000 at the turn of the 16th century to 500,000 by the middle of the 17th. From the mid 16th century until the early 18th century, Polish Jewry was ruled autonomously by the Council of Four Lands (Great and Little Poland, Podolia, and Volhynia), a well-organized instrument for the administration and coordination of the communities belonging to the former principalities. The council's most important functions were the protection of Jewish interests and the distribution of tribute. The council was officially abolished in 1764.

Above: Model of Rabbi Moses Isserles' Rema synagogue, Kraków, 1553 (Museum of the Diaspora, Tel Aviv). An eminent rabbi of his time, Isserles is buried in the cemetery next to this synagogue. An example of the Kraków Renaissance style, the synagogue combined local elements with others from Italian Renaissance architecture that became particularly important in Kraków thanks to the Italian architects and craftsmen who worked in the city. The

synagogue was burned down by the Nazis, but rebuilt after World War II. Above right: Doors of the Kraków Hoyche Schul (High Synagogue) heikhal (late 16th century) in lead on wood, carved by two Jewish artists and featuring temple items (Israel Museum, Jerusalem).

The Chmielnicki Massacres

Life was at its best for Polish Jews in the first half of the 17th century; the situation ended abruptly with the Cossack uprising led by Bogdan Chmielnicki against the Poles of the Ukraine (1648-49). The revolt was caused by the Polish Catholic landowners' excesses and their tyrannical oppression of the Ukrainian Orthodox peasants. In the eyes of the peasants the Jews were representatives of the tyrannical nobility (who were rarely seen on their estates), for with the proceeds from the extremely high rents collected from the peasants the Jews ran inns, mills, and dairies. They were also tax collectors, for which they were equally hated. It was therefore inevitable that Jews should become the insurgents' prime target. When Chmielnicki defeated the Polish army with his Tartar allies, the wholesale slaughter of Jews began, the death toll and cruelty far surpassing the limits reached at the time of the Crusades and the Black Death. A fragile peace was reached in 1649, but war broke out again in 1654. On this occasion, Chmielnicki's ally was the tsar of Russia, who had territorial ambitions

in Poland. As the Russian troops advanced across the eastern regions of Poland, White Russia, and Lithuania, Jews were massacred or expelled. To make matters worse, in 1655 Charles X of Sweden invaded Great and Little Poland. Once the Poles had reconquered the territory, they fell on the Jews, accusing them of treachery, and then committed outrages similar to those perpetrated previously by the Cossacks and Russians. It has been calculated that between 300,000 and 500,000 Jews lost their lives between 1648 and 1658, and that 700 communities vanished or were reduced to a small number of members. As a result of these tragic events, the formerly rich and numerous Polish Jewish community found itself decimated and impoverished, many of its members setting out on an exodus to the Ottoman Empire, Palestine, and even to the same western European countries from which they had been uprooted centuries before.

The horror they had suffered threw the Polish Jews into the arms of mysticism; the yearning for deliverance spread beyond the fron-

72

Top: He Looked and Was Hurt, *oil painting by Maurice Minkowski, 1910 (Jewish Museum, New York). The title is taken from a talmudic story (Tractate Hagigah, 14b) that tells of four rabbis, Ben Azzai, Ben Zoma, Aher (Elisha ben Abuyah), and Rabbi Akiba, who entered Paradise. The first "cast a look and died," Ben Zoma looked and was hurt, Aher strayed from the path, and Rabbi Akiba departed in peace. In his picture, Minkowski reflects the influence* of the Haskalah on talmudic orthodoxy in eastern Europe. Influenced by the new ideas and a consequent secularization, a group of students (right) have ignored the traditional prohibition against shaving and cutting the hair, causing the disapproval of traditional Jews. Above: *Sukkot, by Leopold Pilichowski, Lodz, 1894-95 (Jewish Museum, New York). A group of traditional Jews celebrates the Sukkot festival.*

warning them to guard against the danger of routine and preaching that observance of each precept should be based on spiritual intent. The idea that monotony is an obstacle to devotion and that joy should reign in worship led Besht to incorporate song and dance into religion as a means to ecstatic communion with God. The movement, which attracted thousands of Jews and became the materialization of eastern European Jewry's deep sense of religion, made no attempt to change the basic doctrines of Judaism or the fulfillment of its precepts, but rather sought a new way of serving God according to which absolute piety and one's own actions were more important than wisdom or study. Upon Besht's death, the sect's teachers, known as *zaddikim* ("righteous men"), acted as mediators between God and the Hasidim. Official Judaism under men of the caliber of Elijah ben Solomon, Gaon of Vilna (1720-97), strongly opposed this group, but the Hasidim were never expelled from Judaism, and in time many of their practices and rituals were accepted as orthodox.

tiers of Poland to fill the minds of Jews in Europe and the Middle East with a wave of religious pietism—an ideal climate for false messiahs and for reinforcing the faith of the still numerous followers of the Sephardic Jew Shabbetai Zevi. The most famous of these messiahs was Jacob Frank, who in 1755 revealed himself as the reincarnation of Zevi. When Frank's sect was officially expelled from Judaism, the Frankists turned to the local bishops for support, converted to Catholicism, and revived the ancient accusations against the Talmud. The result was a number of disputations and the burning, yet again, of the Talmud (1757). Forced to leave Poland because the church was suspicious of his sincerity, Frank fled to Offenbach, Germany, where he lived at his own court until his death in 1791.

The other mystical movement of importance to come out of Poland—Hasidism—proved to be more beneficial for the Jewish world. The founder of this movement was Israel Ba'al Shem Tov (known as Besht, 1700-60), who assembled the first group of disciples,

74

Top: Jewish Wedding, *oil painting by Ilex Bellers, c. 1900 (private collection, London). Above:* Villagers Greeting the Messiah, *oil painting by Ezekiel David Kirszenbaum, 1937 (Israel Museum, Jerusalem); the Messiah is wearing Hasidic clothing. Israel Ba'al Shem Tov (1700-60), known as Besht, founder of the Hasidic mystical movement, assembled the first group of disciples, warning them to guard against the danger of routine and preaching that observance of*

each precept should be based on spiritual intent. The idea that monotony is an obstacle to devotion and that joy should reign in worship led Besht to incorporate song and dance into religion as a means to ecstatic communion with God. The movement, which attracted thousands of Jews and became the materialization of eastern European Jewry's deep sense of religion, made no attempt to change the basic doctrines of Judaism or the fulfilment of its precepts, but rather

sought a new way of serving God according to which absolute piety and one's own actions were more important than wisdom or study. Upon Besht's death, the sect's teachers, known as zaddikim *("the righteous"), acted as mediators between God and the Hasidim.*

Who Are the Hasidim?

Contemporary photograph of Hasidim on Fifth Avenue, New York, dressed, as is their custom, according to the fashion of 17th-century Poland. Time seems to have stood still.

The following is one of the most popular Hasidic stories and demonstrates the power of Hasidic faith. "Whenever the great Rabbi Israel ben Eliezer Ba'al Shem Tov saw that misfortune was to befall the Jewish people, he would withdraw to a certain place in the forest, kindle a fire, say a certain prayer, and lo and behold a miracle would take place and the danger be averted. Later, when his disciple and successor to leadership of the movement, Dov Baer, the Maggid of Mezhirech, was obliged to mediate with heaven for the same reasons, he went to the same place in the forest and said, 'Lord of the world, hear me. Though I know not how to kindle the fire, yet I am able to say the prayer.' And lo and behold a miracle took place. Later, in order to save his people, Rabbi Moses Leib of Sasov also went to the forest and said, 'I know not how to kindle the fire, but I can point out the place and that should be enough.' It was enough, and lo and behold a miracle also took place. Then it was Rabbi Israel of Ruzhin's turn to avert the danger, and sitting in a chair he covered his face with his hands and spoke to God, 'I am unable to kindle the fire, I know not the prayer, I cannot even find the place in the forest. All I can do is tell this story, but that should be enough.' And lo, it was enough."

Today, one of the most important Hasidic groups is that of the Habad, or Lubavich, which first appeared two centuries ago under Rabbi Shneur Zalman from the Byelorussian city of Liozna. In 1927, the leader of the group, Rabbi Yosef Yitzchak Schneersohn (of the sixth generation), was sentenced to death by the Soviet authorities, but due to international pressure the sentence was commuted to life imprisonment. Freed later, Schneersohn established himself in Riga and finally in Warsaw, which he fled in 1940 for New York. He lived in the United States until his death in 1950, when he was succeeded by his grandson, Rabbi Menachem Mendel Schneersohn. At the present time, the group is firmly established not only in the United States but also in England, France, and Israel.

Emancipation and Anti-Semitism

In the mid-18th century, the slow and laborious process began that was to lead the Jews of Europe to emancipation. Before this time (and in some countries until the end of the 19th century), however, the panorama in general was one of Jewish communities sunk in the wretched life of the ghettos, overburdened by taxes, without hope or future. For the Jews, hope could not come from the East, where Besht's followers lived absorbed in their own form of religion, their backs turned on the intellect and worldly things. The answer had to come from Western Judaism.

In Germany, the first men to speak out in favor of Jewish rights were the philosopher Gotthold E. Lessing and the writer Christian W. von Dohm, both of whom knew Moses Mendelssohn personally. In France, it was Father Henri Grégoire. (It should be remembered that not all the French Encyclopedists, or *philosophes*, regarded Judaism in the same way; Voltaire, for example, always declared himself totally opposed to it.) In Austria, the Patent of Tolerance (*Toleranzpatent*) granted by Joseph II in 1781 could be taken as a faint sign of change, for with it Austrian Jews saw the severest of the restrictions placed on them lifted, but the under-lying aim of the regulations was the gradual absorption of the Jewish population through conversion to Christianity.

The truly giant step in the emancipation of European Jews came with the French Revolution. In spite of the strong opposition of some members in the national assembly and despite the reaction of the press against the decision, the Jews of France were finally granted equal rights as citizens in 1791. This was to happen wherever the revolution exerted its influence in Europe, the same principles being applied in Holland, Belgium, various parts of Italy (Piedmont, Lombardy, Venice, and Rome, where the ghetto gates were demolished), and in those parts of Germany and Poland that came under French influence or control during the revolution and the time of the Napoleonic Empire. Even in the rest of Europe, the effects of the new order were felt, and in Prussia Jews achieved almost full emancipation in 1812. In France itself, however, Napoleon's attitude toward the Jews was inconsistent; in 1806 he called an Assembly of Notables in Paris to define the position of the emancipated Jew within the modern state, later convoking a Grand Sanhedrin (to support the assembly's decisions) in the manner of the councils that had ruled the destiny of the Jewish people in ancient times. Just one year later, Napoleon forbade the Jews to engage in the arts and in trade and limited their freedom of movement (although these regulations gradually ceased to be applied).

This prelude to liberty was to be short-lived, however. When Napoleon fell, the reactionary elements in Europe raised their heads, and the restoration, the consolidation of the kings—with the return of absolute monarchy—and the church, became the new order of the day, so that, with the exception of France and Holland, the Jews of Europe lost most of their newly won rights.

The Jewish population of 18th-century Italy was approximately 30,000, of which between 4,000 and 7,000 lived in Rome, a smaller number lived in Leghorn, and the rest in approximately seventy other towns. Among those who suffered most under the Restoration were the Jews of the Papal States, where the *ancien*

Liberty, Equality, and Fraternity, *lithograph by Hendrik Roosing, Amsterdam, 1795 (Joods Historisch Museum, Amsterdam). The first man to speak out in favor of Jewish emancipation before the French National Assembly was Abbot Grégoire, although little heed was paid to his words, which received a negative reaction in the press and with public opinion. But the slogan of the revolution was gradually to be* fulfilled, *and from 1790 the Sephardim of Bordeaux, Bayonne, Avignon, and the former papal territories won their civil rights. One year later, the Jews of Alsace won theirs. At this time, too, the Batavian Republic, proclaimed in the Low Countries, granted equal rights to all citizens whatever their religion.*

Below left: Declaration of the Rights of Man and Citizen, 1789 (Musée Carnavalet, Paris). Below right: Napoleon Proclaims Freedom of Worship, popular print from Lyons, 1801 (Bibliothèque Nationale, Paris). During the French Revolution the originally Jewish symbol of the Tables of the Law came to be identified with the declaration of human rights (proclaimed on August 26, 1789) and became a symbol of the principles of revolutionary ideology.

régime was fully restored, with a return to the ghettos, obligatory attendance at church sermons, and other oppressive measures. Furthermore, in the Mortara Affair of 1858, in which the child Edgar Mortara was carried off from his home in Bologna to be brought up as a Catholic, Pius IX refused to capitulate in spite of international public opinion, and the child was never returned to his parents. Indeed, in time Mortara became a priest and missionary.

In Germany, though the Jews were freed from the ghetto, they lost the rest of their rights and were expelled from the towns in which they had settled during the French occupation. Furthermore, from 1819 a serious wave of anti-Jewish riots swept the country in which lives

were lost and property was damaged. In Prussia, although the edict of emancipation was not revoked, it proved to be no more than a worthless piece of paper, for severe restrictions were placed on Jews living in the territories annexed to the country after the Napoleonic Wars. In Austria, the Jews were made to return to the ghettos, special districts were created (some of which they could not leave and others they could not enter), and they were forced to pay all manner of special taxes. Jewish hopes of equal rights were dashed for the time, and it would be necessary to go on fighting a battle that was to last for another sixty years. Thus, the only alternative open to Jews who wished to be accepted into society and into European culture in general was

to convert to Christianity, which many were finally to do. Three of Moses Mendelssohn's four children did just this, as did many others, such as Karl Ludwig Börne, one of the spiritual leaders of the revolutionary Young Germany movement in German literature; the poet Heinrich Heine; the philosopher Eduard Gans; Friedrich Julius Stahl, the Christian constitutional political doctrine theorist; Karl Marx, the chief theorist of socialism and communism (who was baptized by his parents); and Moses Hess, the father of ethical socialism.

In spite of this, a paradox existed, for with the need for large amounts of capital that arose in the wake of the industrial age (for mining, the building of factories and railway lines, etc.), the

77

banking institutions developed by the Jews since the Middle Ages were now at their height. Thus, the banks of the great Jewish financiers became the pillars of European economic life. The list of names is long; one example that can be cited is that of the Rothschilds, a family of financiers who from their head office in Frankfurt am Main established branches in Vienna, London, Paris, and Naples. However, the importance of such private Jewish banks began to decline with the appearance of joint-stock companies in the late 19th century.

The liberal political parties that appeared in the middle of the 19th century took up the cause of Jewish emancipation. The Jews closed ranks around these parties, fighting side by side with them, advancing as they advanced and retreating as they retreated. The revolutionary movements of 1848 that brought victory to liberal groups eager to establish democratic constitutions to govern the different states helped the Jews to achieve their goal. Between the revolutionary period and 1870, liberal constitutions were proclaimed recognizing the equal

rights of Jewish citizens in all the countries of central Europe. With the triumph of the revolution of 1848 in Germany, four Jews were appointed as members of the national assembly, among them Gabriel Riesser, the country's first Jewish judge, who was deputy chairman and the most outstanding figure in the struggle for equal rights. Although such rights were approved in 1849, they never came legally into force; the assembly was dissolved by force soon after, and another twenty years were to pass before full emancipation was granted (1869), when William I and Bismarck signed the so-called Law of Toleration. The law also took effect in the southern states when Bavaria, Baden, and Württemberg became part of the German Empire in 1871 after the Franco-Prussian War. The case was similar in Austria-Hungary, where emancipation was granted by Franz Joseph after the revolution of 1848, although it did not become effective until the signing of the 1867 constitution.

In Italy, Jews participated actively in the ideals of the Risorgimento, a movement that

Above: The Jewish Fiddler's Lunch, *oil painting by Augusto Rizzoni, 1874 (Serpukhov Art Museum, Russia). Above right:* Among the Leaves of the Jewish Cemetery, *oil painting by Sir Jacob Epstein, 1905 (Max Berger Collection, Vienna). Many of the Jews of Europe lived in the most abject poverty, although a large number benefitted from the traditional Jewish sense of philanthropy, as explained by the English author Israel Zangwill in*

his Children of the Ghetto *(1892): "All the Ashkenazic tribes lived very much like a happy family, the poor not stand-offish towards the rich, but anxious to afford them opportunities for well-being. The* Schnorrer *[beggar] felt no false shame in his begging. He knew it was the rich man's duty to give him unleavened bread at Passover, and coals in the winter, and odd half-crowns at all seasons; and he regarded himself as the Jacob's ladder by*

which the rich man mounted to Paradise. But, like all genuine philanthropists, he did not lack for gratitude."

sought to bring unity and freedom to the country. Their claims were supported by such great men as Massimo d'Azeglio, premier under Victor Emmanuel II, and d'Azeglio's successor, Cavour. Jews were granted emancipation as territories were liberated by Victor Emmanuel, who was proclaimed king of all Italy in 1861. The process, which was completed when Rome was taken in 1870 and became the capital of Italy, brought an end to the temporal power of the popes.

From the time of their resettlement, the English Jews enjoyed a status similar to that of the rest of the population, and successive laws passed throughout the first half of the 19th century ensured that they became almost completely equal. Only one obstacle remained—the exclusion of Jews from parliament—summed up in the oath sworn by members before taking their seats: "In accordance with the true faith of a Christian." After a number of lengthy debates, the houses or parliament were forced to make changes to the oath so that Baron Lionel Nathan de Rothschild could occupy his seat as member for the City of London in 1858. There is no doubt that emancipation for British Jews was facilitated by the fact that Queen Victoria's prime minister, Benjamin Disraeli, although baptized into the Christian faith as a child, was of Jewish ancestry and always acted on their behalf. Another extremely important figure in England during this period was Sir Moses Montefiore, who championed the cause of his people wherever they fell prey to persecution or oppression. Indeed, Montefiore accomplished one of his most outstanding feats when he intervened before the sultan on behalf of Jews in Damascus who were accused of ritual murder and had been submitted to torture. For the first time, the Jews of Europe were able to prove that they were strong and well-organized enough to speak out in defense of their persecuted coreligionists. Montefiore also supported Jewish settlement in Palestine, building factories and founding farming communities, schools, and charity associations there.

With emancipation won, 19th-century European Jewry opened the sluices on hitherto unfulfilled skills and capabilities. Jews hurled

79

The Little Jewish Orphan, *oil painting by Ivan Kramskoy, 1837-87 (Russian State Museum, St. Petersburg). Israel Zangwill described the problems posed by emancipation in* Children of the Ghetto: *"Not here in our London Ghetto the gates and gaberdines of the olden Ghetto of the Eternal City; yet no lack of signs external by which one may know it, and those who dwell therein. People who have been living in a Ghetto for a couple of centuries are not able to step outside merely because the gates are thrown down, nor to efface the brands on their souls by putting off the yellow badges. The isolation imposed from without will have come to seem the law of their being. But a minority will pass, by units, into the larger, freer, stranger life amid the execrations of an ever-dwindling majority."*

In Germany, where it had always proved more difficult for Jews to hold high positions in politics, there was Ludwig Bamberger, member of parliament, and, after World War I, Kurt Eisner and Walther Rathenau, who took charge of the German war economy. The fame of German medicine in the 19th century was due largely to the work of exceptional Jewish researchers, such as August von Wassermann, developer of the Wassermann test; Paul Ehrlich, who developed salvarsan; Waldemar Mordecai Haffkine, who discovered the bubonic plague microbe and developed a vaccine against plague and cholera; Sigmund Freud, the father of psychoanalysis; and many more. In the field of science, there was Heinrich Hertz, who investigated electromagnetic waves, and the physicist Albert Einstein, famous for his formulation of the relativity theory. Furthermore, there were many Jewish inventors, including David Schwartz, who invented the dirigible (later commercialized

themselves headlong in pursuit of Western knowledge, swiftly making up for their backwardness vis-à-vis Christian society. Many became prominent figures, and there was not one field of human activity in which they did not become involved: politics, philosophy, finance, industry, the arts, science, and technology. In Italian politics, there was Luigi Luzzatti, who became prime minister of Italy, while in defense there was Giuseppe Ottolenghi, chief of staff, senator, and war minister. In France, Adolphe Crémieux was twice minister of justice and later became a life senator; an active collaborator of Montefiore in the case of the tortured Jews of Damascus, he was one of the founders of the Alliance Israélite Universelle, an association founded in 1860 whose object was to raise the cultural level of Jews and uphold their rights. The alliance was to serve as a model for other, similar groups, such as the Anglo-Jewish Association (founded in England in 1871), the Israelitische Allianz (Vienna, 1873), and the Hilfsverein der deutschen Juden (Berlin, 1901). Among the many other Jewish French politicians, particularly important was Léon Blum, who guided the destiny of France between 1936 and 1938.

by Count Zeppelin); the engineer Edmund Rumpler, who ranks among the fathers of aviation; Siegfried Marcus, who constructed the first petrol engine; Émile Berliner, who invented the gramophone record; Robert von Lieben, whose discoveries led to sound-film cinema and radiotelephony; Gabriel Lippmann, who invented color photography; and Moritz Hermann Jacobi, brother of the mathematician Carl Guistav Jacobi, who was famous for his supposed discovery (1837) of galvanoplastics (his ideas were later shown to be mistaken). Jews were also the driving force behind the economies of their respective countries; they founded the first transport company in Berlin, in various parts of Germany they opened mines, set up shipping companies, and built shoe, weapons, tool, china, and textile factories. The same may be said of the fields of law, philosophy, publishing, the press, and information services (including Israel Beer Josaphat, also known as Paul

81

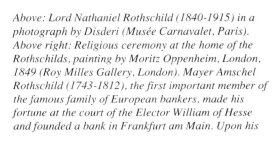

Above: Lord Nathaniel Rothschild (1840-1915) in a photograph by Disderi (Musée Carnavalet, Paris). Above right: Religious ceremony at the home of the Rothschilds, painting by Moritz Oppenheim, London, 1849 (Roy Milles Gallery, London). Mayer Amschel Rothschild (1743-1812), the first important member of the famous family of European bankers, made his fortune at the court of the Elector William of Hesse and founded a bank in Frankfurt am Main. Upon his

death his five sons took over the family business, one remaining in Frankfurt, while the others founded banks in Vienna, London, Paris, and Naples. Lionel Rothschild, from the English branch of the family, was elected to the House of Commons in 1847 but forfeited his seat for eleven years because he refused to take the Christian oath required of all members of parliament. The House of Lords rejected changes in the wording of the oath suggested by the House of

Commons until in 1858 a compromise was reached in which the words "So help me God" were included, thus enabling Rothschild to take his seat. In 1875 Baron Lionel Rothschild financed the purchase of shares in the Suez Canal, which enabled Disraeli to acquire shares from the khedive, Ismail Pasha, and so ensure British predominance in Egypt. In 1885 Rothschild's son, Nathaniel, took his seat in the House of Lords as the first Jewish peer.

Julius Freiherr von Reuter, who set up the telegraphic agency that still bears his name).

The coexistence between a Jewish minority and a Christian majority and the integration of the former into a society in which it was not always easy to observe the strict rules of Judaism led to the rise in Germany of the Jewish Reform movement. Fiercely attacked by Orthodox Jews, this movement was later to spread to other countries.

This period also saw the appearance of the science of Judaism, led by Leopold Zunz (1794-1886), who sought to win respectability for Jewish studies in the German academic community by applying the methods of scholarly investigation to Jewish literature. For the first time, Jewish scholars undertook a scientific study of their own past, with researchers such as Moritz Steinschneider, Isaac Marcus Jost, and Heinrich Graetz delving into medieval Jewish literature and the history of the Jews. These and many others were the first in a new generation of Hebraists who contributed to the revival of Hebrew as a means of scientific and philosophical expression and raised the name of Judaism in the esteem of the Christian world.

It was not long before the great progress made by emancipated Jewry revived the ever-latent ill-will of Christians. In Germany, after the Franco-Prussian War of 1870-71, a period of political upheaval, economic crisis, and social turmoil followed by the collapse of the stock exchange in 1873 served as a setting for the reappearance of organized anti-Jewish activity. A new movement known as anti-Semitism was founded by Wilhelm Marr, a convert whose father had been Jewish. Gaining great popular support in a short time, it was directed against not just all Jews, whether or not they practiced their religion, but also to the first generation of descendants of converts. There is a fundamental difference between the "anti-Jewish" attitude of the medieval church and Marr's "anti-Semitism"; the aim of the former was to convert Jews to Christianity, whereas the latter sought to eliminate Jews altogether. The movement became organized in 1879 within the German Christian Social Party, founded by Adolf Stöcker, chaplain at the imperial court, and

Detail of Lighting the Hanukkah Lights, *painting by Moritz Oppenheim, 1880 (Israel Museum, Jerusalem). The Industrial Revolution provided Jews with a new role in European society. In Germany, for the great mass of the population the standard of living was much less spectacular than that of the great Jewish businessmen, who were never more than a minority. In a world of growing industrialization in which great masses of people were concentrated in the big cities,*

German Jews found unprecedented opportunities not only in business but also in the liberal professions, so that by 1871 60 percent of all Jews belonged to the upper middle class, the German Jewish community being one of the richest in Europe.

Recreation of a Yom Kippur Service at a Camp near Metz (1870) for the 7,000 German Jewish soldiers during the Franco-Prussian War, on cloth, 1871 (Israel Museum, Jerusalem). The picture is fictional; a soldier who was there described the service: "None of us, not even in the most splendid temple that we knew at home, had ever prayed with such passionate devotion as we did in the little low room with a broken door, with windows lacking glass and with walls bored through by grenades. From time to time, a short distance from us, our cannons thundered toward Metz, and we felt the impermanence of our existence, and the need to reconcile ourselves with God, since soon it might be too late. For many of us, for whom the meaning of Yom Kippur until this moment had been inwardly quite strange, it had now become unforgettably clear in the deepest depth of our hearts in a way never before suspected."

attracted the most reactionary elements of the Reichstag, who demanded that Jews be disenfranchised. A pseudoscientific basis for the movement was supplied by Houston Stewart Chamberlain, among others, in writings that compared the "noble Aryan race" to the "depraved Semites." The question was no longer one of the age-old religious-based arguments, which now impressed no one, but rather of secular arguments with a pseudobiological basis: the Jews were a threat to modern civilization because of their "impure" racial characteristics. Such theories, echoed in hundreds of publications and refuted by many liberal social-democratic thinkers (though without much popular support), led to outbreaks of violence in Germany and were taken up in other countries, particularly in Austria, which became another stronghold of hatred for Jews, and in France. The anti-Semitic mottoes, notions, and slogans that gained currency just before the end of the 19th century were later adopted and reshaped within the racist polities of Adolf Hitler and those responsible for the Holocaust.

In France, when a scapegoat was needed for the defeat suffered in the war of 1870-71,

84

Court-martial of Dreyfus, from Le Petit Journal *weekly, December 1894. The first signs of anti-Semitism appeared in France in the 1880s after the collapse of the Catholic Union Générale bank, which was blamed on Jewish capitalists. Anti-Semitic postures were summed up in Édouard Drumont's 1886 book* La France juive *("Jewish France"), hundreds of editions of which were sold, and in the periodical* La Libre Parole, *which Drumont edited.*

Satirical cartoon of the Dreyfus Affair, from the Italian magazine Il Papagallo, *August 1899 (Musée Carnavalet, Paris). The Dreyfus Affair broke out in the middle of an intense anti-Semitic campaign in France. Dreyfus was accused of spying on the flimsy evidence of the similarity between his handwriting and that on a document obtained at the German embassy. Shortly after the trial, Colonel Georges Picquart, chief of the army intelligence section,*

various anti-Semitic newspapers sprang up. These, together with the propaganda of the journalist Édouard Drumont, helped stir up anti-Semitic feeling, which came to a head in the so-called Dreyfus Affair, which brought France to the brink of civil war. In 1894, on flimsy evidence, Capt. Alfred Dreyfus, a French general staff officer—and a Jew—was found guilty of espionage, sentenced to deportation for life, and sent to Devils Island for solitary confinement. The sentence led to a wave of anti-Semitism throughout the country. Although enough evidence soon came to light to prove that Dreyfus was in fact innocent, the reactionary elements within the army refused to reopen the case, and France was split into the opposed camps of Dreyfusards and anti-Dreyfusards for a decade. Famous celebrities, both Jewish and non-Jewish, spoke out on behalf of Dreyfus, among them the writer Émile Zola, who addressed an open letter, *J'Accuse*, to the president of the republic. Finally, in 1900, and after two trials, the first sentence was reversed. Six more years had to pass, however, before Dreyfus was exonerated, reinstated, and decorated with the Legion of Honor.

discovered that the document had probably been the work of Major Ferdinand Esterhazy. But the army refused to reopen the case, and Picquart was first demoted and sent to Tunis and then accused of forgery, dismissed from the service, and arrested. The battle was fought in the press and led to a division in public opinion. French celebrities, both Christian and Jewish, demanded a retrial. The exoneration of Dreyfus in 1906 also absolved Picquart.

Zola in court, from Le Petit Journal, *February 1898. In January 1898 the daily* L'Aurore *published the article* J'Accuse *in which Zola accused the army of undermining the course of justice and shielding the real spy. When the case was reopened in 1899 Dreyfus was again found guilty but was pardoned. Six years later his name was cleared and he was reinstated and decorated with the Legion of Honor.*

Under the Tsars

Practically nothing of the emancipation process taking place in the West affected the Jews of eastern Europe, where, due to the successive partitioning of Poland in the late 18th century, the vast majority of the population now belonged to the Russian Empire. The by no means large number of Jews who had lived within the empire's frontiers until then had had no settlement rights at all and were often submitted to the harshest of treatment. The position was not to change, save only that by the end of the 18th century, the number of Jews living under the tsars had increased considerably.

As part of a policy that tended to exclude Jews from the country's central regions, in the early 19th century a limit was set on the areas in which they were allowed to reside, confining them to the towns of certain border provinces in the south and west in a zone known as the Pale of Settlement. In the reign of Nicholas I (1825-55), anti-Jewish policy reached serious extremes when, by means of approximately six hundred edicts against Jews, the tsar revived the medieval laws of the church. But there was more to come;

Jewish males aged from eight to twelve were obliged to serve a thirty-one-year period of military service. These child recruits, known as cantonists, were trained for six years in garrisons far from their places of compulsory residence and, generally speaking, never saw their parents again.

With the family unit itself under attack, the Jews of the Russian communities turned to the strictest observance of traditional Jewish life as their only form of defense, refusing to have any cultural contact with the outside world. Grouped around their respective *zaddikim,* or religious leaders, who were not always on good terms with one other, the Hasidim were involved in constant disputes with those rabbis who opposed their movement. However, both sides joined in bitterly opposing Moses Mendelssohn's Haskalah movement and its distinguished Berlin circle. Despite this opposition, the movement managed to gain a foothold in Russian Judaism; one result of this was a nonreligious form of literature in both Hebrew and Yiddish subscribed to by important figures in the rebirth of Hebrew as a literary language.

Postcards from the turn of the century featuring Jews from Russian Poland (William L. Gross Collection, Ramat Aviv, Israel). In the first fifteen years of this century, the Jews of Russia underwent a sharp process of urbanization that affected the Jewish way of life. The concentration of Jews in big cities brought cultural assimilation and undermined the importance of traditional ways of life, but it also reinforced the sense of solidarity among Jews. The economy became urban-based, and Jews played a particularly important part in the food industry, especially in the sugar factories, the Brodsky family producing almost a quarter of the sugar consumed by the country and founding the syndicate that handled exports. In addition to controlling exports of timber and many other agricultural products, Jews controlled many of the country's flour mills and tobacco plants and played an active part in the textile industry.

The reign of Alexander II (1855-81) brought a process of modernization that led to a considerable improvement in the lot of Russian Jews. The period of compulsory military service was reduced to five years; Jews were admitted to universities and centers of higher education and were allowed to practice as lawyers and doctors; furthermore, the wealthier artisans and merchants could engage in activity anywhere within the country; Jews were entrusted with creating a banking system; and on rare occasions distinguished Jews, such as Samuel and Lazar Poliakoff—who built a railway linking Russia from east to west—were accepted into the nobility.

The assassination of the tsar by terrorists in 1881 dashed all Jewish aspirations, for the discovery that a Jewish woman was among those involved in the plot led to a wave of brutal massacres known as pogroms.

In 1882, the Provisional Regulations were put into effect. These were the core of the so-called May Laws (issued in May 1882), an anti-Jewish code that from that time on ruled

the lives of Russian Jewry—by the 1880s, 5 million souls. All Jews thus became subject to the whims of the local authorities and were barred from higher education and most of the liberal professions, leaving any chance of self-improvement beyond their reach. Confined to urban ghettos in the western limits of the empire or living out a wretched existence in a *shtetl* (Yiddish for "small town"), they somehow managed to hold on to their dignity by turning to the values of a traditional way of life; the deeply religious way of life so wonderfully described by Shalom Aleichem in his works. In the face of such a concurrence of disasters, Russian Jewry sought salvation in flight. Beginning in 1881 and continuing over the next thirty years, there was a major wave of migrations to western Europe, particularly to England, and to countries overseas, such as Australia, New Zealand, South Africa, South America (mainly Argentina), Canada, and particularly the United States, which saw the arrival of over 400,000 Jews between 1881 and 1890.

87

Top: Street in the Vilna ghetto, c. 1905. Above: Polish Jew on a donkey (lower left), c. 1900. (Postcards from the William L. Gross Collection, Ramat Aviv, Israel.) Vilna has been called the Jerusalem of Lithuania, having become an important center of rabbinic studies in the early 17th century. The 1897 census revealed a Jewish population of 63,831—42 percent of the total population. Vilna was also a focal point of the Haskalah movement, attracting large numbers of Hebrew writers, and an important center of political activity, first for the Jewish Socialist organizations (late 19th century) and later for the Russian Zionist movement (early 20th century). Hebrew and Yiddish literature also flourished in Vilna, the greatest Jewish cultural development taking place between 1922 and 1939, when Vilna belonged to Poland and with the establishment of a group of secondary schools, one of whose main teaching languages was Hebrew. Vilna *was also a world center of Yiddish culture and produced a large number of periodicals; in 1919 the Jewish Historical and Ethnographic Society created a museum and archive, and in 1925 the YIVO institute of Yiddish language and culture was founded.*

Pograms in Tsarist Russia

Right: *Birth of the Jewish Resistance,* oil painting by Lazar Krestin, 1905 (Judah L. Magnes Museum, Berkeley, California); this is based on a pogrom that took place in Lithuania in April 1903. Below: Members of the Odessa Jewish self-defense forces who died in the pogroms of 1905 (Museum of the Jewish Diaspora, Tel Aviv). Opposite top: Jewish street after the pogroms of 1881 (Central Zionist Archive, Jerusalem). Opposite bottom: *After the Pogrom,* oil painting by Maurice Minkowski, c. 1910 (Jewish Museum, New York).

Anti-Jewish sentiment in Russia became rampant after the assassination of Tsar Alexander II in 1881, turning to violent riots in the Ukraine that affected almost one hundred and sixty communities in southern Russia. The word *pogrom* ("devastation") was a new term for something much older—the organized hunting down of Jews—and was to become a commonplace event endorsed by local authorities. Nothing changed under Tsar Nicholas II, violence against Jews reaching a climax in 1903 with the Kishinev pogrom in

which, according to official sources, over fifty Jews were killed, five hundred were injured, and hundreds of houses and shops were plundered and destroyed. In response to the pogrom protest meetings were held in cities throughout the world, and the U.S. Congress passed a resolution of sympathy with the Jews. Such brutality also brought about a change of attitude in those affected, and the Jewish victims of the Gomel (White Russia) pogroms of 1903 opted for resistance. The only action taken by the local police was to interfer with the efforts of the Jews to defend themselves, and the rioters were free to go on killing. When the so-called Black Centuries supported by army and Cossack units were brought in in 1905, there was little the self-defense organizations could do, and further pogroms took place, as in Odessa, where hundreds died.

The revolts ended in 1907 with Stolypin's dictatorial government, when popular agitation and uprisings were put down in an attempt to curb anti-Semitic policy and restore the confidence of the international financial markets in Russia.

"If You Really Wish For It, It Will Not Be a Dream" (T. Herzl)

The idea of the return to Jerusalem and to *Eretz Israel* ("Land of Israel") had been present in the minds of the Jewish people since the first day of the Diaspora. Jews have repeated the saying "This year here, next year in Jerusalem" since the earliest of times at the ritual Passover supper, and over the centuries the desire to return to the Promised Land served as inspiration for numerous literary works, one example being the lovely *Zionides*, poems written in the 12th century by Judah ben Samuel Halevi. Furthermore, there have always been Jews in Palestine, and there is a long history of aged people setting out for the Holy Land in order to die there and be laid to rest.

In the 19th century, however, to add to this religious type of Zionism, a political form of Zionism arose almost simultaneously in both eastern and western Europe. There were several reasons for this. Russian Jews had become aware of the anomaly of their own economic structure, a structure from which any physical contact with the land had been completely eradicated. It would seem that the idea of devoting their lives

to farming—an activity that for centuries had been forbidden to them—had taken shape as the solution to their problems. After the first vain attempts in southern Russia to set up farming colonies, more earnest experiments were carried out in Argentina and Palestine. The Argentinean project began in 1891 thanks to the generosity of the financier Baron Maurice de Hirsch, who had reached the conclusion that the country's immense virgin plains were the perfect place for a form of colonization that would accommodate a million eastern European Jews. However, by the end of the century the project had begun to founder, as only 30,000 Jews had emigrated to the new settlements, and not all of these were engaged in farming.

Settlement in Palestine, on the other hand, was to prove more successful in the long run as it laid the foundation for the birth of the state of Israel. One of the first ideologists to suggest that the problems of the Jews would not come to an end until Israel had become a "normal" nation with its own territory was Leo Pinsker, born in Odessa, who in 1882 expounded his theories in a

Top: The Promised Land, *color lithograph, Breslau, 1880. Above: Portrait of Theodor Herzl (1860-1904) and allegorical and idyllic scenes of the return of the Jews to the land of Israel, color lithograph, Vienna, 1925. (Both from the William L. Gross Collection, Ramat Aviv, Israel.)* "The emigration of the Jews should not be seen as a sudden emigration, but rather as a gradual one lasting for decades. First the poorest will leave and these will make the land workable. According to a preconceived plan, they will build roads and bridges, railways and a telephone system; they will redirect the rivers and build homes. Their work will bring trade, and trade will bring markets which in turn will attract new settlers who will come by their own means. The work then done on the land will raise the value of the country. The Jews will soon see that their hitherto hated and despised determination has opened up a new and prosperous age." (From Der Judenstaat, by Theodor Herzl, 1895.)

language, a language that was to become the new community's common tongue.

The Jews of western Europe, on the other hand, were by now convinced that no matter how hard they tried, they would never be fully accepted by Christian society, whether Catholic or Protestant. In spite of having in many cases renounced their cultural past and their traditional language, having reduced their form of Judaism to no more than a few more or less symbolic practices, having been assimilated by and even converted to Christianity, having time and time again proved themselves to be good and even exemplary patriots, they found themselves yet again victims of anti-Semitism, as if the centuries had not passed and the darkest days of the Middle Ages had returned to the pulpits, faculties, and palaces. It was therefore obvious that the only way to win freedom was to become an independent nation, much as the peoples of the many Balkan countries who were beginning to recover their own identity had done. The difference, however, was that these countries had a geographic area of their own, whereas the Jewish people did not.

pamphlet entitled *Auto-Emancipation*. That same year and in the wake of the pogroms of 1881 and 1882, various groups of Russian Jews, who were later to be joined by more from Poland and Rumania, set out for Palestine to found farming colonies. Despite the hostility of the Turkish authorities, the resentment of the Jews who had lived in Palestine since the earliest of times, the harsh conditions of the new life, and malaria, they managed to put their plan into practice. At the same time, *Hovevei Ziyyon* ("Lovers of Zion") groups sprang up all over Russia to form an organized movement known as *Hibbat Zion* ("Love of Zion"), which set up a settlement fund. The experiment would have failed due to lack of resources had it not been for the aid of Baron Edmond de Rothschild. By the end of the 19th century there were thirty farming colonies in Palestine with a total population of almost 6,000. They had no common language, but this problem was solved by the astonishing determination of Eliezer ben-Yehuda, who had emigrated to Palestine with his family in 1881. Untiringly Yehuda labored to revive Hebrew as a spoken

91

Top: Keren Kayemet poster in Hebrew, Polish, and Yiddish inviting settlers to the Valley of Jezreel in Palestine, Poland, 1930. Above: Keren Hayesod poster in Yiddish on colonization in Palestine by Jews, Jerusalem, c. 1925. (Both from the William L. Gross Collection, Ramat Aviv, Israel.) The Keren Kayemet, the World Zionist Organization fund for the acquisition and development of land in Palestine, was founded in 1901 at the fifth Zionist Congress (Basel),

its headquarters being set up successively in Vienna (1902-7), Cologne, The Hague (1914), and Jerusalem (1922). The first land purchased was Kefar Hittim (Lower Galilee), followed in 1908 by Ben Shemen and Huldah in Judaea and Kinneret-Deganyah near the Sea of Galilee; but the first large-scale purchase of land—11,000 acres in the Valley of Jezreel—did not take place until 1921. The Keren also aided urban development through loans to the founders of Tel Aviv

and acquired the Bezalel Academy of Arts and Design building in Jerusalem and land for the Herzliyyah High School in Tel Aviv and for the Technion in Haifa. Founded in 1920 to finance immigration and colonization projects in Palestine, the Keren Hayesod was the financial organ of the World Zionist Organization. Its main office was in London until 1926, when it was transferred to Jerusalem.

One positive result of the unfortunate Dreyfus Affair was the appearance of the man destined to become the greatest ideologist and proponent of political Zionism. Born into a considerably assimilated Budapest family, Theodor Herzl (1860-1904) studied law in Vienna, but chose writing and journalism as a career (as a Jew, it would have been impossible for him to practice as a jurisconsult). Herzl was in Paris, working as correspondent for a Viennese newspaper, when the scandal of the French captain accused of spying broke out. He was deeply affected by the attitude of the French populace toward the Jews; in the streets of that supposedly civilized city, he heard the cry "Death to the Jews!" Convinced that the creation of a state was the only solution, Herzl wrote Der Judenstaat ("The Jewish State"), in which he proposed a return to Palestine, an ideal to which he dedicated enormous energy during the rest of his short life. Although his plan was greeted without enthusiasm and even with suspicion and derision by the assimilated Jews of central and western Europe, Herzl received the support of numerous well-known figures, among them the critic and essayist Max Nordau, the English writer Israel Zangwill, David Wolffsohn, a Cologne businessman, and the majority of the Hovevei Ziyyon groups in eastern Europe. Herzl convened the first Zionist Congress at Basel (1897), founded the World Zionist Organization, and drew up the movement's program. His aims were to take shape many years later with the creation of the state of Israel.

When a proposal put forward in 1903 by the British government to set up an autonomous Jewish colony in British East Africa (Uganda) was rejected by the sixth Zionist Congress—Herzl himself called it no more than an "asylum for the night"—the practical sector of the movement advocated purchasing land in Palestine.

Between 1904 and 1914, and after the arrival, mainly from Russia, of a new wave of immigrants inspired by Socialist ideals, the number of new colonists in Palestine reached 12,000.

Shortly before the end of World War I, intensive diplomatic activity took place in which the Jewish chemist from England Chaim Weizmann, an ardent Zionist ever since Herzl's day, played an important part. Weizmann's efforts led to the Balfour Declaration, signed in 1917 by the British foreign secretary Arthur James Balfour, in which His Majesty's government endorsed the idea of creating a "national home for the Jewish people." In 1920, the League of Nations approved a British mandate over Palestine with Herbert Samuel, an eminent English Jew, as high commissioner.

Above: The Wailing Wall in a photograph, c. 1900 (Museum of the Jewish Diaspora, Tel Aviv). Opposite: The Wailing Wall, oil painting by Jean-Léon Gérome, 1880 (Israel Museum, Jerusalem). In a Zionide (12th century) Judah Halevi wrote about his future in Jerusalem:
My dwelling I exchanged for the shade of bushes, the strength of my door for a fence of branches; on fragrant aromas my soul was sated, but my syrup I exchanged for the smell of brambles... on the bosom of the sea my paths I have set until the footstool of my Lord I find and there pour out my soul and my sighs. I shall sit on the threshold of the Sacred Mountain and build my iron gates opposite the gates of heaven. With water from the Jordan I shall make my spikenards bud and in Shiloh my trees grow.

The Struggle for Autonomy

A series of events during and immediately after World War I gave rise to considerable optimism among European Jews, leading them to believe that, in one way or another, their position would finally return to normal. Once again, however, harsh reality was to dash their hopes—hopes based on the Balfour Declaration of 1917, by which it finally seemed possible that the creation of a Jewish national homeland in Palestine was within reach; based also on the Russian Revolution, in which a large number of Jews had participated, some holding prominent positions, and which, through the abolition of all discrimination, recognized Jews as equal citizens with full rights; and on the clauses relevant to the autonomy of minorities drawn up at the Versailles Peace Conference and affecting the new states that had arisen with the disappearance of the European multinational empires (Austro-Hungarian, Ottoman, and Russian), namely Estonia, Latvia, Lithuania, Poland, Rumania, Czechoslovakia, Hungary, Yugoslavia, Austria, Greece, and Turkey. It should be noted that several of these new countries had the highest Jewish populations in the world after the United States; in Poland there were over 3 million, in Hungary half a million, in Rumania 750,000. Furthermore, the Jews of the Soviet Union numbered over 2.5 million.

Jewish groups and institutions worked hard on the political front during the period prior to the Versailles Conference, with the result that the 1920 Peace Agreement included a treaty regarding minorities according to which not only Jewish rights but also Jewish autonomy and representation as a nation were guaranteed; that is, Jews must be represented as a national group in the institutions of central government in the new countries, being free to lead their own way of life, particularly in matters relating to religion, education, and charitable institutions. In spite of still having no territory of their own (as had been their situation since the Middle Ages), self-rule within each country would enable Jews to maintain their identity as a nation and ensure against assimilation.

Believing that such clauses placed limits on their national sovereignty, the new states strongly opposed enforcement from the very begin-

Top: Jewish emigrés from Germany at a settlement in Montana, 1890 (Montana Historical Society, Helena). Above: The German Jew Julius Meyer visiting Indian chiefs, c. 1880 (Nebraska State Historical Society, Lincoln). The number of Jewish emigrés from central Europe to the United States increased in the middle of the 19th century. The German Jews adopted the same organization as that in their country of origin, forming a closely knit group. Aid funds were created

to help the new settlers, some, in time, becoming banks. From the very beginning, Nebraska, which became a territory in 1854 and was admitted as a state in 1867, was chosen as a settlement site by Jewish emigrés mainly from central Europe (Alsace-Lorraine, Germany, and Bohemia). From 1881 these were joined by others from Russia. Most made clothing or opened businesses, and some dealt with Indians. Such was the case of Julius Meyer, who

settled in Omaha in 1866. Meyer, who is believed to have learned as many as six Indian dialects, was adopted by the Pawnee tribe. He accompanied a group of Indians to the Paris International Exhibition as their official interpreter.

ning, so that (except in Czechoslovakia) sooner or later the clauses became ineffective or the Jews' autonomous and civil rights were drastically reduced. Thus, in Rumania and Poland all manner of obstacles were placed in the path of Jewish citizenship, so that virtually nowhere were Jews allowed to join the civil service or were Jewish languages officially recognized. Furthermore, a limit was set on the number of Jewish students admitted to higher education, and in many of these countries severe restrictions were placed on Jewish businesses; for example, Jewish craftsmen in need of apprentices were required to take a language test, Jewish-owned businesses applying for credit had to include Christian partners, state subsidies were granted to competitors, Jews were excluded from the huge state monopolies formed by government companies, and so on. Indeed, a large number of small Jewish businessmen and craftsmen would not have been able to avoid bankruptcy and the confiscation of their goods had it not been for the credit cooperatives set up with the aid of the American Jewish Joint Distribution Committee and other Western Jewish organizations. Other important institutions contributed to plans to train youths for manual labor, including the Jewish schools belonging to the ORT, a company founded in Russia in 1880 to further the teaching of farming and the trades.

In many of the new countries fresh waves of pogroms accompanied the birth of independence, resulting in several thousand Jews slaughtered in Poland, Hungary (particularly after the abortive Communist coup of 1919), and Rumania.

The disillusionment that came with the loss of all hope for the future led many Jews to join wide-ranging political parties, both Jewish and non-Jewish. Supported by the Hasidim and the majority of rabbis and religious dignitaries, the ultra-orthodox parties, such as *Agudat Israel*, were in favor of collaborating with even the most reactionary and anti-Semitic of governments; the various factions of the Zionist movement—the religious *Mizrachi*, the General Zionists, and *Po'alei Zion*—became extremely active, some of them turning to Socialism and Communism; the left-wing ideological movements that were grow-

95

Top: The Danish Jewish Besbroda family celebrating the Passover seder, Copenhagen, 1917 (Museum of the Jewish Diaspora, Tel Aviv). Above: Austrian Jewish soldiers celebrating the seder in Russian Poland, c. 1915 (Österreichisches Staatsarchiv, Vienna). Unlike the Jewish communities of eastern Europe, those in western Europe did not engage in any struggle for recognition of autonomy, as they considered themselves to be protected by the laws of

equal rights and had no difficulty in becoming fully integrated with their surrounding cultures. Nor were there Jewish political parties like those in the east, which is not to say that Western Jews did not play an active part in the politics of their countries. In England, Jews formed part of Liberal governments and during World War I even became cabinet ministers in Lloyd George's coalition government. Later, some became important members of the Labor

Party. In France, Jews belonged to the Republican, Radical, and Socialist parties, some holding government office. In Germany and Italy, too, Jews led the Socialist and Communist parties and were even among the parties' founders.

in schools, some private, others supported by different organizations, which offered them a nonreligious education in Hebrew and Yiddish. In Vilna, the Yiddish Scientific Institute (YIVO) was founded in 1925, its syllabus being the history, language, and culture of the Ashkenazic Jews. Furthermore, Jewish historiography developed considerably during this period, its most important representative being Simon Dubnow (1860-1941). Although he was not against the creation of a Jewish homeland in Palestine, Dubnow did not believe that the Jewish people needed a separate territory of their own; instead, he presented a theory of "autonomism" based on Diaspora nationalism. He believed that Jewish survival had resulted from the communal and spiritual independence of Jews in the Diaspora and that Jewish nationalism would be best served if the Jews were given cultural autonomy within the many and varied communities of the Diaspora. Dubnow taught history in St. Petersburg, where he helped found the Jewish Historico-Ethnographical Society; he moved to Berlin in 1922 and then went to Riga, Latvia,

ing in Europe proposed a new society based on principles of universal justice. The latter were to open up new horizons for many young Jews who, eager to see their dream of universal brotherhood come true, played an active part in the development of the European Socialist parties and even more in the Communist parties of the Third International. These Jewish revolutionaries, most of whom were assassinated, included Kurt Eisner, the first republican premier of Bavaria in 1918; Béla Kun, who led the Communist uprising in Hungary in 1919; Rosa Luxembourg, a veteran German revolutionary; and Hugo Haase, leader of the German Independent Social Democratic Party. Other Jews joined nonextremist parties, such as the German Democratic Party, whose members included such men as Hugo Preuss (instrumental in the Weimar Constitution), and Walther Rathenau (assassinated by anti-Semitic fanatics in 1922).

The new social and cultural order influenced a whole generation of Jews. Indeed, in Hungary, Czechoslovakia, Lithuania, and eastern Poland a large number of young people studied

Top: The Synagogue of Dzialoszyce, Poland, c. 1915 (Österreichisches Staatsarchiv, Vienna). Above: Shops in the Prague ghetto, late 19th century (Museum of the Jewish Diaspora, Tel Aviv). It was the policy of many eastern European governments to ruin Jewish citizens (heavy taxation on companies, compulsory language examinations for craftsmen, accountants, servants, coach drivers, etc.). In Austria the economic crisis of 1929 led to the closure of

various Jewish banks, while in the late 1930s, the bankruptcy of the Phoenix insurance company ruined hundreds of Jewish customers and employees. In the period between the two world wars, the Jewish craftsmen and small traders of Poland, Rumania, Lithuania, and Latvia were ruined by the large-scale expansion of the peasants' cooperatives and increasing state intervention in economic activities. In Poland the state possessed a large number of

monopolies (on tobacco, wine, salt, matches, mines, timber, the chemical industries, and army supplies) that excluded Jews from employment. In Latvia one third of all property belonged to the state, and in Lithuania 40 percent, as well as a third of all trade and industry and all forests, with the result that the large number of Jews who worked either as foresters or in the timber industry lost their only means of livelihood.

The Altneuschul Synagogue, built in 1270, and the Jewish quarter town hall, in a photograph, c. 1920 (Museum of the Jewish Diaspora, Tel Aviv). Czechoslovakia was the only country to acknowledge Jews as a national minority. Although a large number of Jews of German and Hungarian origin lived in Czechoslovakia, conserving their own languages and cultures, the authorities preferred to consider these actually as Jews. If they had been considered as *groups who spoke a particular language, it would have been necessary to take the linguistic autonomy of German and Hungarian into consideration, for according to the constitution, minorities that numbered over 20 percent of the local population could build their own schools and classes could be held in their language.*

when Hitler came to power in 1933. He was killed there by the Nazis in 1941.

Other factors exerted considerable influence on the Jews of Europe in the period following World War I. Natural growth declined swiftly, due, among other things, to a large sector of the Jewish population turning away from the traditional way of life and also to a sharp increase in mixed marriages (a new and far-reaching phenomenon) in which the children were not brought up as Jews. Furthermore, the worldwide depression of 1929 brought an intensification of discrimination against Jews. The number of emigrés also declined considerably between the two world wars; between 1901 and 1914, over 1.5 million Jews had emigrated, whereas in the latter period scarcely more than a million left their countries, with an increase in emigration to Palestine and a sharp fall in emigration to the United States. Furthermore, between 1926 and 1938, just when flight meant survival for many European Jews, severe restrictions on immigration came into effect in the United States.

In the early 1930s, the situation for the Jews of eastern Europe took a turn for the worse. The rise of the Nazis in Germany inflamed anti-Semitic sentiment, particularly in Poland and Rumania, where attacks on Jews, their homes, and businesses intensified and demands were made to deprive Jews of their civil rights. Discriminatory race laws (and those who upheld them) also increased in the Baltic countries, Hungary, and Austria.

The Russian Revolution and Its Aftermath

Until the outbreak of World War I, the Russian Empire was not only the greatest center of Jewish life in the world, but also the largest potential source of new populations for Jewish communities. But this situation soon changed. The defeat of Russia led to the Revolution of 1917, giving rise to high hopes for the future, as it seemed that for the first time in their history Jews would be free to lead their lives as they wished. The idea of Jewish national and cultural autonomy met with the support of such political parties as the Socialist Revolutionaries, the Mensheviks, and the Constitutional Democrats, but not of the Bolsheviks, despite the party's large number of Jewish members. Consequently, when the Bolsheviks came to power, all the plans that had been made by the Jewish organizations came to nothing.

During the civil war between the Red communists and White anti-Bolsheviks that devastated the country from 1918 to 1920, the sufferings of the Jews reached a new peak, particularly in the Ukraine, where the cruel pogroms of the White armies claimed the lives of over 60,000 Jews. When the civil war ended, all Jewish parties and indeed all forms of independent organization were obliterated, and in 1919, the Zionist parties were dissolved. With thousands of their members in prison or deported, these parties went underground. Moreover, all religious communities were declared bourgeois institutions and closed down. With the antireligious propaganda campaign of the 1920s, many rabbis, butchers, and Jewish teachers were expelled or arrested, synagogues were closed down, and the printing of religious literature, including prayer books, was forbidden. As an alternative to their traditional Hebrew culture, the Jews were made to accept a nonreligious alternative with Yiddish as its only language.

"War Communism," the name given the first period of Bolshevik government, brought wrack and ruin to the already poor masses of Jews who lived in the small town communities of the old Pale. Large numbers of young Jews drifted to the larger towns and to areas of central Russia, where, as they struggled to survive in competition with thousands of other dispos-

Poster for the Socialist Zionist youth group Hasomer Hasair with the Hebrew slogan "Long live the October Revolution, Long live the Soviet Union's struggle for the freedom of the peoples and Socialism" (Central Zionist Archive, Jerusalem). The movement first appeared in Vienna in 1916, when two previous groups from Galicia that had formed before World War I merged; these were the Seire Zion group, which took charge of cultural activities, and the Hasomer group, which was organized in the manner of the British Boy Scouts. Its aim was to educate Jewish youth in preparation for life in the kibbutzim in Israel. The movement was founded secretly in Russia in 1922, its purpose being to prepare the way for settlement in Palestine. Its numbers reached 20,000 throughout the Soviet Union and the first groups left for Palestine in 1924.

sessed souls like themselves, anti-Semitism yet again raised its head. In the late 1920s, however, a plan was proposed for a permanent new autonomous Jewish region in Birobidzhan (Siberia), near the Chinese border. Although the first contingents set out in 1928, the plan was not to prove as successful as had been expected, due mainly to the new opportunities offered elsewhere to young people by the five-year plans. Russian Jews also underwent a rapid process of proletarianization and cultural and linguistic assimilation in the 1920s, the number of manual workers trebled, and the proportion of Jews admitted to centers of higher education increased. In the 1930s, Jews tended to forsake farming to become skilled workers in industry, so that more and more chose to take up technical activities and the liberal professions, working in teaching, medicine, and the arts and sciences. At this time, too, Jews were admitted into the civil service. Consequently the concept of Jewish identity began to fade, mixed marriages increased, and the new generation drifted away from its cultural tradition—and indeed, from the Jewish world in general.

In the late thirties, when Russia annexed large areas of territory—eastern Poland, the Baltic countries, Bessarabia, and Bukovina—some 2 million Jews were added to the 3 million who already lived in the Soviet Union. This vast community, which suffered Stalin's purges in the late thirties, was finally to be handed over to the Nazis for extermination on the very day that Germany invaded the Soviet Union.

Above left: Postage stamp dedicated to the Jews of Birobidzhan, issued by the Soviet Mail in 1933 (Biblioteca Macías, Madrid). Above right: "Make Communist life grow in the fields of Russia," lithograph in Yiddish urging Jews to support collectivization of the land, Moscow, 1926 (Israel Museum, Jerusalem). With industry in ruins in the 1920s, the Soviet regime ruled that in order to save the population from famine the land should be worked. *In 1924 the Soviet Presidium appointed a commission to study the feasibility of settlement by Jewish workers in the countryside. The number of settlements grew, and by 1930 10 percent of the Jewish population lived from farming, which gave rise to the notion of creating an autonomous Jewish territory—necessary in any case as the settlement of Jews in the Ukraine, White Russia, and Crimea had met with opposition from local farmers. The region* chosen was Birobidzhan, near the Chinese border. *The first groups arrived in 1928. After five years the settlers' numbers had increased to 20,000, but 60 percent of these eventually left the area due to the harsh climate, poor soil, and lack of outside aid. In spite of all this, and although less than 20 percent of the population was Jewish, the area was declared the Jewish Autonomous Oblast in 1934.*

Western Europe Between the Two World Wars

Anti-Jewish poster issued by the German Ministry of Propaganda, Berlin; in German from 1940 (below), with the slogan "Behind the enemy: the Jew," and in French from 1942 (below right), with the slogan "And behind: the Jew" (private collection). After the Communist Revolution, aristocrats who had fled to the West from the Baltic countries distributed the Protocols of the Elders of Zion, a document written at the end of the 19th century in Paris by members of the Russian secret police who copied and adapted a political satire against Napoleon III written by the French lawyer Maurice Joly and published in 1865. The document attracted no attention when it was published in Russia at the beginning of this century or when it was reedited during the revolution of 1905, but it had a strong impact in versions distributed after World War I in Germany, France, Great Britain, and even in the United States.

The Jewish communities of western Europe, including those in Germany and Italy, did not take part in the eastern European Jews' struggle for recognition as a national group, for they felt that laws guaranteeing equal rights already protected them as members of the societies in which they lived. Indeed, in England, Jews had played, and continued to play, an active part in politics as Liberal and Labor members of parliament, while in France, many Jews belonged to the Republican, Radical, and Socialist parties. Furthermore, in Germany and Italy, Jews held important positions in the Socialist and Communist parties. In religious matters, Jews were particulary active in organizations set up to help their persecuted coreligionists and in charitable institutions; in all other activities, they could not be distinguished from non-Jews. As far as Zionism was concerned, many Jews in these countries were interested in it only as a means by which to overcome the difficulties of Jews in eastern Europe, North Africa, and other countries—but not their own difficulties.

In western Europe, there were no Jewish

political parties similar to those in eastern Europe, the Zionist organizations existing rather as groups with ideological tendencies and even as educational and cultural associations. However, after World War I, young Western Jews began to take a certain romantic interest in the Orthodox Judaism of eastern Europe. Furthermore, growing anti-Semitism eventually intensified the search for historic roots and adherence to the Jewish heritage.

Established after the war, the Weimar Republic in Germany made a wholehearted attempt to erase anti-Semitism; but the idea began to take root in the minds of a German nation exasperated by the humiliation of defeat, inflation, and postwar unemployment that the Jews and the left-wing political parties were to blame for all the country's ills. Furthermore, anti-Semitic sentiment was often whipped up by members of the Russian tsarist aristocracy who had fled to Germany after the 1917 revolution and now took it upon themselves to spread anti-Bolshevik and anti-Semitic propaganda, one example being the Protocols of the Elders of Zion, a fraudulent doc-

ument purported to be the minutes (protocols) of a meeting held by prominent Jews early in the 19th century in which they planned the destruction of Christian civilization so they might eventually take control of the world. The Russian exiles claimed the Russian Revolution had been only the first step in this plot and that the Soviet government and Communist International were led by Jews.

In postwar France, extreme right-wing factions blamed Jewish Masonry for all the country's woes, and even in England the influence of the *Protocols* made its mark on Catholic circles. In the United States the *Protocols* was praised in the industrialist Henry Ford's newspaper, the Dearborn *Independent* (in 1927 Ford admitted the work was slanderous). In part as a result of the *Protocols*, the Ku Klux Klan included Jews on their blacklist of enemies of the United States.

The outbreak of civil war in Spain in 1936 served to aggravate the antagonism between Left and Right in the western European countries. The Liberal, Socialist, and Communist groups support-

Poster by René Peron advertising the anti-Jewish exhibition The Jew and France, held in Paris in 1941 during the German occupation (private collection, Paris). Anti-Semitism grew stronger in Europe after World War I. Although Communism proved to be disastrous for Russian Jewry, the fact that Jews were among the leaders (Lenin's mother may have been Jewish, and Trotsky, Zinoviev, Kamenev, Sverdlov, Joffe, Radek, Sokolnikov, and others were Jews) was used as a pretext to equate Jews with Communism and led to charges that Jews were responsible for its creation.

Jews and the Spanish Civil War

Right: Machine-gun unit of the Lincoln Brigade on the Ebro front during the Spanish civil war (Abraham Lincoln Brigade Archives, Brandeis University, Boston). Below: Commemorative plaque dedicated to the Jews who fought in the International Brigades and died defending Madrid (Fuencarral Cemetery, Madrid).

A large number of Jews joined the International Brigades; of the 40,000 volunteers, around 10,000 were Jews from Africa, Canada, the United States, Palestine, and Europe (Great Britain, Austria, Belgium, France, Italy, Scandinavia, Germany, Hungary, Czechoslovakia, Poland, Yugoslavia, Rumania, and Russia). There were also Jews who simply happened to be in Spain at the outbreak of the military uprising and who did not hesitate to join the people's militias. Among these were Emmanuel Link, who led the Botwin unit, 22 Palestinian athletes of the Hapoel sports association who were in Barcelona for the Workers' Olympics, and two Jewish tailors from London who happened to be in the south of France taking part in a bicycle race. Others actually lived in Spain, as did Benjamin Balboa, a Sephardic Jew

from Morocco and a petty officer with a Spanish navy communications unit. Balboa broadcast the alert to the sailors of the naval units in the Mediterranean to take control of their ships.

The Jewish Brigade members were scattered among various battalions—including the Chapiaev Brigade, over 60 of whose 389 volunteers were Jews, and the Dombrowski Battalion (later the 13th Dombrowski Brigade), where the proportion of Jewish officers was very high—and in brigades, such as the Lincoln Brigade, 40 percent of whose number were Jewish. Also extremely important were the large number of Jewish doctors—49 of the 50 Polish volunteers, 27 Americans, and many of the nurses from the United States, Belgium, and France. One company, the Naphtali Botwin belonging to the Palafox Battalion, was made up almost exclusively of Jews, their number at one point reaching 152; this company, which fought on the Extremadura, Teruel, and Lérida fronts, published its own newspaper in Yiddish and even formed its own theater and sports groups. One of its members, Pinkus Kartin, was among the Jews who later organized the Warsaw ghetto uprisings.

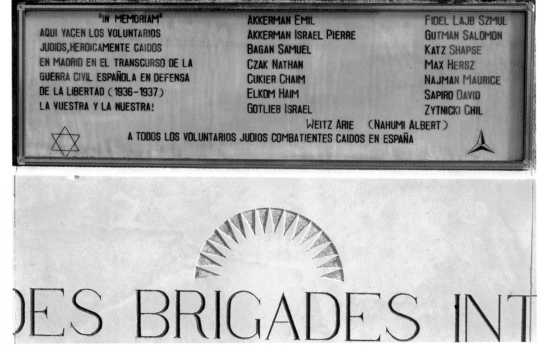

"IN MEMORIAM"
AQUI YACEN LOS VOLUNTARIOS JUDIOS, HEROICAMENTE CAIDOS EN MADRID EN EL TRANSCURSO DE LA GUERRA CIVIL ESPAÑOLA EN DEFENSA DE LA LIBERTAD (1936-1937) LA VUESTRA Y LA NUESTRA!

AKKERMAN EMIL	FIDEL LAJB SZMUL
AKKERMAN ISRAEL PIERRE	GUTMAN SALOMON
BAGAN SAMUEL	KATZ SHAPSE
CZAK NATHAN	MAX HERSZ
CUKIER CHAIM	NAJMAN MAURICE
ELKOM HAIM	SAPIRO DAVID
GOTLIEB ISRAEL	ZYTNICKI CHIL

WEITZ ARIE (NAHUMI ALBERT)
A TODOS LOS VOLUNTARIOS JUDIOS COMBATIENTES CAIDOS EN ESPAÑA

DES BRIGADES INT

ed the elected Republican government, while the Right favored nonintervention, which in France led to the fall of Léon Blum's Popular Front government. Many Jews joined the International Brigades that went to Spain to fight for the Republic, and according to some estimates, between a quarter and a third of all the Republican troops were Jewish volunteers. Indeed, a large number of generals were also Jews.

When the Nazis came to power in Germany, Western Judaism awoke from its lethargy and was forced to begin to organize itself for its own political battle. The World Jewish Congress met in Geneva in August 1936, and various resolu-

tions were passed on propaganda, a boycott of German products, the fight against discrimination, and methods to aid refugees. In France and England, anti-Semitic propaganda increased when in 1938 the two countries signed an agreement with Hitler in Munich believing they had thus secured peace; in consequence the suffering of the Jews became no more than an uncomfortable fact, and subsequent waves of Jewish refugees found the doors to all the Western countries closed, while the British authorities suspended immigration to Palestine. This situation paved the way for the greatest disaster ever to strike the Jews of Europe.

102

Above left: German Jewish wedding in Fort Worth, Texas, 1924 (Institute of Texan Culture, University of Texas, San Antonio). Above: Mural by Ben Shahn at the Homesteads Roosevelt, New Jersey, 1938-39, featuring Jewish emigrés led by Albert Einstein. After World War I growing anti-Semitism in the United States led to immigration restrictions based on quotas that varied according to the country of origin; in 1921 the annual limit was fixed for each country at

103

3 percent of the immigrants who were resident in the United States in 1910; in 1924 this number was lowered to 2 percent of the 1890 figures. Thus the number of Jewish immigrants fell from 150,000 to 49,000 and then to 11,000. Anti-Semitism intensified with the crisis of 1929 and Hitler's rise to power, its most conspicuous exponents being the German-American Bund, the "Silver Shirts," and the Catholic priest from Detroit Father Coughlin, who in 1938 launched an anti-Semitic campaign in the press and on radio. Discrimination became commonplace, jobs were offered only to Christians, and some universities set limits on the number of Jews they would accept while others refused to accept them at all. The banks, large companies, and the majority of the industrial consortiums would not employ Jews, and some clubs, hotels, and recreational centers barred them from entry.

The Holocaust

In January 1933, with Germany deep in economic crisis and 6 million unemployed, Hitler became chancellor of the Reich. Once in power, he replaced the parliamentary system with an iron-fisted National Socialist dictatorship. Terror swept the Jewish communities, and to the indifference of the Western world Jews were excluded from public and intellectual activities and their businesses boycotted. Anti-Jewish laws took shape in Nuremberg in 1935, defining Jews as a race apart and describing as "Jewish" anyone, whatever his or her religion, with at least one Jewish grandparent. Among the many measures taken against them, Jews were stripped of their German citizenship and the right to vote—they were confined to the status of "subjects"—they were barred from virtually all professions, and mixed marriages were prohibited. The Western countries paid little heed, however, and

in spite of everything met in Berlin for the 1936 Olympic Games.

Jews had been leaving Germany for several years, and now the stream of refugees increased. The German authorities had no objection to their leaving, as long as they took nothing with them. By the outbreak of World War II, over 300,000 Jews had left the country, a further 70,000 managing to do so over the next two years. Troubled by the fate of the thousands of refugees, the Western powers met for a conference in Evian, France, in 1938, but not one was prepared to take in these Jews who had no country of their own.

When Austria was annexed to the Third Reich in 1938, a fresh wave of anti-Semitic violence broke out, above all in Vienna. On November 7, a seventeen-year-old German Jewish refugee by the name of Herschel Grynszpan—

seeking to avenge the deportation of members of his family and the persecution of Jews in Germany—shot and mortally wounded an official of the German embassy in Paris, Ernst vom Rath. The Nazis used this as the excuse for the worst pogrom that had yet taken place in the Third Reich. The organized violence of the so-called *Kristalnacht* ("Night of Broken Glass," November 9-10, 1938) raged rampant all over Germany. Six hundred synagogues were burnt down or demolished, Jewish shops and houses were sacked, and 30,000 Jews were sent to concentration camps.

The Nazi invasion of Poland in September 1939 led to the outbreak of World War II. Within weeks areas in which almost 2.5 million Jews lived were devastated. Polish Jews were made to wear a yellow badge (the common practice in all the countries that fell to the Germans) and were herded into ghettos, the largest of which, in Warsaw, at one point contained half a million Jews. In 1941 Germany invaded the Soviet Union, massacring all the Russian Jews they encountered as they advanced; in Babi Yar near Kiev, over 30,000 were shot in two days. In the course of the next few years, Germany occupied or controlled almost all of Europe, from the Arctic Ocean to the Mediterranean and from the Pyrenees to the Caucasus. Virtually nowhere did the Nazi Jewish policy meet with strong opposition; indeed, in some countries, such as Poland and Rumania, certain sectors of the population actively collaborated with the Germans. There were, however, certain worthy exceptions, as in Denmark and Holland, where in general everything possible was done to save the Jewish communities, and in Finland, where no kind of restrictions were tolerated. To these must be added the individual actions of certain Belgians, the French men and women of the Resistance, consuls—among them Spaniards who issued Spanish passports to both Sephardic and non-Sephardic Jews—and of charitable souls in general, both priests and laymen.

Until 1941, Jews in the occupied countries were immediately separated from the rest of the population and transferred to concentration camps in a special area set up by the Germans in Lublin (Poland). But in 1942, the decision was

The Frankfurt Börneplatz Synagogue (built in 1882) in flames after being set on fire during the "Night of Broken Glass," November 9-10, 1938 (Museum of the Jewish Diaspora, Tel Aviv). The Nazi machine was in motion. Blamed for the fire and destruction, the Jews of Germany as a group were fined a billion marks and made to repair the damage done to their own shops and factories by the rioters. Next, Jews were excluded from financial companies and management positions.

They were also forbidden to take part in cultural activities, their organizations were suppressed, their publications were banned, and Jewish children were refused entry to schools. German Jewish cultural and economic life was brought to an end, and it was not long before the Jews lost even their lives.

death toll, but the number of victims of the "final solution" alone stands at around 4.5 million. The total of almost 6 million was the equivalent of two-thirds of European Jewry, and in some countries, such as Poland, Greece, and Czechoslovakia, only a tenth of the Jewish population survived.

The Jews, the only surviving ancient people of Europe, who settled there not through choice but because of the political requirements of the Roman Empire—a European empire—have for centuries been like an indispensable and ubiquitous thread in the fabric of European historical reality, sometimes for the good of Europe—furthering cultural change, as, for example, in the medieval Hispanic kingdoms or in the cultural birth of central Europe after emancipation—and sometimes for the bad, by serving as a catalyst for Europe's demons and neuroses—as when religious fanaticism (a sentiment having nothing to do with the tolerant teachings of the Jew Jesus Christ, but of the intolerant interpretation of his church) or anti-Semitic fanaticism (a sentiment having nothing

taken to implement the so-called final solution, entrusted to Adolf Eichmann. Extermination camps with gas chambers and crematoriums were built in Majdanek, Belzec, Treblinka, Auschwitz, and Sobibor, among other places in Poland, Mauthausen in Austria, and in Dachau, Bergen-Belsen, and Buchenwald in Germany. In eastern Europe, mass executions by firing squad under Latvian, Ukrainian, and White Russian police became the order of the day.

On some occasions attempts were made to resist, many of the Jews who managed to escape joining the Russian or Polish guerrilla movements or organizing their own guerrilla forces. But the most glorious page in the history of Jewish resistance was written in the Warsaw ghetto, where, starving and virtually weaponless, men, women, and children of all ages rose up against the Germans in April 1943, holding out for five weeks and finally obliging the German army to take the ghetto house by house.

When the war ended, the Allies discovered to their horror what had been taking place. It will never be possible to calculate the exact

105

Top: Survivors of the Warsaw ghetto revolt being led off to the death camps, April 1943. Above: Suitcases belonging to Jews deported to the Auschwitz-Birkenau concentration camp (Auschwitz Camp Museum). Of all the Jewish resistance movements, the most famous was that led by Mordecai Anielewicz in the Warsaw ghetto. Starving and virtually weaponless, men, women, and children of all ages held out for five weeks, finally obliging the German army to take the ghetto house by house. Purely symbolic and doomed to failure from the start, this display of resistance served to affirm that neither the Nazi terror nor the indifference of the world had served to break the spirit of a people who continued to practice their faith and believe in the future. Over 7,000 Jews died in the revolt.*

to do with the Christian cultures of Europe) has led to the spilling of Jewish blood on its soil. And this because the Jew is the *alien*, notorious and closest at hand. Torn from their natural geographic environment, the Jewish people never exercised political or territorial power in Europe and so always lay at the mercy of Europe's governments. Effortlessly and in the most natural way, they were granted Roman citizenship in the 3rd century by emperors who did not gauge the efficiency or goodness of their subjects by their pedigree; yet all their rights were denied them during the centuries in which the Catholic Church governed Europe, controlling princes and monarchs alike under its iron rule, and also when its teachings—harsh, implacable, and with virtually no chinks in its armor—added to the ill-will of both Orthodox and Protestant. Since the Holocaust, the nerve center of Judaism is no longer Europe, and some Europeans who find it hard to accept this fact now walk abroad in search of new minorities on which to blame their woes.

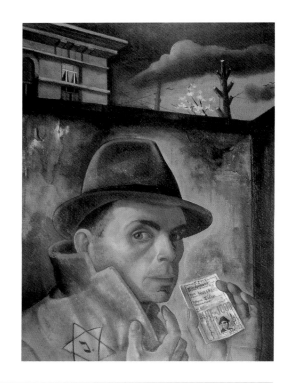

Top left: Self-portrait with Jewish Identity Card, *oil painting by Felix Nussbaum, 1943 (Kulturgeschichtliches Museum, Osnabrück). In spite of the artist's efforts to evade the Nazis by constantly changing his whereabouts he was finally arrested with his wife in 1943. Both died in Auschwitz. Above left: Students visiting the ovens of Auschwitz, where the bodies of over 70,000 human beings were cremated (photomontage). Above:*

Evidence of the Prosecution, *oil painting by Joseph Kukrynsky, 1967 (State Tretyakov Gallery, Moscow). The Russian painter here presents a scene of the Nuremberg war crimes trials.*

Man is a traveler who wanders in the dark;
his soul is the monarch his mainstay the body.
Death appears and reaches out with the scythe
and the shadow shatters over the well
of desolation.
—*Solomon ibn Gabirol, 12th century*

Rites and Customs

Opposite: The Last Night of Hanukkah, by Charles
Spencelayn (Christie's Gallery, London). Above:
Looking for hamez, by Bernard Picart from
Cérémonies et coutumes réligieuses de tous les peuples
du Monde, 1725 (Biblioteca Nacional, Madrid).
Arise, chosen soul,
to the house of God and its threshold
and turn thy song to myrrh before His face.
—Judah Halevi, 12th century

Religion

Below: A father blessing his children on leaving the synagogue in a Haggadah from Aragon, c. 1350-60 (Bosnia and Herzegovina National Museum, Sarajevo). It is common practice for a father to bless his children on Sabbaths, festivals, and certain other occasions. The father places his hands on the child's head and says, "God make thee as Ephraim and as Manasseh" (Gen. 48:20) if the child is a boy, and "God make thee as Sarah, Rebecca, Rachel, and Leah" in the case of a girl, followed by the priestly blessing (Num. 6:24-26).

Judaism is not only the oldest of the world's monotheistic religions; it is also their source. It is not enough to see Judaism as a strictly religious phenomenon, for, theological and ritual aspects apart, it rules every moment of Jewish life, revealing itself no less in adherence to beliefs than in certain individual, social, and cultural forms of conduct.

Belief in a single God of Creation whose unity is indivisible is essential to the Jewish faith; God is immaterial and therefore cannot be depicted; He is eternal and therefore immortal; He is infinite and therefore too great for the human mind.

Men have the freedom to choose between good and evil and receive the reward or punishment that their choice merits.

Although intangible, the God of Judaism revealed Himself on Earth and in history: on Earth because His providence rules the world through the continuous renewal of His work of creation; and in its history as it was He who chose Israel as His people to serve Him and bear witness to Him on Earth. This choice was sealed

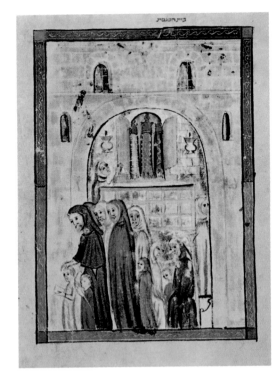

with a *berith* ("covenant") in which Israel received the Torah and accepted the responsibility of its fulfillment.

The source of Jewish doctrine is the divine revelation contained in the *Torah* ("teachings" or "learning"), the Hebrew word for the five books of Moses—the Law of Moses or the Pentateuch—which by extension refers to the entire content of Judaism—the Scriptures, their oral tradition, and their inspired interpretation. Jewish law thus forms a vast sea whose intimate knowledge requires time and dedication. Since the origin of the Torah is divine, its study is considered an ethical virtue. For this reason, the assiduous student (*Talmud hakham*) is held in the highest esteem within traditional Judaism.

The rabbi is an expert on the Torah who has studied deeply to attain the position he holds. His task is to lead in worship, ensure that the precepts are fulfilled, and to teach, interpret, apply—and above all study—the Torah. He may be the spiritual leader of a synagogue, a community, or a group of communities, yet whatever his position, his authority is determined not by a centralized hierarchy but by the prestige he has gained through his knowledge and the recognition of such knowledge by Jewish society.

The Torah is also a guide and a set of rules in life. Study and erudition in the law do not achieve their goals if they are not accompanied by practice, which, far from being limited to worship and the liturgy, finds expression throughout a Jew's life from birth to death. The Torah concerns all levels of human existence, from the most trivial everyday actions to the most sacred liturgical ceremonies, so that whatever situation a Jew finds himself in, there will always be a *halakah,* or law, to determine what he must do or a precept (*mitzvah*) to be fulfilled so that he may act in accordance with the Torah.

The 613 precepts (*mitzvot*) of Judaism, both positive (commands) and negative (prohibitions), refer to one's obligations to God, to one's neighbor, and to oneself.

Certain precepts govern social content, examples being the institution of a day of rest during the week and, in certain circumstances, of freeing one's slaves.

Fulfillment of the precepts is not limited to any specific place; in many cases these are fulfilled in the home, as when the table is blessed, or at the Passover supper. It is here where the woman's role in traditional Judaism is decisive, especially in relation to the extremely complex Jewish dietary laws.

The extent to which the precepts are complied with varies within traditional Judaism, but they are followed to the full by the Orthodox Jew, whose whole life is governed by the *halakah*. However, the different branches of Reform Jews attach more importance to other religious values than to strictly and literally obeying the precepts. The Conservative movement, or "historical school," has elaborated a middle position, maintaining most of traditional Judaism while accepting certain changes in accordance with contemporary considerations. While the lines drawn between the three positions are distinct, the more moderate members of each express tolerance toward one another. There are, of course, secular Jews who do not belong to any organization but adhere to Jewish values and culture, sometimes seeking a religious life outside the synagogue.

Rabban Gamaliel and his pupils in two miniatures from the Passover Haggadah. Above left: Haggadah from Aragon, c. 1350-60 (Bosnia and Herzegovina National Museum, Sarajevo). Opposite: Haggadah from France, 14th century (private collection). Considered a primordial religious duty, the study of the Torah is one of the basic principles of rabbinic Judaism. The times in a child's life when he must begin to study the religious texts are set out in the talmudic tractate Pirkei Avot ("Chapters of the Fathers," 5.21). According to the treatise, five is the appropriate age to begin studying the Scriptures, ten the Mishnah, thirteen the observance of the precepts, and fifteen the study of the Talmud. In the Kiddushin talmudic tractate (30a), on the other hand, it is stated that a man's time should be divided up in such a way that a third is dedicated to the Scriptures, a third to the Mishnah, and a third to the Talmud.

The Synagogue

Of Greek origin, the word *synagogue* means "assembly" or "house of assembly" and is an accurate translation of the Hebrew term *bet kenisa*. Together with the temple it is the most important institution in Judaism, and yet little is really known of its origin.

Historians have offered several theories; some believe that the synagogue existed at the time of the First Temple, before 587 B.C.; others hold that it originated with the Babylonian Exile; while for another group it is an institution dating from a later period, in the Hellenistic Diaspora.

Whatever its origin, by the 1st century A.D. it had become a firmly established institution that in both Palestine and the Diaspora communities was the center of social and religious life for the Jewish people and in Israel stood alongside the temple.

As the Gospel proves, there were numerous synagogues in the villages of Galilee at that time, and the New Testament also contains references to the synagogues of the Diaspora communities. Furthermore, the Acts of the Apostles relates that Paul preached in various synagogues

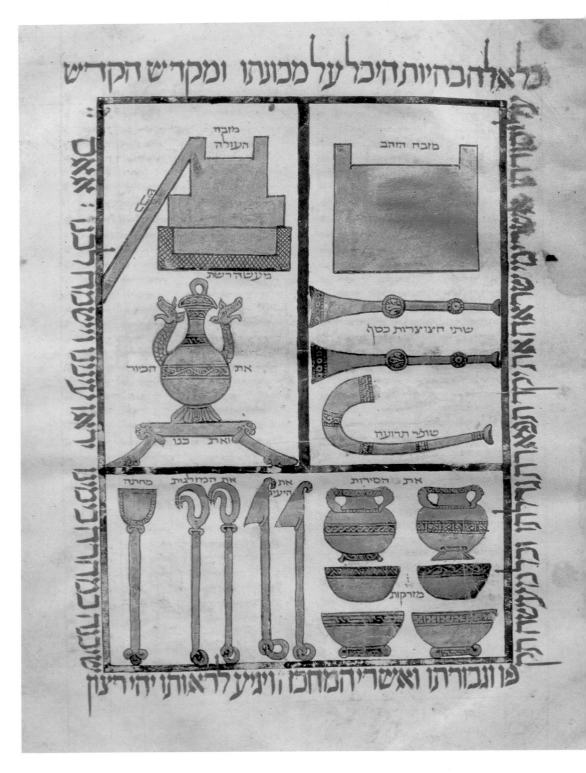

112

Illustrations of temple implements. Above left: Regensburg Pentateuch, *c. 1300 (Israel Museum, Jerusalem). Above and opposite left:* Bible, *Perpignan, 1299 (Bibliothèque Nationale, Paris). Opposite right:* Bible, *Catalonia, 14th century (Biblioteca Palatina, Parma). The seven-branched candelabrum, or menorah, was one of the liturgical implements made by Moses according to God's instructions (Exod. 25:31-40; 37:17-24). Kept in the* Temple of Solomon, *it disappeared when Jerusalem was conquered by the Babylonians, although according to legend it was hidden and later returned to Jerusalem by the exiles who built the Second Temple. During the reign of Antiochus Epiphanes IV it disappeared again, but Judas the Maccabee made another, which remained in Herod's Temple until the building was destroyed by the Romans. It was then taken to Rome and placed in a special temple. There*

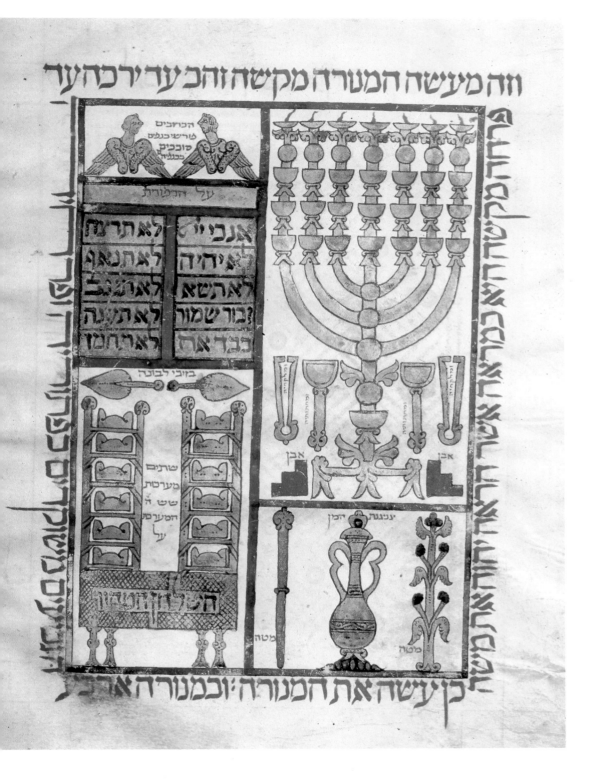

in Damascus, and mention is also made of the synagogues in the towns he visited in Asia Minor and Cyprus.

After the destruction of the temple, the synagogue became the center and focal point of Jewish religious life, inheriting many temple customs and rites. Other rites and customs were explicitly forbidden, as they were exclusive to the temple, so that prayer, for example, replaced sacrifice, and the officially appointed priest was replaced by a cantor or reader.

Since the earliest of times and due to certain historical circumstances—as, for example, when Jews were made to live in ghettos—the synagogue was not only a place for prayer, study, and teaching, but also served as a community center and a house of assembly that dealt with matters relating to life within the community. The officials of the local synagogue served as community leaders, law courts met within the synagogue, and communal funds were often deposited there.

In the synagogue, official decrees were read out to the people, scholars and students spent whole days and sometimes whole nights

113

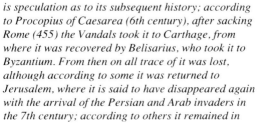

is speculation as to its subsequent history; according to Procopius of Caesarea (6th century), after sacking Rome (455) the Vandals took it to Carthage, from where it was recovered by Belisarius, who took it to Byzantium. From then on all trace of it was lost, although according to some it was returned to Jerusalem, where it is said to have disappeared again with the arrival of the Persian and Arab invaders in the 7th century; according to others it remained in

Byzantium until the city was sacked during the Fourth Crusade in 1204. The menorah has been the most important symbol of Judaism since earliest of times; during the Middle Ages it was depicted in the decoration of synagogues, tombstones, lamps, amulets, and manuscripts.

The Religious Service

absorbed in the Torah, and the local synagogue was the first place a Jew from another town visited. Moreover, everything necessary for Jewish life was to be found in the synagogue or its adjacent buildings—the rabbinic law courts, the ritual bath, or *mikveh*, and the hospice for travelers.

Religious service, as established in the Talmud, has continued to exist without any fundamental changes for 2,500 years, and only with the passage of time have certain modifications, which vary from one community to another, been made.

Communal prayer is held in the synagogue three times a day—at nightfall, dawn, and midday—before a *minyan*, a prayer quorum of at least ten males over thirteen years of age.

With the congregation following him, an officiant reads aloud, chanting traditional or psalmodic melodies at the beginning and end of (and sometimes throughout) the paragraphs in the book of daily or holy day prayer (*siddur* and *mahzor*). Prayer may be led by anyone of those taking part, providing he is familiar with the ritu-

114

Ritual flagellation in Amsterdam's German Synagogue, from an engraving by Bernard Picart. Flagellation was practiced by certain highly religious Jews on the eve of the solemn commemoration of Yom Kippur, the day of atonement, penitence, and fasting during which repentance for sins is the order of the day.

Objects for liturgical use from an engraving by Bernard Picart. A., b., and c. are short talliths with fringes, or zizit, *and the loose* zizit; *d. is a Sabbath lamp; e. is* matzo shmurah, *special unleavened bread for the Sabbath; f. is* matzo, *or unleavened bread; g. is a* lulav *branch for the Sukkot festival; h. is a bitter orange for Sukkot; i. is a shofar; k. is a* mezuzah, *a container for verses from the Bible hung from the doorpost.*

with the recitation of the doxology (kaddish), the content of which bears a close relationship to the Lord's Prayer, although its liturgical function is different.

During prayer, males cover their heads with a yarmulke, or skullcap, or any kind of hat and their shoulders with a shawllike tallith. For daily prayer in the synagogue phylacteries, also known as *tefillin*, must also be worn on the forehead and left arm. These are small black leather boxes that contain pieces of parchment inscribed with verses from the Shema.

Communication with God is not limited to communal prayer in the synagogue; there are prayers for the home and others that can be said anywhere, hence the eulogies (*berakhot*, "benedictions")—a tradition hundreds of years old—that are used to communicate with God while carrying out all mundane actions—eating fruit, smelling a flower, admiring a beautiful landscape, receiving good or bad news—so that God is constantly invoked and acknowledged as the origin of all creation.

al, but it is normally led by the cantor (*hazzan*) or the rabbi.

Prayer, praise, and petition to God, which are all said in Hebrew with a few sentences in Aramaic, consist of passages from Psalms and other books from the Bible mixed with further passages dating from the Second Temple and later. The essence of the liturgy lies in the biblical passages that form the Shema, the Jewish confession of faith (Deuteronomy 6:4-9 and 11:3-21 and Numbers 15:37-41), the benedictions (*berakhot*) that accompany them, and the Eighteen Benedictions (*Shemoneh Esreh*), recited while standing (*amidah*).

The Torah is read out in services on Mondays, Thursdays, Sabbaths, holy days, and festivals; a passage dealing with a single topic (*parashah*, meaning "explanation") is read every week, so that the Pentateuch is read from beginning to end in the course of one year. The parashah is followed by a passage from the Books of the Prophets (*haftarah*, meaning "conclusion") that has some relevance to the parashah reading. Communal prayer alternates

115

The Calendar: Festivals and Commemorations

In the Hebrew calendar, the months begin with the new moon and are 29 or 30 days in length, while the year is solar and is normally of 12 months. In order to adjust the difference between the solar year (365.25 days) and a year of 12 lunar months (354 days) certain "leap" or embolismic years—7 in every cycle of 19—have 13 months instead of 12. Furthermore, years may be regular, defective, or perfect, which gives rise to six possible periods of duration; the common regular year has 354 days, the common defective year 353, and the common perfect year 355 days, while the regular embolismic year has 384 days, the defective embolismic year 383, and the perfect embolismic year 385 days.

In a regular year, the odd months (Tishri, Kislev, Shevat, Nisan, Sivan, and Av) have 30 days, while the even months (Heshvan, Tevet, Adar, Iyyar, Tammuz, and Elul) have 29. In a defective year, a day is removed from Kislev, while in the perfect years, Heshvan has one day more. In embolismic years the 29-day month of Adar Sheni (or Veadar) is intercalated between Adar and Nisan, and Adar has 30 days.

The succession of regular, defective, and perfect years does not follow a consistent pattern, so the years are determined by means of complicated calculations whose purpose is to avoid Yom Kippur, the "Day of Atonement" considered the Sabbath of Sabbaths, falling on a Friday or a Sunday (as there would then be two consecutive Sabbaths), or Hoshana Rabba (the seventh day of the Sukkot festival) falling on the Sabbath itself.

In ancient times, the Sanhedrin announced the beginning of the new month when at least two witnesses had reported to the judges that they had seen the New Moon in the sky, but in the time of the Second Temple, when a part of the Jewish people lived in Babylonia, the Sanhedrin announced the coming of the New Month by lighting bonfires on the peaks of a number of mountains between Judaea and Mesopotamia. Later, word was sent by messenger. When the Christian state made normal life difficult for the Jews in the mid-4th century A.D., Hillel II, then president of the Sanhedrin, revealed the manner way in which the Hebrew calendar was calculated (until then a secret) so that all Diaspora Jews should be able to calculate the calendar for themselves. One custom from ancient times remained effective; in order to cover all eventualities, Pilgrim Festivals were observed for one day more in the Diaspora communities than in Israel.

As far as the calculation of the years is concerned, Judaism takes as its starting-point the creation of the world, which, according to rabbinic tradition, was the year 3760 B.C. Days do not begin in the morning but at sunset and last until the sunset of the next day.

Panel illustrated with the days of Omer (Old Cemetery Museum, Prague). Omer is the 49-day period between the morning of the second day of Passover, during which a measure of barley, or omer, was offered in ancient times to the temple, and the first day of the Shavuot, or Pentecost, festival, when the earliest crops were also offered. In order to keep count of the days, it was common to have calendars like this one in the household.

Hebrew calendar from Mantua, 1594 (William L. Gross Collection, Ramat Aviv, Israel). The Jews have rejected all attempts to adopt the world calendar and instead use a more accurate system than the current Gregorian calendar. Their day of rest depends on an indivisible sequence of six working days followed by the Sabbath, which is not only a day of prayer but is also fundamental to the Jewish faith. Any change could affect the sequence.

Announcing the Sabbath, *postcard based on an oil painting by Moritz Oppenheim, Germany, 1894. At dusk on Friday, shortly before the Sabbath begins, the housewife lights at least two candles, saying a special prayer as she does so. As she makes the final preparations for the Sabbath supper, her husband and children go to the synagogue for the Kabbalat Shabbat ("Reception of the Sabbath"), during which additional prayers to the usual eventide ones are said.*

The Sabbath Eve, *oil painting by Isidor Kaufmann, c. 1920 (Jewish Museum, New York). From the Babylonian Talmud, in the Tractate Shabbat, 119b: "Two ministering angels accompany a man on the eve of the Sabbath from the synagogue to his home, one a good [angel] and one an evil [one]. And when he arrives home and finds the lamp burning, the table laid, and the couch [bed] covered with a spread, the good angel exclaims, 'May it be even*

thus on another Sabbath [too],' and the evil angel unwillingly responds, 'amen.' But if not [if everything is in disorder and gloomy], the evil angel exclaims, 'May it be even thus on another Sabbath [too],' and the good angel unwillingly responds, 'amen.'"

Festivals have a twofold significance in Judaism, religious and historical. Moreover, some festivals commemorate the original agricultural organization typical of the society in which they came into being. A common characteristic is the sanctification of the holy day through the transformation of the various elements of the celebration into *mitzvot* ("precepts").

On the ritual calendar, the most important Jewish institution is the Sabbath (Saturday), which once a week commemorates God resting on the seventh day; just as God rested from his work of Creation, so must Man rest from his work of transforming nature, so that activities like kindling fire, operating machines, bearing burdens, and walking more than a certain distance may not be performed, unless by doing so a life will be saved or a sick person can be attended to. Consequently, everything necessary for the Sabbath—such as meals and the fire on which to heat them—must be made ready on the eve. Celebration of the Sabbath begins before sunset on Friday, when one or two Sabbath candles are lit. As on the other holidays, meals

begin with a prayer of sanctification (*kiddush*) recited over a cup of wine, followed by another blessing over two loaves of bread. As night falls and the holy day comes to an end, another prayer is recited to mark the distinction (*habdalah*) between the Sabbath and the new weekday that is beginning.

The liturgical year begins with the Solemn Days, dedicated to repentance and penitence. The first of these, *Rosh Hoshana* ("New Year"), lasts for two days and usually falls in September or at the beginning of October. During Rosh Hoshana the creation of the world is commemorated, the most distinctive observance in the synagogue being the sounding of the *shofar* (ram's-horn trumpet). The shofar was also sounded in the temple to announce important events, such as the crowning of a king or the beginning of a Jubilee. On this day, God judges the actions of all men, who will be rewarded or punished accordingly in the coming year. However, until the arrival of Yom Kippur it is possible to avoid an unfavorable decision through repentance, prayer, and good deeds.

117

Habdalah, *postcard based on an oil painting by Moritz Oppenheim, Germany, late 19th century (private collection). Once three stars have been sighted in the sky, the Sabbath comes to an end, and evening prayer is said in the synagogue. The Habdalah ceremony is performed both in the synagogue and the home to celebrate the end of the holy day and the beginning of the next, ordinary day. During the ceremony the aroma of spices is inhaled*

from a special container, a candle is lit, a glass of wine is drunk, and the candle is then extinguished in drops of wine spilled onto a dish. All these actions are accompanied by special prayers.

Yom Kippur ("Day of Atonement"), the most solemn—and the most highly respected—of the Jewish holidays, is the culmination of the Ten Days of Penitence that begin with the New Year. It is a day of fasting, dedicated to repentance and prayer for the expiation of sins committed against God, oneself, and also against one's neighbor; in the latter case it is necessary to repair damage to obtain forgiveness—though when the neighbor is a Gentile, such reparation and repentance must not be sufficient. The religious services held in the synagogue go on all day, beginning with the Kol Nidre prayer, in which release from vows imposed upon oneself yet unfulfilled is sought, and ending with the sounding of the shofar.

There are three festivals of pilgrimage to Jerusalem that date from Biblical times. The first, *Pesah* ("Passover"), takes place in March or April and in the Diaspora lasts eight days. It marks the beginning of the new agricultural cycle with the arrival of spring and commemorates the merging of the descendants of the patriarch Jacob into one people who gained their freedom with

the Exodus from Egypt. With the destruction of the temple and the dispersion of the Jewish people, the festival lost its agricultural character, and its significance as a celebration of freedom faded so that it finally became associated mainly with dietary laws. The only kind of bread that may be eaten at *Pesah* is unleavened bread (matzo), in commemoration of the flour and water that did not have time to ferment, as the pharaoh ordered the Jews to leave Egypt immediately. It is also forbidden to eat or have within the household any food containing *hamez*, that is any food or drink made through the fermentation of certain cereals (wheat, barley, rye, oats, etc.) or which contain leaven. Consequently on the eve of Passover the house is carefully cleaned so that not even the smallest crumb of bread remains. All crockery, cutlery, and cooking utensils that have come into contact with leavened food throughout the year are also scrupulously cleaned. The celebration in the home begins with the *seder* ("order of service"), or ritual supper. A tray is placed on the table containing a symbolic assortment of foods, such as unleavened bread (matzo), bitter herbs

Two illustrations from a 15th-century Spanish Haggadah (Musée Condé, Chantilly, France): at the Passover table (top) and roasting the lamb (above). The following passages from the Haggadah explain why the text is read year after year and the children are told of the events that took place. "And thou shalt shew thy son in that day, saying, This is done because of that which the Lord did unto me when I came forth out of Egypt" (Exod. 13:8). "And he brought us out from thence, that he might bring us in, to give us the land which he sware unto our fathers" (Deut. 6:23).

(*maror*, which symbolize the bitterness of slavery in Egypt), a shank bone (*zeroa*, recalling the lamb sacrificed in the temple), *haroset* (a type of sweet paste commemorating the mortar that the Jews were forced to make for the bricks of the pharaoh's cities), a hard-boiled egg, and a few vegetables, which are also symbolic. Four cups of wine must also be drunk. At the seder the Haggadah—the story of the Exodus—is read. It contains texts from different ages whose purpose is to explain the significance of the festival to the children. The children themselves play a prominent part in the celebration, as the youngest present must ask a ritual question prior to the reading of the Haggadah, and some of the poetic and semipoetic passages with which the reading ends are addressed specifically to them.

Seven weeks after the beginning of Passover, in May or June, the two-day festival known as *Shavuot* ("Pentecost") takes place. In temple times, this served as an opportunity to offer the early wheat and first ripe fruit to God. Shavuot also commemorates the revelation of the Ten Commandments on Mount Sinai.

The Feast of Tabernacles is one of the oldest and most joyous of Jewish holidays. In the Bible it is called the Feast of Ingathering; today it is often called *Sukkot* (Hebrew for "Booths"). The holiday lasts nine days (eight in Israel) during which Jews must reside in or at least take their main meals in specially constructed booths in gardens or terraces. It commemorates the forty years of wandering in the desert before the people of Israel reached the Promised Land. There is a procession every day in the synagogue during which hoshanas are sung and a citrus fruit (*etrog*) and a palm branch (*lulav*), bound up together with myrtle and willow branches, are waved. On the seventh day of Sukkot, known as *Hoshana Rabba*, there are seven circumambulations of the synagogue and the scroll of the law is shown to the congregation. This procession is reminiscent of those once made around the altar in the temple of Jerusalem.

Sukkot is followed by *Simhat Torah* ("Rejoicing of the Law"), during which the annual cycle of public readings from the Pentateuch comes to an end, and a new cycle begins. This is celebrated in the synagogue by

119

Preparations for Passover and kneading and baking the matzoth, or unleavened bread, in a Haggadah from the Rothschild Miscellany, *northern Italy, c. 1470 (Israel Museum, Jerusalem). Written by no single author, the Haggadah text is not a literary composition in the normal sense but rather a collection of passages from the Bible, the Mishnah, and the Midrash interspersed with the ritual elements of the celebrations, tales, and songs also gradually being included. It appears that the Haggadah was compiled in the 7th or 8th century, but the oldest existing version is that which forms part of the 10th-century prayer book of Saadiah Gaon (882-942), an important leader of Babylonian Jewry.*

Minor Celebrations

parading the scrolls of the Torah in joyous procession. It is considered a great honor to read out the last passage from the Torah in the old cycle or the first in the new cycle, and those who receive such a distinction are called Bridegrooms of the Law (*Hatan Torah*) and of the Genesis (*Hatan Bereshit*) respectively.

Hanukkah ("Festival of Lights" or "Festival of Dedication") in December commemorates the rededication of the temple of Jerusalem in 165 B.C. after the victory of the Maccabees. It lasts for eight days, the main ceremony consisting of lighting a candelabrum of nine candles (*menorah*) in the home to commemorate the miracle of Hanukkah in the time of the Maccabees. The lamp oil used in the temple menorah was of a special type that remained ritually pure in sealed jars, or cruses. When the time came to light the lamp, the Jews saw that only one cruse of pure oil remained and that the small amount of oil it contained would be enough for no more than one day. The lamp miraculously burned for eight days, giving the priests enough time to make more oil.

Tu Bi-Shevat ("Fifteenth of Shevat") or the "New Year for Trees," which normally falls in January and occasionally at the beginning of February, was originally related to tithing purposes for the temple: all that ripened before this date was considered to belong to the previous year, whereas whatever came after that day was considered as part of the new harvest. However, with the passage of time, the holiday came to be an exaltation of the life of the landworker and his bonds with nature.

The Festival of Esther or *Purim* ("Lots," from the casting of lots by Haman in Esther 9:24-26) is usually celebrated in March, although it sometimes falls at the end of February. It commemorates an event that took place in the middle of the 5th century B.C.—the deliverance of the Jews from their enemies in the Persian kingdom of King Ahasuerus, whom some historians have identified with Xerxes. The story is told in the Book of Esther, which is read in the synagogue from a parchment scroll, or *megillah*. Being the most festive of the Jewish holidays, it has a certain carnival air about it; alms are given to the poor, gifts, particularly

Dismountable wooden sukkah *from the Deller family of Fischbach, southern Germany, 1825 (Israel Museum, Israel). Over the centuries, many ways of building the* sukkah *have been devised in accordance with religious regulations, demands of climate, available materials, and the owner's own taste. Specific requirements are that it should stand in the open air, have at least three walls, and that the roof be of foliage so that the sun can shine through and the* stars be seen. This unique sukkah—only one other of its kind is known—is decorated with paintings combining religious themes—left, Jerusalem, the temple, the west wall, Moses on Mt. Sinai, etc.—and secular themes, such as hunting scenes. It was in use until 1910.

mourning, the congregation sit down on the synagogue floor or on low stools instead of on pews or chairs. It is also customary to chant laments on the expulsions (such as the expulsion from Spain), persecutions, and massacres that took place in medieval Europe, during the Crusades, and on other occasions, as when the ten elders were tortured on Hadrian's orders at the time of the Bar Kokhba revolt.

sweet things, are exchanged, and there is even a certain degree of overindulgence in eating and drinking. Games of chance are also played at this time. Purim is also associated with costumes and traditional farces in which episodes from the Bible, particularly the hanging and burning of a dummy representing Haman, are performed. Such performances have taken place since earliest times and are common in numerous European communities, both Sephardic and Ashkenazic. With the passage of time, the content of the celebrations grew to include singing and dancing. Indeed, the germ of Jewish theater may be observed in this celebration.

Apart from these festivals, the Jewish calendar also contains days of fasting, all of which commemorate sorrowful events in Jewish history. The most important of these is *Tishah be-Av* ("Ninth of Av"), which falls in July or August and recalls, among many other sorrowful events in Jewish history, the destruction of the two temples of Jerusalem, the first by Nebuchadnezzar, king of Babylonia, in 586 B.C., and the second, by fire on Titus's orders in A.D. 70. As a sign of

121

Top: A wealthy Amsterdam family dining in a sukkah, *engraving by Bernard Picart from* Cérémonies et coutumes réligieuses de tous les peuples du Monde, *1725 (Biblioteca Nacional, Madrid). Above: Building a* sukkah *(right) and blessing the wine inside it, wood engraving, Poland, 19th century (Jewish Museum, New York). The Talmud states that for the rest of the year Jews should eat and sleep in the* sukkah *instead of in the house, but in practice it is now used only as a*

place in which to eat the main meals. In the communal sukkot *the faithful are normally given a cup of wine and a mouthful of bread, over which blessings are said, after the religious service.*

Rites of Passage

The Torah governs the life of each individual from the cradle to the grave. The first ceremony in life for a male is circumcision (*Berit Milah*), which takes place on the eighth day after birth as a sign of the covenant (*berit*) with God.

At the circumcision ceremony, which must be carried out by an expert (*mohel*) with the necessary practical and religious knowledge, the child is given a Hebrew name (among the Sephardim, he is usually named after one of his grandfathers). At the moment of circumcision, one of the close relatives of the child acts as godfather or *sandak*, sitting on a special seat known as the Chair of Elijah (after the prophet) and holding the child on his knees. A month and a day after the birth of the firstborn (who, according to the Law, must be dedicated to God), the *Pidyon ha-Ben* ("Redemption of the firstborn") ceremony takes place, in which the father places the child in the arms of the *kohen* ("priest") and "redeems" the child by paying a symbolic sum of money.

The Jewish male comes of religious age at thirteen, that is he becomes *Bar Mitzvah* ("son of

122

Above: Circumcision instruments and a book of prayers and regulations for the occasion. Above right: Book with circumcision regulations, copied and illuminated in ink and gouache by Aaron Wolf of Gewitsch, a distinguished Austrian scribe and illuminator and the author of a number of Hebrew manuscripts outstanding for their fresh approach, Vienna, 1728 (State Jewish Museum, Prague). According to God's instructions to Abraham (Gen. 17:11-12), *all Jewish males must be circumcised in a ceremony that is to take place eight days after birth, provided the child's health allows it. It is usually performed in the synagogue, and the* mohel's *instruments, all of which are richly ornamented, include knives, protective pegs, a flask for the astringent powder, and a bag in the shape of a lyre that serves as a case.*

the Commandment") and from then on is responsible for his own actions. At the celebration, the boy dons the tallith and the tefillin for the first time, and it is customary for him to be invited to the synagogue to read an appropriate text from the Torah.

Until relatively recently, Jewish marriages were arranged by marriage brokers, the couple having little say in the matter and sometimes seeing each other for the first time at their wedding. Indeed, marriage brokers sometimes began planning suitable matches even before the parents knew about it. Settlement of the dowry and trousseau was also arranged exclusively by the parents. Very often well-to-do families sought to marry their children into the families of rabbis, that is into the intellectual class—a son-in-law studying Jewish law became a privileged person free from all financial worries who lived at the expense of his father-in-law. The couple became officially engaged several years before the marriage ceremony actually took place.

On the day of the wedding the bride, her mother and future mother-in-law sit under a

Top: Wedding Ceremony of Portuguese Jews, *from an engraving by Bernard Picart; the groom is about to break the glass by throwing it against a tray. Above left: Scene from an Ashkenazic wedding in Amsterdam, also by Picart. The engravings demonstrate some of the differences between Sephardic and Ashkenazic wedding rites. The Sephardic couple stand under a canopy, or* huppah, *in the home (as in the engraving) or in the synagogue,*

while in the Ashkenazic ceremony, which is preferably held in the open air and generally in the synagogue court, a tallith *is placed over the bride and groom's head and shoulders. Furthermore, the Ashkenazim of central Europe usually throw the glass against a wall, rather than break it with the foot, while those of eastern Europe follow the same custom as the Sephardim. At all marriages a small orchestra plays music for the occasion.*

Above: Ketubbah, *or marriage contract, Padua, late 18th century (William L. Gross Collection, Ramat Aviv, Israel). In most Jewish communities it was customary to illuminate and decorate these contracts. Certain examples from Germany (1392) and the Hispanic kingdoms date from the Middle Ages. The most noteworthy, however, come from 16th-century Italy, certain communities in Sepharad, and the Near and Far East.*

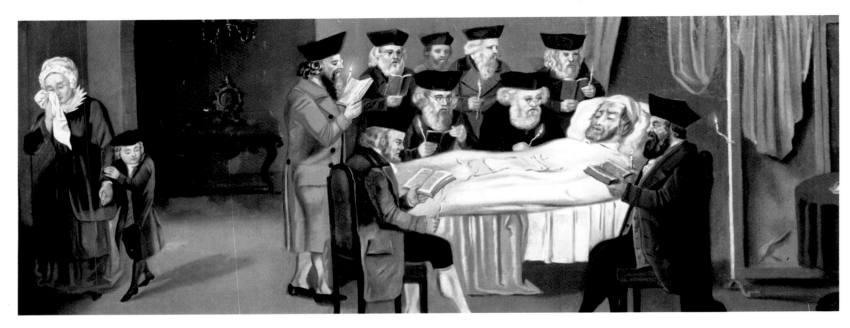

canopy (*huppah*) symbolizing the bridal bower. The marriage ceremony is in two parts; during the betrothal and sanctifications (*kiddushin*) the groom places a gold ring on his bride's finger, and the marriage contract (*ketubbah*) is ritually read, including the responsibilities the groom will take upon himself as a husband and the

compensation he must pay his wife in case of divorce; secondly, the marriage itself (*nissu'in*) consists of the reciting of the seven marriage benedictions. The groom must then break a glass with his foot in evocation of the destruction of the Temple of Jerusalem.

The Jewish burial ceremony involves an

institution that has always existed in Jewish communities, the holy society (*Hevra Kaddisha*), which prepares the body for the grave, attends to cemeteries, and so on. The body of the deceased is ritually washed and wrapped in a white shroud; then, accompanied by the bereaved, it is borne to the grave on a type of stretcher or on a bier and is

The institution of the Hevra Kaddisha *("Holy Society") is unique to Jewish communities and appeared as the result of the rabbinic prohibition that forbade capitalizing on death. For this reason profit-making companies are not allowed to take charge of burials. The Hevra Kaddisha appeared in Germany and the medieval Hispanic kingdoms at the beginning of the 14th century, attending to the dead among their own numbers and carrying out the prescribed funeral*

rites. In the Sephardic world the group also received the name of "Society of Washers," a term derived from the funeral rite of washing the corpse. Composed of volunteers, the first societies appeared in the 16th century as community charitable organizations, carrying out the sacred duty of attending to the burial of community members. The first known organization of this type appeared in Prague, founded in 1564 by Eleazar Ashkenazi.

The Prague Hevra Kaddisha at their annual banquet; this picture and the one below belong to a series of oils painted in Prague, c. 1840 (State Jewish Museum, Prague). The Hevra Kaddisha meets as a society on various occasions, the most important being the annual celebration, whose date varies from one community to another, although it is most commonly held on the seventh of Adar, the day on which, according to rabbinic tradition, Moses died.

The day begins with fasting in atonement for any lack of respect shown inadvertently by the society toward the dead and ends with the banquet, which is considered one of the community's most important occasions.

buried. The eldest son of the bereaved family recites a prayer (*kaddish*) that is repeated during the period of mourning and on each anniversary of the burial. The Talmud mentions the hiring of professional mourners skilled in the art of provoking grief and weeping by means of gestures and funeral chants; this custom has existed in

Jewish communities for centuries. The period of mourning (*abel*) consists of three stages: *shivah* ("seven") the traditional seven days of deep mourning, which begins immediately after the funeral, followed by two further periods of modified mourning; during the second stage the bereaved males do not shave or cut their hair for

thirty days; and in the third stage, on the first anniversary of the bereavement, the funeral monument is raised—normally a marble tombstone inscribed with the Hebrew name of the deceased, the date of his or her death, and an epitaph. All signs of mourning are put aside one year after the bereavement.

125

Above: Leaders of the Prague Hevra Kaddisha at the grave of Judah Löw in the city's Jewish cemetery. This famous rabbi, who lived in the 17th century, devised the takkanot, *or ordinances, of the Prague Hevra Kaddisha. These were later ratified by the Austrian authorities. The* takkanot *state that the society's services are to be extended to all Jews within the community, even if they are not members of the society and have not paid any dues.*

Dress

Classical Jewish sources contain a wealth of references to clothing and ways of dressing. Examples are the detailed descriptions of priestly clothing and adornment in the Bible and the importance attached by the Talmud to the wearing of clean clothes: "A student on whose clothing there is a stain deserves death" (Babylonian Talmud, Tractate Berakoth, 43b). Rabbinic literature, which also contains a large number of rules on dress, insists on the wearing of garments that reflect decency and humility and the use of fine clothing on Sabbaths and festivals only. Such rules have, to a certain extent, contributed to the fact that Jewish clothing may seem oldfashioned. However, the large number of rabbinic regulations that attempt to place a limit on the wearing of finery suggests that Jews, like all other human beings, are not immune to the attraction of jewelry and fine clothing.

The self-imposition of restrictions in dress has always had a dual purpose; on the one hand, it makes differences in financial status within Jewish society less obvious, and on the other it means that the attention of non-Jews is not attracted by ostentatious clothing—at certain times perhaps a means of survival in a frequently hostile and watchful Gentile environment.

In the synagogue the male must wear a tallith, the prayer shawl worn over the rest of his clothing. Usually made of wool, it is adorned with white or colored stripes and has white fringes (*zizit*) at each of its four corners. It is interesting to note that on the talliths worn by Polish Jews, the part that fits around the neck (*atarah*) is adorned with embroidery executed in flat, silver threads in what is known as the Spanish style (*spanier*). The short tallith is for more general use, as it is not limited to the synagogue. It is worn beneath the shirt and consists of a rectangular piece of material with an opening in the middle for the head and has a *zizit* at each corner hanging outside the clothing.

Jews wear some kind of head-covering on all occasions, be it a hat or skullcap (yarmulke, or *kappel*). This became customary in the 17th century. Married women cover their heads when in the street, although there is no compulsory type of headgear.

In some communities the rabbi wears special

Judici de Crist davant dels sacerdots jueus ("Judgment of Christ before the Jewish Priests"); detail from the predella of the Maestre de Rubió altarpiece, second half 14th century (Museo Episcopal de Vich, Spain). The following passage is taken from Alfonso X's Siete Partidas ("The Seven Divisions of Law," 7:24.11) and deals with the mark to distinguish Jews from the rest of the population (Law XI): "Jews must bear a sign so that they may be recognized: Much damage and many outrageous things take place between Christian men and Jewish women and Christian women and Jewish men as... the ones dress as do the others. And to avoid any damage and ills which might take place for this reason... we hereby order all Jews and Jewesses that live in our realm to wear some special sign upon their heads and that the sign be such that the people may know immediately who is a Jew or a Jewess."

clothing. In general, Jews have always followed the customs of the societies in which they lived in terms of nonreligious clothing. Little is known of Jewish clothing in the early Middle Ages, except for a few references to the use of belts and the so-called *judaicae peluciae*, garments trimmed with fur. It is therefore reasonable to assume that no specific clothing was worn exclusively by Jews. Furthermore, the beards and side whiskers so characteristic of later times were not common during this period.

The difficulty of telling Christians from Jews troubled church leaders throughout the Middle Ages, and the subject was included in the proceedings of the Fourth Lateran Council, which Pope Innocent III convened in 1215 to crown the labors of his pontificate. Generally considered by church historians to be one of the most brilliant councils ever held, its various canons—which include a statement of faith and a definition of transubstantiation—sum up Innocent's ideas for the church. The council's Canon 68 addresses the problem of distinguishing Jews from their Christian neighbors: "In several provinces, a difference in vestment distinguishes the Jews or the Saracens from the Christians; but in others the confusion has reached such proportions that a difference can no longer be perceived. Hence, at times it has occurred that Christians have had sexual inter-

Above and above right: Depictions of Jews in the Passion of Christ altarpiece in the Correa de Vivar Parish Church, Burgos, late 15th century (Varez Fisa Collection, Madrid). The following are passages on Jewish clothing from the takkanot, *or ordinances, of Valladolid of 1432 (Chapter V): "For in many* kehilloth... *there are dishonest and prejudicial rules and customs due to... the clothing of the women and their jewels... and they do wear clothing of great*

value and of great show as well as rich fabrics of great value and trains and jewels of gold and silver and pearls... which give reason for much ill... and for this reason from time to time they dictate decrees concerning us and we have never even been considered completely innocent; and that is the reason for making great takkanot *and being strict on this matter." These considerations are followed by a list of prohibited adornments and clothing, after*

which the ordinance continues: "But this has been said; this is not to be understood for clothing worn at times of celebration nor when lords or ladies are received, nor at dances, nor on similar occasions."

course in error with Jewish or Saracen women and Jews or Saracens with Christian women. That the crime of such a sinful mixture shall no longer find evasion or cover under the pretext of error, we order that they [Jews and Saracens] of both sexes, in all Christian lands and at all times, shall be publicly differentiated from the rest of the population by the quality of their garment." These laws, which, with the occasional lapse, remained in force in Europe for the next seven hundred years, served the purpose of both humiliating Jews and making them immediately distinguishable from non-Jews. From this time on, it became possible to speak of "typical Jewish clothing," although this, in fact, varied from one country to another, as the council did not specify which badge Jews were to wear and left it to each country to decide if and how to enforce such legislation.

In England, a piece of yellow taffeta in the shape of the Tables of the Law (considered symbolic of the Old Testament) was chosen, but in most areas a yellow circle (said to represent a coin) was used. Called the *rodela, rouelle,* or

Clothing of a Salonica Jewess, 19th century (Israel Museum, Jerusalem). For the head, the complicated coif that left the hair at the temples visible. She wore a large garment of silk or brocade with a square neck fastened below the chest and covered by a piece of fine embroidered cloth. Over the skirt she wore a rectangular pinafore held below the chest with a cord. On top of all this she wore a wide-sleeved gown open at the front.

Woman's (above left) and man's (above right) ceremonial tunics, Ottoman Empire, 19th century (Judah L. Magnes Museum, Berkeley, California). The technique of embroidery was highly developed among the Sephardim of the Ottoman Empire, woolen and satin garments embroidered with gold and silver threads being particularly important and reserved for sultans and courtiers in the 16th and 17th centuries (although toward the end of the 18th century they

rotella, in some countries it took the form of a complete circle, at times partially colored. In France the *rodela* was of red felt or saffron-yellow cloth and was worn on the back and chest; in Germany the authorities preferred the yellow *rodela*; while in Hungary and southern Poland, Jews wore a red circle of woolen cloth. To all these must be added the yellow six-pointed "Star of David" which the Nazis obliged the Jews to wear.

In many countries, such marks were not considered sufficient, and other ways of distinguishing Jews were sought. These included the beard, which became common in many countries, and the wearing of special clothing. In the medieval Hispanic kingdoms, Jews were occasionally obliged to wear a wide, black tunic under a cloak with a pointed hood. In the 13th century, the Jews of the Germanic kingdoms, England, and France wore a pointed hat, known as the *Judenhut*, of their own free will; in time, however, the hat became compulsory. In 1267, the Jews of Vienna were compelled to wear the *cornutius pileus*, a long, cylindrical hat with

were worn by the middle classes, especially in Istanbul). In the 19th century specialized companies employed hundreds of workers. This type of embroidery was also used on ceremonial clothing for festive occasions, as on wedding gowns. Tunics of blue or purple velvet or satin in pastel colors were embroidered with gold and sequins, the entire garment covered with patterns, particularly of flowers.

A Jewish cloth-seller wearing clothing typical of the 17th and 18th centuries, ink and gouache, Istanbul, 19th century (I. Einhorn Collection, Tel Aviv). He wears a hat in the shape of a truncated cone that ends at the bottom in a yellow turban. His wide-sleeved tunic is cut diagonally and held at the waist by a sash. Over this, he wears a dark-colored open coat. Wide trousers are visible under the tunic.

Oriental Fashion

horns, which died out in the 15th century to be replaced, according to the laws of Frankfurt, by a cap with a pompon. In many parts of Germany and central Europe Jews were made to wear a round black hat of wool or felt, and in Poland, too, they wore a special hat. The headgear ordered by the church for use in the Papal States and the rest of Italy was a yellow hat, which remained in force until the French Revolution. From the 13th century on, in many parts of Europe Jewish women were made to wear a veil with two blue stripes (*oralia* or *orales*). This was later replaced by a pointed veil (*cornalia* or *cornu*).

Nowhere in rabbinic tradition do stipulations exist as to any particular type of clothing for rabbis themselves. The Ashkenazic Jews have always tended to put on special garments when studying the law, and in the 19th century rabbis wore long beards and dressed in the Polish style with a tunic and a fur-trimmed hat that was replaced on the Sabbath and festivals by a wide-brimmed fur hat known as the *streimel*. The rabbis of western Europe, for their part, were less

strongly influenced by tradition in their dress; the clothing of those in England and Holland in the 17th century, for example, was practically the same as that of the Christian clergy. More striking was the clothing worn by the Sephardic rabbis of the Ottoman Empire, who in the 16th century wore a cloak on the Sabbath in the Spanish manner; in the 19th century they wore a dark blue felt hat that had a strip of white material with thin blue stripes around the base, in the manner of a turban, or else a type of cap worn only by doctors and priests.

In eastern Europe, where Jews were considerably less influenced by Christian fashions, the typical Jewish garment of early times was the Byzantine tunic. In the 15th century, the Oriental caftan, Persian in origin, open at the front and held at the waist with a sash or cord, was adopted as the main garment. In the 16th century, garments similar to those used shortly before by the Polish nobles were worn, such as the long caftan and round fur hat. The adoption of Christian fashions in this way led many authorities to pass regulations obliging Jewish men to wear yellow

caps and women to wear head scarves of the same color. Women were also forbidden to wear jewelry and fine clothes. During the 18th and 19th centuries, the Jews of eastern Europe continued to wear their distinctive clothing, although in Russia and Lithuania a certain Oriental influence led to the appearance of multicolored silk garments for women and turbans for men.

In the 16th century, the Romanita Jews of the Ottoman Empire wore a yellow turban, while the Sephardic Jews wore a conical red hat. Sometime later, clothing became more standardized in a violet turban known as the *kaveze*, a black or violet habit, and slippers of the same color. Normal clothing in the 18th century consisted of a type of striped cotton kimono known as the *antari*, which was crossed and held at the waist by a wide sash of white or printed material, and a small waistcoat of white or black satin known as the *capitana*, open at the front. In the winter, a fur-lined caftan or a cotton-padded topcoat was worn. The *antari* was later replaced by the *jubbah*, a type of cape of striped or printed

Two Hasidim in traditional dress in Vienna, photograph from 1915. The Hasidic way of dressing is a perfect example of how the wearing of certain garments can become traditional while local climate is ignored. In this case the type of clothing worn by the Polish nobility of the 16th century can be seen in cities as different as New York and Jerusalem.

cloth held at the waist by a belt. A red fez with a black tassel was usually worn on the head. During the 19th century the Jewish women of Salonica and Smyrna wore wide Turkish trousers under two or three tunics adorned with wide flowery fringes and slit from the hip to the hem. When in public they wore a long dark red pelisse and covered their heads with a *maraman*, a type of long, white head scarf of thick material. In Constantinople women wore a short, loose jacket instead of a pelisse. The headgear worn by the Jewish women of the Ottoman Empire also included a type of large cushion covered by a white muslin veil known as the *hotoz*.

Since the beginning of the 20th century, clothing worn exclusively by Jews has tended to disappear, except in some of the more ultra-Orthodox Ashkenazic communities, where the style of the Polish Jews of the 18th century is still in use for daily wear and the *streimel* and the long caftan are worn on the Sabbath and festivals. Except in Orthodox circles, the custom of Jewish married women covering their heads has also died out.

131

The Bearers of the Law, oil painting by Sir William Rothenstein, 20th century (Bradford City Art Gallery and Museums, England). The tallith is a rectangular shawllike garment whose four corners end in zizit, or fringes (as dictated in Num. 15:38-41). In ancient times it was the usual garment of Jewish males, but with the passage of time its use became limited to liturgical occasions. It can be made of wool, linen, cotton, or silk and is normally white with blue or black stripes. The piece that fits around the neck and over the shoulders is often loose material sewn on to the shawl with silver thread. Jewish males wear it during the morning service and on Yom Kippur.

Cuisine

In their dispersion throughout the world, the Jews adopted the dishes, ingredients, and cooking methods of the different peoples with whom they came into contact. This, together with the Jewish dietary laws, led to the appearance of the diverse culinary traditions of the Jewish people.

All vegetables are fit (*kosher*) or acceptable for consumption. Of the land animals, the meat of all ruminants with cloven hooves (bovids) may be eaten, which excludes animals such as the pig, the hare, the camel, etc. As regards fowl, the meat of all birds except birds of prey may be eaten. Of sea creatures, all fish with scales and fins are fit for consumption. As regards meat, however, it is not enough for the animal itself to be included among what is permitted; it must have been slaughtered in accordance with all the rabbinic laws by an expert butcher (*shohet*). But even this is not enough, for in preparation and consumption all meat products must be kept apart from dairy products, and the utensils used to prepare the two must not come into contact.

The economic factor must also be taken into account when considering matters of traditional Jewish cuisine. For centuries the poverty of the Jewish masses set severe limitations on culinary possibilities. In general, meat and fish were eaten only on the Sabbath and holidays, and so the dedicated Jewish housewife was obliged to resort to legumes, eggs, green vegetables, and dairy products when preparing food for her family.

Subject to the same dietary laws and local influence, the special holiday dishes were linked to symbolic connotations typical of each festival, so that the meaning of the celebration itself was

132

Below: Meal of consolation, from the Rothschild
Miscellany, northern Italy, c. 1470 (Israel Museum,
Jerusalem). This is the name given to the first meal eaten by
the relatives of the deceased after a funeral. According to
talmudic regulations, it must be made by friends and
neighbors (it is forbidden to eat bread on the first day of
mourning). In the foreground are the deceased's closest
relatives, who, according to custom, must sit on the floor or
on low seats.

available ingredients according to dietary laws
and by the integration of certain ingredients on
Jewish festivals due to the symbolism attributed
to them by Jewish tradition. Consequently, the
dishes that can be considered truly Jewish are
those which, through tradition, have become typical of certain festivals.

The festivals were celebrated in the Temple
of Jerusalem until its destruction, but afterward
Jewish homes and communities inherited the
temple's role in such matters. The rabbis empha-
sized the sanctity of the home, so the table
became the altar and the father of the household
the priest who gave thanks to God.

Two great traditions stand out in European
Jewish cuisine: the Mediterranean Sephardic,
which has become enriched by a combination of
the Arabic, Persian, and Turkish cultures; and
the central European Ashkenazic, based mainly
on German, Polish, and Russian cuisine. The
former made abundant use of spices and olive
oil, its main ingredients including green vegetables, legumes, and lamb, and, due to the
extremely wide range of pastries and confec-

often reinforced with one particular kind of food.
The clearest case of this is the Passover supper,
where the ritual foods laid out on the seder tray
symbolize and commemorate at one and the
same time the sufferings of the children of Israel
in Egypt. As during the Passover, certain fruits
and vegetables are also compulsory for the Rosh
Hoshana celebration. Thus, religious tradition
dictates which ingredients must be used not only
on these holidays, but also (with variations from
one region to another) on all the other holidays.
This may even be extended to the preparation of
the entire dish according to recipes often passed
down from one generation to the next. In this
way, such ingredients or even entire typical dishes, without which no celebration would be complete, serve a quasi-liturgical purpose. Thus, fish
is eaten on the Sabbath, sweet things at Purim,
dairy products at Shavuot, and sweet things or
fried things made with flour and potato at
Hanukkah.

Jewish cuisine can be said to be the result of
the adaptation of the non-Jewish cuisine of the
134   specific environment in two ways: by processing

Top right: Scene from the Passover seder in a
Haggadah from Aragon, c. 1350-60 (Bosnia and
Herzegovina National Museum, Sarajevo). Above: A
Sephardic family from Amsterdam celebrating the
Passover, from an engraving by Bernard Picart in
Cérémonies et coutumes réligieuses de tous les
peuples du Monde, 1725 (Biblioteca Nacional,
Madrid). The ritual foods at Passover are three
matzoth, or unleavened bread; a boiled egg; a shank

bone commemorating the lamb sacrificed in the
temple at Passover; a bowl containing water and salt
(symbolic of the tears of the Israelites), in which the
"herbs" (normally lettuce and celery) are dipped;
and haroset, a paste made with almonds, apples, and
wine that is symbolic of the mortar made by the
Israelites for the pharaoh's cities during the time of
slavery in Egypt.

tionery, almonds also became an essential ingredient. The main ingredients belonging to the Ashkenazic tradition include vegetables, ox meat, potatoes, dairy products, flour, and fish.

The two traditions can be illustrated by describing a Sephardic dish—*adafina* (or *dafina*)—and an Ashkenazic dish—*gefilte* fish (stuffed fish).

Just as *hamin* is the Sabbath meal par excellence for the Jews of the Ottoman Empire and *cholent* for the Ashkenazic Jews (both are made with beans, fat meat, and potatoes), for the Sephardic Jews of the area around the Strait of Gibraltar it is *adafina*. What they all have in common is that they are cooked for the Sabbath in accordance with the law that states that fire may not be kindled on that day. *Adafina* is a type of stew whose recipe dates from the time of the medieval Hispanic kingdoms. Its origin is known to be medieval because it is mentioned in both the *Libro de Buen Amor* and the *Lozana Andaluza*. As it is known today, the dish is made with chick peas, potatoes, meat, marrow bones, eggs, onions, and a variety of spices (pepper, nutmeg, cloves, and cinnamon). Before sunset on Friday (when the Jewish Sabbath begins) the food is placed in a pot over a type of portable stove with live coals to cook slowly on a very low heat until the lunchtime of the next day. Nowadays, an electric ring is normally used instead of the traditional stove.

Gefilte fish is a special holiday meal devised to bring more taste to river fish. It is normally served cold with *khreyn*, a horseradish and beetroot sauce. It is made with balls of minced fish (usually carp) blended with onion, parsley, eggs, and flour and cooked in a stock made with fish, carrots, onions, and celery.

135

Beautifully decorated ceremonial objects for the Passover seder (Wolfson Museum, Jerusalem): china plate (rear) for the unleavened bread with the word matzo *in the middle, from England, 19th century; glass wine flagon (left), from Bohemia, 19th century; silver wine goblet (center) with a wing-shaped handle and the inscription "Passover Cup," from Russia, 19th century; hammered-silver engraved goblet (right) reserved for the prophet Elijah, which is filled with wine and may not be drunk from, from England, 19th century; engraved silver plate (bottom left) for the symbolic foods with the inscription "And I will take you to me for a people" (Exod. 6:7) and family emblems, from Italy, 17th-18th century; and (right) small silver container for* haroset, *from Germany, 19th century.*

Art

*Opposite: Ceiling of the Chodorow Synagogue
(Ukraine, formerly Poland, 1652), painted by Israel
ben Mordecai Lissnitzki in 1714 (from a model in the
Museum of the Jewish Diaspora, Tel Aviv). The
synagogue was destroyed by the Nazis. Above: Seder
plate with scene of the exodus from Egypt based on
engravings of the Amsterdam Haggadah, 1695, and
depictions of the ten plagues, Lemberg, 1805
(William L. Gross Collection, Ramat Aviv, Israel).*

Architecture

Opposite: Detail of the decoration of the south wall of the El Tránsito Synagogue of Toledo, built in 1357 on the orders of Samuel Abulafia, treasurer to Peter I. It is considered a masterpiece of the Mudéjar style because of the outstanding beauty and craftsmanship of its pinewood coffered ceilings (richly decorated with mocarabs, pinecones, and Arabic inscriptions) and the meticulous Hebrew inscriptions and magnificent plasterwork decoration on its walls.

In general terms, it is not possible to speak of "Jewish" architecture, but rather of a selection of preexisting ideas and their adaptation to certain needs. Only in the period from the 16th to the 18th century did the Jews of eastern Europe succeed in creating an architectural concept of their own. Thus, Jews have always made use of the construction materials, fashions, and styles that were typical of the ages and regions in which they lived, giving rise to a wide variety of architectural forms throughout the length and breadth of Europe.

Since European Jews have never wielded political power, the only sumptuous construction that can be called truly their own is the synagogue, with its dual role of prayerhouse and community center. Its use as the former was the most decisive factor in its inner structure, for as the successor of the temple it responds to a concept of worship based on the participation of the entire congregation in group liturgy.

Whatever the differences in architectural features, all synagogues have certain things in common in those elements determined by religious practice. They must all be oriented toward Jerusalem, while inside, two points, or centers of attention, meet the requirements of the liturgy: these are the *heikhal* or *Aron Kodesh*, a type of cabinet, ark, or niche in the wall containing the scrolls of the law and oriented toward Jerusalem; and the *tevah* or *bimah*, a type of desk usually standing on a platform for use by the officiant who leads prayer and reads out designated portions of the Torah. A synagogue must also contain some kind of seating for the congregation, generally in the form of pews, and an *azara*, an area reserved for women. This area existed in some 14th-century Judeo-Spanish synagogues and began to take on relevance in the Ashkenazic world in the 15th century, when women were allowed to enter the synagogue. Since nothing dictates the actual arrangement of these elements, the methods used in this respect characterize the different architectural styles of European synagogues.

Synagogues have not been influenced only by rabbinic laws, for Muslim and Christian legislation—always in conflict with the former—have also played their part. Dictated vis-à-vis life in Palestine and Babylonia and under conditions of much greater freedom, rabbinic law required the synagogue to be built on the highest land in any given area. The Muslims and Christians, however, passed laws that tended to limit the external grandiosity of the synagogue, its ornamentation, and also its height (which could not surpass that of mosques and churches). Furthermore, during certain periods the building of new synagogues or the restoration of old ones was forbidden. As the result of all this and since it was often in the interest of the Jews not to draw the attention of the outside world toward themselves, it can be said that until emancipation the majority of European synagogues tended to be austere and even poor in external appearance, being hardly distinguishable from the buildings around them. As for the problem of height, this was solved symbolically by building part of the synagogue below ground level, thus gaining height inside, or by placing a pole on the roof to increase the overall height of the building. Moreover, until well after the beginning of the Middle Ages those who built and decorated synagogues were Muslims or Christians, as Jews were normally excluded from the guilds. Most medieval synagogues consisted of no more than one room. However, we do know of the existence of other, larger synagogues, that housed the school, rabbinic court, ritual bath, communal oven, offices, and travelers' hospice, or had outbuildings that served such purposes.

As far as interior ornamentation was concerned, the rabbis of the earliest times tended to be tolerant, so that the inclusion of mosaics and frescoes was not forbidden. Representational decoration, however, met with a certain amount of opposition as it was argued that it could distract the attention of the congregation. In the Middle Ages—at first because of Islamic influence, which did not permit figurative representation, and later because of Christian asceticism—the Jews tended toward sobriety in the decoration of their synagogues and refrained from using figurative elements.

Although scarce in the case of synagogues built in Europe before the 6th century, archaeological remains dating from this period (among

Interior of the Santa María La Blanca Synagogue, Toledo, mid or late 13th century. Toledo Mudéjar in style, the synagogue stands on a basilica ground plan and has five aisles. According to tradition, it was consecrated by Friar Vincent Ferrer in 1411. Though for some years it was used as an army barracks, it was restored in 1798 and again in 1851 when it was declared a national monument.

Ancient Synagogues

them the extremely beautiful frescoes of the clearly Hellenistic synagogue of Dura-Europos), have in the last few decades proved to be abundant in Israel, Egypt, and Syria. The synagogues of the Greco-Roman period generally stood on a basilica ground plan and had columns around a central area. Ornamentation consisted of mosaics and frescoes with Jewish symbols and geometric and plant figures. Decorative elements also included human figures in scenes from the Bible or from Greek mythology. The ark does not appear to have permanently occupied any one area within the synagogue, and it is thought that the scrolls of the law were kept in a kind of mobile cabinet that was brought into the main assembly hall on the days when the law was to be read out.

Noteworthy among the most ancient synagogues that still stand are those of Asia Minor, in Priene, Miletus, and especially that of Sardis (2nd century A.D.), while in Europe those of importance include the Greek synagogues of Delos (2nd century B.C.) and Aegina on the Gulf of Piraeus (5th or 6th century A.D.), that of Stobi in the former Yugoslavia (1st century A.D.), and the remains of the synagogue of Elche (c. 4th century A.D.) on the eastern coast of Spain near Alicante. Virtually nothing remains of the numerous synagogues of Rome referred to in literary sources, since with the Christianization of the empire they were either destroyed by fire or converted into churches. The oldest remaining synagogue of this kind is in Rome's old port of Ostia. It stands on a basilica ground plan, and although part of it was built in the 1st century A.D., it contains a large number of elements dating from the 4th century A.D. Other synagogues have been discovered in southern Italy; that of Reggio di Calabria dates from the 4th century A.D. but was raised on a 2nd-century A.D. structure.

Above: The smooth marble decoration of the reconstruction of the ruins of the synagogue of Sardis, capital of ancient Lydia (western Anatolia), discovered in 1962. Architecturally, it is one of the most imposing of the ancient synagogues. Opposite: The synagogue courtyard and in the background the entrance to the prayer hall (from a model in the Museum of the Jewish Diaspora, Tel Aviv). The synagogue was built around the 1st century as part of an architectural complex in the city center containing baths, a gymnasium, and a number of shops owned mainly by Jews. The appearance of the basilica indicates that it was completed in the 4th century; it was originally used for civic affairs but was later assigned to the Jewish community, although precisely when it came into use as a synagogue is not known. It has a spacious courtyard with three gates that lead to a large prayer hall with a capacity for 1,000 people.

*The apse on the east side contains a pew that seats
seventy and was probably intended for use by the
community elders; on the opposite wall is a large
marble table flanked by lions. There is evidence,
however, that the* bimah *once stood in the middle of
the hall. The walls are adorned with marble and
frescoes, while the floor contains mosaics with
geometric decoration and inscriptions, most in Greek,
with details on members of the congregation.*

Hispano-Jewish and Sephardic Synagogues

Some towns in the Hispanic kingdoms had comparatively populous Jewish communities and a considerable number of synagogues. For example, there were over twenty synagogues in Seville and nine in Toledo. When the Jews were expelled, most of these synagogues were converted into churches and dedicated to Christian saints. Of those still standing, only four can be considered monumental. Two of these—the Santa María La Blanca (12th century) and the El Tránsito (14th century, built by Peter I's treasurer, Samuel Halevi Abulafia)—are in Toledo, one is in Córdoba (14th century), and the other, the Corpus Christi (15th century), is in Segovia. To these must be added the synagogue of Tomar in Portugal (15th century).

The synagogues of the Hispanic kingdoms are usually Mudéjar in style and contain certain elements of Gothic influence. Inside, the decoration is also Mudéjar and usually based on *mocarabs*, stucco arabesques with plant and geometric motifs, to which fringes with inscriptions in Hebrew were added. Two types of structure exist in the Iberian Peninsula; one divided up

into several sections by rows of octagonal columns (the Santa María La Blanca with five sections and the Corpus Christi in Segovia), and the other consisting of one main area (El Tránsito and that of Córdoba). In these last two, an open gallery on the upper floor overlooking the assembly hall served as the women's area. The Hispanic Jews solved the problem of achieving a balance between the two centers of attention by using a bipolar system, with the raised platform against the west wall and directly opposite the ark in the east wall. Reminiscent of the pulpit in Christian churches and Islamic mosques, the platform was usually situated at a considerable height on tall columns and was reached by stairs.

Important among the Sephardic synagogues are those in Holland, particularly the Spanish-Portuguese in Amsterdam. Begun in 1670, it was the largest in the world, with a capacity for almost 1,200 men and over 400 women. Architecturally it reflects the contemporary Dutch style with Protestant baroque influence. Around its large court stands a group of buildings

Top and above: Exterior and interior of the Corpus Christi Church in Segovia, Spain, which served as a synagogue until 1410. Its architectural layout and decorative elements remained virtually unchanged until 1899, when it was damaged by fire. Subsequent restoration left the structure greatly changed. Its original layout can be observed in a watercolor made by Ricardo Madrazo in 1883 in which the similarity between it and the Santa María La Blanca Synagogue in Toledo can be seen (the same architect probably worked on both). In the manner of the Almohad mosques, it is made up of three sections separated by two rows of five horseshoe arches resting on octagonal pillars whose capitals are decorated with interlacing pinecones. Over these stood two arcades of twenty-six arches.

Italian Synagogues

Below: Rue de la Synagogue, *anonymous watercolor of the Piazza delle Scuole in Rome, 1837 (Israeli Community, Rome). Once a church, its two wings served the five main congregations of Roman Jews after the papal decree of 1555, according to which each ghetto was allowed only one synagogue. It continued to be used as a synagogue for 350 years but was demolished after a fire in 1893.*

that includes the school, the communal office, the rabbinate, and the famous Etz Hayyim library. This synagogue was a model frequently imitated by the architects of Sephardic synagogues in England, such as the Bevis Marks in London, and the large number of synagogues built by Dutch Sephardim in the Caribbean (as in Surinam, Curaçao, and Jamaica).

Little is known of Italian synagogues before the 16th century. In the centuries up to the 13th the Jewish population was concentrated mainly in the south, and from the time of the northward exodus, the vast majority of the abandoned synagogues were either destroyed or converted into churches. Such was the case of those in Trani near Bari, Trapani in Sicily, and Cagliari in Sardinia.

In the 15th century, the Italian Jews who had settled in northern Italy were joined by Ashkenazic Jews from France and Germany, and after 1492 and 1496 by a large number of Spanish and Portuguese exiles. A short time later, these were joined by Jews known as Levantines, the majority of whom were

144

Above and opposite: Interior and exterior of the Scuola Grande Tedesca, the great Ashkenazic synagogue of the Venice ghetto built between 1528 and 1529 (from a model in the Museum of the Jewish Diaspora, Tel Aviv). Remodeled several times over the centuries, it is the oldest of Venice's five main synagogues. In contrast with the exterior, its interior is beautifully decorated, the ark and other items being covered with gold foil that, with the red of the curtains, *produces a splendid effect. The ark is reached by four stone steps and is flanked by the pews of the community leaders. The long inscription with the Ten Commandments over the women's gallery is unusual in Italian synagogues. There is evidence that the reader's platform originally stood in the center, in the Ashkenazic manner, but that subsequently and in keeping with the Italian custom it was moved to the west wall. The women's gallery is elliptical and laid*

Sephardim from the Ottoman Empire who settled mainly in Venice and Ancona. Each group brought with it its own special liturgical forms and architectural traditions to which the Renaissance influence of the surrounding culture was then added.

Many Italian synagogues are unique in that they occupy the upper floors of communal buildings of several stories. Particular attention was paid to the decoration of the ark and the officiant's platform, and the walls and ceilings were usually covered with elegantly ornamented fancy woods. From the 16th century on, the bipolar arrangement of the two centers of attention in the manner of the Hispanic synagogues, that is the ark in the east wall and the often elevated platform in the west wall, became commonplace. The pews ran parallel to the north and south walls, leaving a large open area in the center. Among the loveliest synagogues of this kind are those of Venice, which date from the 16th century and were later remodeled. A different interior arrangement is found in the synagogues of Piedmont, such as those of Casale Monferrato (late 16th century), and in others where the platform occupies the central area in the Ashkenazic manner. According to the age, Renaissance, baroque, mannerist, and rococo elements were used in the decoration of the interiors. The walls and ceilings were covered without the use of representational forms.

In 1555, when Pope Paul IV decreed that each ghetto was to be allowed only one synagogue, many such buildings were demolished. In the Papal States over one hundred and fifteen were closed, thirteen of them in Rome alone. Thus the rites of the different synagogues were celebrated in a single building, with one area set aside for the Castilians and Italians and another for the Catalonian-Aragonese and the Sicilians and non-Roman Italian Jews. This situation remained unchanged for a further three and a half centuries until the building was destroyed by fire in 1893.

Ashkenazic synagogues adopted a different system from that used by the Sephardic Jews to solve the problem of the two centers of attention. As always, the ark, often flanked by seats reserved for important persons, was situated on

145

out in the style of the Sephardic synagogues. It did not form part of the original building but was added at a later date. Seen from its unassuming exterior, the synagogue area on the upper floor can be distinguished only by the elongated windows.

the wall that faced Jerusalem, but the officiant's platform was situated in the center. The most common kind of ornamentation was one of murals with figures of animals and plants—in spite of the opposition by a number of rabbis to the inclusion of floral decoration. Decorative art did not, in fact, flourish in the German synagogues until after 1648, coinciding with the arrival of a large number of Jewish craftsmen fleeing the Polish massacres.

Dating from the 12th century, the most ancient architectural remains prove that for centuries two types of structure coexisted, as may be seen in the synagogue of Speyer, of one body, and that of Worms, of two equal sections divided by two columns with decorated capitals, the plat-

form set between them and thus the main center of attention.

From the 12th to 16th century, this type of structure was adopted throughout the Ashkenazic world. One of the most noteworthy examples of this is the strongly Gothic-influenced Altneuschul Synagogue in Prague, most of which dates from the 14th century and which is, along with the El Tránsito in Toledo, among the most imposing synagogues of the Middle Ages. According to legend, Rabbi Judah Löw (16th century), creator of the *golem*, a type of mechanical monster devised to defend the Jews of Prague, once prayed in the Altneuschul. On the Night of Broken Glass (November 9, 1938) the Nazis systematically burned and sacked

most of the synagogues in Germany, Austria, and the Sudetenland. Others were destroyed during World War II. Thus, few synagogues still stand in central and eastern Europe, and where they have survived, there is no Jewish community to use them.

In Poland, different types of synagogues date from the 14th to 16th century, when the center of t h e

Above left: Interior of the Altneuschul, a Gothic-style synagogue built around 1280 in the Jewish quarter of Prague (from a model in the Museum of the Jewish Diaspora, Tel Aviv). Above: The Gothic tympanum over the entrance. Opposite: The Rashi Chapel, a study room next to the old synagogue of Worms (from the same model), built in 1624 on the orders of Oppenheim, a local Jewish community leader. Its name commemorates the illustrious medieval French

Ashkenazic world transferred to Poland from Germany. The oldest of these follow the model of the synagogues in Worms and Prague, but in time, as the raised platform took on ever greater importance, four pillars were positioned in the center of the assembly hall to support the roof or dome, the raised platform between them.

With the advent of the baroque style—mainly in the towns near the Russian and Ukrainian borders—the fortress-synagogue began to make its appearance, being used not only for worship, study, and assembly, but also for defense and indeed becoming an important factor in a town's defensive system. Such synagogues are monumental buildings with adjacent towers on one side and thick walls with parapets and loopholes for cannon on top. Once again, there are four central pillars inside, and the ark is larger in size, being richly decorated with floral and animal motifs and even with human figures.

Another original type of structure found all over Poland from the mid 17th century on is that of the wooden synagogue, generally of pine although occasionally of oak. Due to their structure and ornamental systems, these buildings occupy a unique place in the history of synagogal architecture. Before World War II nearly one hundred such synagogues could be found in Poland, but all were destroyed by the Nazis.

In the interior, the distribution of space was similar to that in all other Ashkenazic synagogues, the focal point of attention being a central platform at times framed by four pillars that served no actual structural purpose. The ark, walls, and ceilings were usually richly adorned with carvings and paintings, motifs being varied—plants, animals, human figures, scenes from legend and the Bible, instruments for syna-

147

rabbi who studied in Worms some five centuries earlier, and the stone chair against the back wall is said to have been his. The chapel was rebuilt in 1855. Destroyed by the Nazis during the "Night of Broken Glass," it was again rebuilt in 1961 by order of the Federal German government.

Jewish Prague

Right: Renaissance vault of the Alta Synagogue (1568), which forms part of the Jewish town hall and dates from the time of the growth of the Prague ghetto during the reign of Rudolf II. Below: Clock tower of the Jewish town hall (16th century); the hands on the dial with Roman numerals turn clockwise; those on that with Hebrew numbers (which dates to 1754) move counterclockwise. Right: The old cemetery, which was used as a burial place until 1787; its oldest tombstone dates to 1439. Illustrious figures buried there include the printers Mordecai Katz (d. 1592) and his son Bezaleel (d. 1589); David Gans (d. 1613), mathematician, philosopher, doctor, and a pupil of Galileo's; Joseph Solomon Delmedigo (d. 1655), and Hendel (d. 1628, grave in the foreground), wife of Jacob Bassevi, the courtier Jew who was probably the first Jew outside Italy to be ennobled. Opposite right: Buildings in the Jewish quarter on the banks of the Moldau River (18th century). The Prague Jewish community is the oldest not only in Bohemia but also in Europe, its first settlements dating from Roman

times. According to documentary evidence, a firmly established Jewish community existed in the city as early as 1091 (and was decimated by crusaders in 1096). During the siege of Prague in 1142, the old Jewish quarter below the castle and its synagogue were destroyed. A new quarter was founded, and in 1270 the synagogue later known as the Altneuschul was completed. In the Middle Ages the city was an important study center, Prague's Hebrew printing presses, which existed from 1512, becoming famous. When Christians were legally allowed to lend money at the end of the 15th century, the Jews of Prague were obliged to engage in other forms of activity, such as trade and crafts, thus competing with the Christians. This led to various attempts at expulsion (1501, 1507, 1517, and others), which bore fruit in 1541 and 1557 when King Ferdinand I signed edicts that remained in force for several years (until 1545 and 1562 respectively). The reigns of Rudolf II (1576-1611) and his successor, Matthias (1611-19), brought a golden age for the Jews of Prague, their economy and cultural activity flourishing. The Empress Maria Theresa expelled them yet again in 1745, but they were allowed to return in 1748, having agreed to pay

high taxes. With Joseph II and the Patent of Tolerance, restrictions placed on Jews were gradually lifted; when businessmen were allowed to live outside the ghetto, families such as the Porges, Dormitzes, and Epsteins took the lead in the textile industry. The Jews of Prague were finally granted full civil rights in 1848, and due to the insalubrious conditions within it the ghetto was demolished in 1896. When Hitler came to power a tide of refugees fled to the city from Germany, Austria, and the occupied areas of Czechoslovakia, with the result that by the time the city fell to the Nazis on March 15, 1939 (with deportation to the death camps beginning immediately after), the Jewish population stood at 56,000. A total of 77,297 Jews died in the Bohemia and Moravia area. After the city was liberated in 1946 only 10,338 Jews remained in Prague. The Nazis pillaged 153 Jewish communities in the area and assembled the plunder (5,400 religious objects, 24,500 prayer books, and 6,070 items of historical importance) in Prague with the intention of setting up a central museum of the extinct Jewish race. After the war this large collection of objects was acquired by the local Jewish museum.

Opposite: Interior of the great synagogue of Vilna (from a model in the Museum of the Jewish Diaspora, Tel Aviv). Built in 1572, it is a noteworthy example of the type of synagogue with four central pillars, between which stand the officiant's platform and, to the left, the ark, also raised. Originally of wood, it was destroyed by fire during anti-Semitic riots in 1592 and was rebuilt in stone and brick around 1630. It was destroyed by the Nazis.

gogal use, imaginary scenes of the Holy Land and Jerusalem, signs of the zodiac, and rabbinic and biblical texts within medallions. The ceilings of these buildings became particularly important as greater height was achieved.

Of the few changes that can be observed in the synagogal architecture of the 18th and 19th centuries, the most important is that exteriors tended to gain in splendor. Over a long period that ended with World War II, synagogues lost their nature of community centers to become, like churches, places for prayer only. In some buildings a renaissance of Greek, Gothic, Romanesque, and even Islamic styles may be observed, the latter appearing first in Germany, then in Russia and the United States.

At the end of the 19th century, architects began to react to the stylistic exuberance of the previous period, tending toward simplification and later functionalism, the best examples of this being the Liberal Synagogue in Hamburg and the Dollis Hill in London.

In present times, new technologies and freedom of form have opened up unlimited pos-

sibilities in architecture, and new synagogues have appeared in Germany, England, France, Italy, and Spain, some with advanced architectural designs. Since 1945, synagogues have once again become buildings with communal centers containing, as in medieval times, schools, the community administrative offices, and assembly halls.

Top: Synagogue-fortress of Lutsk, Poland, 1626-28. Above: Wooden synagogue of Zabludow. (Models in the Museum of the Jewish Diaspora, Tel Aviv.) The Lutsk Synagogue is an excellent example of the type of synagogue that also served as a fortress. When work began on it in 1626 the local Christian clergy raised objections to the construction of such a solid structure. The licence issued by the king specified that the building should have loopholes on its four sides, that weapons be paid for by the Jews, and that it should be defended by men capable of repelling enemy attacks. The Zabludow Synagogue, originally built in the mid 17th century, was remodeled on various occasions, its final outer appearance dating from 1756 and reflecting the style of the Wolpa wooden synagogues. It was destroyed by the Nazis during World War II.

Ceremonial Art

Given that life in the Diaspora communities was mainly sheltered and perhaps also because of the reservations of some rabbis regarding plastic art, Jewish art has focused primarily on the decoration of synagogues and the creation of ceremonial objects. However, such objects were used not only in the synagogue but also in the home on the Sabbath and festivals and for the rites of the life cycles. Among the most common ornamental items are the menorah, or nine-branched candlestick, the Tables of the Law, the temple instruments, the two wreathed columns, the crown, the lions rampant, and the eagle; and above all, in the Ashkenazic world, the figures of Moses and Aaron. To these must be added geometric and floral motifs and the use of Hebrew script as ornamental elements.

In the interior of the synagogue, the ark and the officiant's platform are the two points to which woodcarvers dedicated their skills, the Renaissance and baroque carvings of the Italian synagogues being the most beautiful. The platform usually has a balustrade of carved wood or wrought iron, and there is often a canopy above resting on columns.

Pre-16th-century Jewish ceremonial objects are rare, and few such items from the 16th or 17th centuries have survived. Consequently it can be said that the vast majority of objects on display in synagogues and museums were made in the last three hundred years. The most highly prized object is the *Sefer Torah*, or scroll of the law, and synagogues often possess more than one. The scroll is a roll of parchment made up of several pieces stitched together and attached at each end to a rod. It is kept in either a wooden case covered with leather or metal (usually engraved silver) or is wrapped in a mantle (*mappah*) usually made of silk or profusely embroidered velvet, closed at the top and open at the bottom. The scrolls are held by a long strip of linen or silk. In Germany and eastern Europe it was customary for mothers to make this strip from the piece of linen used at the circumcision of their sons. Upon his first visit at the age of four or five, the boy donated the strip—on which his name and traditional prayers wishing him virtue were embroidered or painted—to the synagogue.

Glass vessel with gold-decorated base found in the Jewish catacombs of Rome, 4th century (Israel Museum, Jerusalem). The decoration, based on Jewish symbols, includes the open ark (top) with the scrolls of the law visible inside, flanked by two lions representing the reign of David and the future reign of the Messiah; below this are two candelabra, the shofar, the lulav, *the* etrog, *and two pitchers. This is a fine example of the development of decorative art on glass by the Christian and Jewish craftsmen of Rome in the 3rd and 4th centuries. Most of the examples found appear to have been deliberately broken, and no truly convincing reason for such a custom has yet been found.*

Bronze menorah, 6th century (Israel Antiquities Authorities, Israel Museum, Jerusalem). This is from the synagogue of En-Gedi, an oasis on the western shore of the Dead Sea and one of the most important archaeological sites in the Judaean desert. Excavations carried out in 1970 unearthed a synagogue with a beautiful mosaic, this bronze candelabrum, and 5,000 coins and shed light on this Jewish community as it was during Byzantine times.

festivals. For the Sabbath, the beginning of the day is marked by the lighting of lamps, and for this purpose there are bronze and silver hanging lamps with richly ornamented branches or candelabra decorated with figures of animals and flowers. Other objects used on the Sabbath include chalices for the kiddush blessing of the wine, made of a variety of materials, from glass to precious metals and usually bearing floral motifs, the name of the owner and words in Hebrew from the ritual blessing; and receptacles for the aromatic spices used in the Habdalah ceremony at the conclusion of the Sabbath or festival. These receptacles are without doubt the favorite object of Jewish craftsmen, who have lavished their creativity on them, usually making them of silver and in all shapes and sizes and in imitation of such objects as towers, flowers, fruit, fish, birds, and windmills.

The other special object in Jewish ceremonial art is the menorah, the nine-branched candelabrum typical of Hanukkah and made of a wide variety of materials—clay, stone, bronze, brass, pewter, copper, china, ceramics, glass,

On the *Sefer* cover and encrusted in the ends of the rods are other adornments of brass and engraved silver. These are the *keter* ("crown") and *rimmonim* ("pomegranates") or *tappuhim* ("apples"), generally adorned with small bells. A "breastplate," normally of silver and at times adorned with semiprecious stones, is usually hung on the cover. For the reading of the sacred text, the officiant uses a pointer ending in a hand (*yad*) that has an extended finger and is made of silver, wood, or ivory often incrusted with semiprecious stones. A permanently lit candelabrum usually hangs before the ark, and the ark itself has a curtain (*parokhet*) made of velvet or profusely embroidered brocade. The Sephardim usually place this curtain inside the cabinet, while the Ashkenazim place it on the outside and over the doors. On the solemn festivals of the New Year and the Day of Atonement, the customary brightly colored curtain is replaced by a white one.

Some of the most beautiful ceremonial objects, found not only in the synagogue but also in the home, are used on the Sabbath and

Above: Sefer Torah *ornaments (Wolfson Museum, Hechal Shlomo, Jerusalem). Large gilded silver crown set with precious stones, a piece of amber suspended in the center, Poland, 18th century; crown of gold and precious stones, Amsterdam, 19th century; engraved silver crown partially gilt and set with precious stones, Ukraine, 18th century; partially gilt filigree silver pointer, or* yad *("hand"), Poland, 19th century.*

and silver. There are two clearly differentiated types of lamp: the candelabrum type, which holds candles; and the wall lamp, which is vertical with a receptacle at the base that usually contains oil. Either can be profusely ornamented with motifs depicting trees, animals, scenes from the Bible, and historical events.

At the Purim festival the congregation reads the Book of Esther from the megillah scroll, which is smaller than the *Sefer Torah* and is attached to one rod instead of two. Profusely ornamented cylindrical cases of wood, ivory, and precious metals have been made to contain this scroll. During the festival the children sound rattles each time the name of Haman, the perverse minister of King Ahasuerus, is uttered during the reading. These rattles are usually made of wood, but they can be of ivory.

The seder, or ritual Passover supper, has also given rise to a number of ceremonial objects, including the plate on which the symbolic foods are served. Decorated with pictures and inscriptions alluding to the *Sefer*, in Italy they are made of majolica and in Germany of

Opposite: Ark of the Sephardic synagogue of Prague with three sefarim, *or scrolls of the law, all of which are ornamented: the one in the middle has a crown at the top, while the others have* rimmonim. *They are covered by* mappah, *richly embroidered with symbols, adornments, and inscriptions; over these are pointers (as an aid to the reading of the sacred text) and breastplates.*

For Festivals and Festivities

Below: Torah binders from the Ottoman Empire, probably dating to the 19th century (Israel Museum, Jerusalem). From left to right: Satin, with metal thread embroidery; reversible linen with multicolored silk embroidery; silk with silk embroidery; brocade; brocade.

(16th-17th century). Particularly beautiful and original are the thick Italian rings made of enamel or gold with exquisite filigree and sometimes adorned with a kind of small castle symbolizing both the temple and the future home.

The main doorways of Jewish houses must display a *mezuzah* (from a Hebrew word for "doorpost"). The Bible twice (Deuteronomy 6:9 and 11:20) directs that "Thou shalt write them [the words of God] upon the posts of thy house, and on thy gates," and evidence indicates that *mezuzahs* have been used since the period of the Second Temple. The *mezuzah* consists of a piece of parchment on which are written the biblical passages (Deuteronomy 6:4-9 and 11:13-21) in which the command appears. This parchment is rolled and inserted in a case with a small opening. It is customary for pious Jews to kiss the *mezuzah* or touch it and kiss their fingers on entering or leaving a house. The case itself can be made in a great variety of shapes and designs and of many materials, from the rarest to the most common—precious metals, wood, and even porcelain.

pewter. Extremely interesting is the design of the German three-tier plate for the unleavened bread. In other communities the plate is covered with an embroidered cloth with three folds that serve the same purpose.

Among the ceremonial objects related to the cycle of life, of great importance is the chair or throne of the prophet Elijah, used in the circumcision ceremony (which, according to tradition, is attended by the prophet himself). Chairs with two places, one for the godfather, the other for the prophet, are commonly found. Particularly interesting are those in the synagogues of Provence, being very small and fixed at a height in the same wall as the ark. The instruments used during the circumcision ceremony are normally decorated with scenes from the life of Abraham, such as the sacrifice of Isaac, and other scenes related to the ceremony.

The *huppah,* or canopy, under which the bride and groom stand during the wedding ceremony is also profusely decorated. Among Jewish wedding rings, especially interesting are those from Italy (16th-19th century) and Germany

156

Parokhet, *Prague, 1602 (State Jewish Museum, Prague); one of the oldest European examples in existence. The inscription at the top begins with the donor's name, "Nathan bar Issachar, called Karpel." Made of silk, it is embroidered with gold and silver threads and has silk appliqué. The crowns are those of the 14th-century Hapsburgs, and the medallion, at top center, is that of the Stifter family.*

Velvet parokhet *embroidered with silver and gold thread, Poland, 1716 (Wolfson Museum, Hechal Shlomo, Jerusalem). Hidden underground, it escaped pillage by the Nazis. Both this* parokhet *and that on the left include the frequently used columns of the Temple of Solomon as a decorative motif.*

Finally, the greatest variety of Jewish household and synagogue objects, particularly textiles, are also the subject of meticulous handiwork. These include tablecloths with pictures and inscriptions relating to the Sabbath and Passover, embroidered cloths for covering bread, and velvet cases for the prayer shawl and phylacteries embroidered with the name of the owner and a variety of patterns. Among the items for use in the synagogue are plates and boxes for collecting the money that is sent to charity organizations, lamps—with oil in the Sephardic and candles in the Ashkenazic synagogues—embroidered cloths for covering the officiant's table, and many other objects.

Above left: Silver filigree spice box for the Habdalah ceremony decorated with precious stones and eight enamels with miniatures of scenes from the Bible, Germany or France, late 17th century (Wolfson Museum, Hechal Shlomo, Jerusalem). Above right: Partially gilt silver Hanukkah lamp, Germany, 18th century (Israel Museum, Tel Aviv); here traditional Jewish elements, such as the menorah, crown, figures of Moses, Aaron, Judas Maccabee, Judith, and the

lions rampant, are combined with others used less frequently in Jewish iconography, such as the bears rampant that flank the top edge of the menorah. The inscriptions on the sides include the blessing for the lighting of the Hanukkah candles.

Goldwork

Examples of Jewish goldwork (except for the first and fifth, which are from the Judah L. Magnes Museum, Berkeley, California, all are from the William L. Gross Collection, Ramat Aviv, Israel). Above, left to right: Pair of silver *rimmonim,* with small bells, decorated with floral, animal, and symbolic motifs, Leghorn, 1837; octagonal kiddush cup, Augsburg, Germany, 1763-65; silver cup for the prophet Elijah, Ukraine, c. 1800. Below, left to right: Pewter Sabbath plate, with inscription of the blessing for wine, perhaps Germany, c. 1780; silver filigree spice box for the Habdalah, Galicia, Poland,

18th century; engraved silver case for the scroll of Esther, Poland, 18th-19th centuries. Since biblical times, Jewish craftsmen have been particularly skillful as gold- and silversmiths. The Jews' great craftsmanship in such work, the general demand for objects made of precious metals, and the widespread ceremonial use of such objects over the centuries are among the main reasons for the blossoming of Jewish gold- and silverwork everywhere in the Diaspora communities. In the Middle Ages, such crafts were common among the Jews of the Muslim and Christian kingdoms in the Iberian Peninsula as well as in many other Mediterranean countries. In 1415, the antipope Benedict XIII was obliged to

forbid the Hispanic Jews from making chalices, crucifixes, reliquaries, and other Christian objects in violation of their own laws. The exiled Jews of Spain took their crafts with them to the Ottoman Empire, Safed (Israel), and Italy, where important silversmiths are known to have settled in Ferrara, Venice, and Rome. Jewish goldsmiths flourished in Bohemia and Moravia from the 16th century on, and in the 18th century Jewish silversmiths played an active part in the precious-metal and stone trades centered around Amsterdam. In 17th-century Poland and Lithuania the craft grew as the Christian guilds declined, some Jewish silversmiths being appointed official suppliers to the king.

Ceramics

Plates for the Passover seder (except for the first, all are from the William L. Gross Collection, Ramat Aviv, Israel). Above, left to right: Majolica plate, probably made by a non-Jew since the Hebrew inscription contains errors, Spain, c. 1450 (Israel Museum, Jerusalem); painted china plate, Alsace, 18th century; china plate decorated with Chinese motifs, Hungary, 1930, made by the Herend company, the most famous china factory in Hungary, which was founded by a Jew named Fischer (mid 19th century) and is still in operation. Below, left to right: Painted china plate from a

factory managed by the Jew Sussman, western Ukraine, 1880; painted china plate, Budweis, Bohemia, 1858; hand-painted china plate, Lorraine, France, 1900. The most important ritual object found on the Passover table is the plate for the ritual foods, in use at least since the 12th century. The oldest of those still in existence appear to have come from the medieval Hispanic kingdoms. Particularly outstanding among china plates of this kind are those from northern Italy (16th-18th centuries), which were made of a variety of materials. It seems that the Hispanic Jews also used small wicker baskets, and although the vast majority are made of pewter, they have also been made of wood, copper,

bronze, china, faïence majolica, and even plastic since the Renaissance. A variety of motifs were also used for decoration, including Jewish symbols (the menorah, Star of David); motifs from heraldry; scenes from Exodus and other Bible stories; episodes from the Haggadah—the rabbis of Bene-Berak, the four sons, characters from the song *Had Gadya* ("An Only Kid"), which is chanted at the end of the seder, etc.; the names and shapes of the symbolic foods; the key words of the seder ritual; inscriptions in Hebrew (the blessing of the wine, the Aramaic words *Halahma aniyya*, "This bread of affliction," etc); pictures of holy places; and the signs of the zodiac.

The Art of the Book

Hebrew writing techniques date from the earliest times and developed to a large extent according to religious requirements. Veritable artists in calligraphy held in high esteem within Jewish society, the scholar-scribes (*soferim*) wrote out the synagogal *Sefer Torah* according to strict rules common to the whole of the Jewish world (for example, the *Sefer* cannot contain corrections or additions, and the parchment upon which it is written must be flawless).

For centuries the most highly prized biblical codices were those from the Iberian Peninsula, particularly from the school of scribes in Toledo, famous throughout Europe for its faithfulness to the original text and also because some codices were copied directly from the extremely accurate *Codex Hilleli*. A venerated (and now lost) codex, the *Hilleli* is believed to have been copied in León around the 10th century by Moses ben Hillel, from whom it takes its name. It was seized by the Almohads in 1197, but was later recovered and taken to Toledo. In his *Sefer Yuhasin* ("Book of Genealogies"), the astronomer Abraham Zacuto (who prepared the astronomical tables Columbus used in his voyage) wrote that it still existed at the time of the expulsion.

Hebrew script varies from one region to another. Like their counterparts in the Middle East, the Sephardic copyists used a stylus, whereas the Ashkenazic and Italian copyists used a pen. The vertical and horizontal lines in Sephardic scripts are therefore of the same width, while in Ashkenazic script the vertical lines are thin due to the pen's greater flexibility. It is interesting to note the imitation of the characteristics of local script in many Jewish documents from Germany in which Hebrew characters are very similar to Gothic script.

There is no way of knowing when the technique of manuscript illumination began to spread throughout the Jewish world. The oldest existing examples date from the 9th century and originated in Islamic countries, but there is evidence that illumination existed in the Hellenistic period and that motifs from Jewish tradition may have influenced early Christian painting. In Europe, the oldest known illuminated Hebrew manuscripts come from 13th-century Germany. Much more numerous, however, are those from the 14th cen-

160

Haggadah, Aragon, c. 1350-60, an illuminated manuscript until recently in the Bosnia and Herzegovina National Museum, Sarajevo (this reproduction and those opposite come from a facsimile edition published in Ljubljana in 1985 that belongs to the Museo Sefardí in Toledo). Over the generations, the Passover Haggadah has been one of the most widely diffused works of Jewish religious literature. Manuscripts exist dating from the 13th to 15th century from all the countries in which there have been Jewish communities, and nearly 3,000 editions dating from the 15th century on are known. Since the earliest times the Haggadah has been translated into the Jewish vernacular languages— Judeo-Spanish, Yiddish, Judeo-Greek, Judeo-Arabic, and Judeo-Persian—because the Haggadah must be read in the local language on the second night of the festival.

Twelve examples of illuminated Haggadoth from the medieval Hispanic kingdoms exist; of these, the Sarajevo Haggadah, an illuminated parchment manuscript, is one the best known and most frequently reproduced. It contains a large number of miniatures of scenes from the Bible (some based on the Midrash*), scenes of preparation for the Passover, illustrations, and the Aragonese coat of arms. Particularly important is the illumination depicting a group of*

Jews leaving a synagogue somewhere in Aragon (see page 110). Its iconography is derived from the Latin Franco-Hispanic biblical and has specifically Jewish elements. In style it is Italian Gothic, common in Catalonia and, in fact, similar to the 1343 chronicle of James II.

minators were Jewish. The names are known of a number of illuminators from the Spanish, Portuguese, Ashkenazic, and Italian schools who adorned manuscripts between the 14th and 16th centuries, as are those of the majority of the artists of the 18th-century Bohemian and Moravian schools. However, the possibility that some artists were Christians working under the guidance of Jews cannot be ruled out.

During the Middle Ages, no religious restrictions of any kind were placed on representational illumination, and when opposition arose it was often as the result of the more intransigent attitudes of non-Jewish environments. Such was the case in Muslim countries, where the representation of the human form was forbidden, and in the Byzantine Empire during the iconoclastic period (c.720-843). Moreover, as a result of the Christian ascetic movements in Germany and northern Italy during the 13th century, the Jews restricted representation of the human form, giving rise to an ascetic movement of their own, during which time the illuminators depicted misshapen figures with human bodies and animal

tury, while by the 15th century such manuscripts were commonplace throughout Europe. By the end of the 15th century and with the invention of the printing press, manuscripts began to decline, although Jewish schools of illumination continued to appear, the greatest being in central Europe around the end of the 17th century. The most important schools of all were in Spain, Provence, Portugal, and Italy and, in the Ashkenazic world, particularly in northern France and southern Germany.

Over the centuries, Hebrew manuscripts reflected the changing styles of the schools of illumination of different areas, making it difficult to speak of a typically Jewish style. However, certain features became traditional in Hebrew illumination, remaining constant in Europe despite changes during the Middle Ages. Depending on the creativeness of the artist, some styles may at times seem obsolete or old-fashioned. It is reasonable to assume that due to the deep knowledge of religious regulations, customs, and themes from Jewish legend displayed in the illustrations, the vast majority of the illu-

heads. Such figures became one of the main motifs of Jewish illumination in southern Germany during the 13th and 14th centuries.

Another characteristic of illuminated Hebrew manuscripts is the use of letters themselves as a decorative element. Since Hebrew script has no capitals, the first letter is not illuminated (as in Latin manuscripts), but the first words and, in Bibles, entire verses are. Indeed, when the Jews of Europe finally began to illuminate first letters, it was directly through the influence of Latin illumination. The ornamental rhythm of Hebrew signs is interrupted, at times deliberately, by letters that are large in size, the upper and lower features of certain letters being used as decoration. Another characteristic feature of Hebrew illumination is the use of microwriting, characters so small as to be practically invisible to the naked eye. This was used to form geometric or floral shapes as a frame for texts written in characters of normal size, to serve as a background for whole pages, to form animals or grotesque figures, and even to serve as an illustration to the text. Microwriting is commonly

161

The Sarajevo Haggadah was almost certainly taken out of Spain at the time of the expulsion. From notes made on it, it is known that it was sold in Italy in 1510 and that in 1609 it had to pass church censorship. In 1894 it reappeared in the possession of a Sephardic family that had settled in Sarajevo who then sold it to the Bosnia National Museum. In 1941 the museum's director succeeded in recovering the manuscript from the Nazis.

Following pages: Temple objects and the scrolls of the law in Hebrew in a Latin manuscript with miniatures from the Historia Escolástica, *by Pedro Comestor, Aragon, 15th century (Biblioteca Nacional, Madrid). The Christian illuminator, who was born in Rosellón or at least lived there, followed the model of the Hebrew Bibles illuminated in Perpignan around 1300; the architectural elements are 15th-century Italian Gothic in style.*

found in the *Masorah magna*, which are summarized linguistic commentaries written in the margins of conventional bibles and contain repeated lexical lists of grammatical forms and irregularities in the writing, spelling, and reading of the canonic text.

Jewish illumination also has special characteristics in terms of its themes. The Jewish illuminators' main source of inspiration was the Bible, whose motifs and themes were used to illustrate even nonbiblical texts. Legendary midrashic commentaries are also used, and these are reflected in the illumination of all the European schools from the 13th century on. Certain motifs are exclusively Jewish; for example, in Christian art the creation of the world normally includes the image of the creator, whereas in Jewish works the hand of God only or even various lines are used to indicate his presence. In the majority of liturgical manuscripts, Jewish domestic and synagogal rites and customs are depicted, while another recurrent motif is that of temple implements.

The Jewish illuminators worked mainly on bibles, prayer books for daily use and for festivals—particularly in the Ashkenazic world—and on the Haggadah, a text that is always read during the ritual Passover supper. The Haggadah usually contains a number of full-page miniatures depicting scenes from the Bible as well as others that reflect what is prescribed for the

164

Above left: Illustration from The Rothschild Miscellany, *a manuscript that contains over fifty works, both religious and secular, and some 300 illustrations, northern Italy, c. 1470 (Israel Museum, Jerusalem). This illustration corresponds to the text of the historical chronicle entitled* Sefer Josippon *and depicts Judith holding the head of Holofernes. Above right: Haggadah, perhaps from Catalonia, 1320 (Sassoon Collection, Israel Museum, Jerusalem). This*

miniature illustrates the passage that begins with the words "This is the bitter herb"; the man holds the herb in his right hand, while with his left hand he seems to be pointing to his wife, rather than to the herb—which has been interpreted as a humorous allusion to the verse in Eccles. 7:26: "And I find more bitter than death the woman."

Passover in the home and the synagogue. Certain individual books from the Bible have also been illuminated, such as Psalms and the Book of Esther, as have Bible interpretation, books on philosophy, and religious regulations—particularly Maimonides' *Mishne Torah* and *Moreh Nevukhim*, and the *Sefer Milhamot Adonai* by Levi ben Gershon (Provence). In Spain and Italy a large number of secular works were also illuminated, particularly in the fields of science and medicine, and these normally contain diagrams and explanatory drawings. Examples of such works are Ptolemy's *Almagest* and Avicenna's *Canon of Medicine*. To all of these must be added the illumination of nautical charts. As regards the Ashkenazic world, one of the few secular books to have been illuminated is the *Meshal ha-Kadmoni*, a book of *maqāmāt*—narratives in rhymed prose interlaced with short metrical poems—by the 13th-century Hispanic poet Isaac ibn Sahula, although not one illuminated copy remains in the Iberian Peninsula. Of special interest among illuminated Hebrew manuscripts are the *ketubboth*, or marriage contracts, which, though having existed previously, seem to have become particularly predominant, above all in Italy, after the invention of the printing press.

These schools were highly influenced by the ancient decoration of the Middle East, although it is true to say that they also developed their

The School of Sepharad

Opposite: Full-page miniature from the Cervera Bible depicting the candelabrum of seven branches according to Zechariah's vision (Zech. 4:2-3): "I have looked, and behold a candlestick all of gold, with a bowl upon the top of it, and his seven lamps thereon, and seven pipes to the seven lamps, which are upon the top thereof: And two olive trees by it, one upon the right side of the bowl, and the other upon the left side thereof."

own techniques. Western techniques also exerted a certain influence. Reaching their greatest heights in the 14th century, they declined sharply after the massacres of 1391, when the Jewish communities virtually disappeared from the kingdom of Aragon (and with them some of the most important schools of illumination). The Catalonian school is the oldest known, its Oriental-style decorative elements (carpeted pages, depiction of temple implements, the use of microwriting, and Mudéjar filigree of fine, rolling volutes in patterns of Persian origin) combining with Italo-Byzantine influences (use of dark colors, perspective, coffered ceilings,

and so on) and others from French and Italian Gothic (such as ornamental page borders).

Two interesting novelties made an appearance in the Hispano-Hebraic Bibles: perpetual calendars for the twelve lunar months of the Jewish year, generally circular in shape, some with movable disks; and decorated pages whose ornamental borders contained linguistic observations and even treatises and grammatical dictionaries, as in David Kimhi's *Sefer Mikhlol* (such pages having ornamental borders with scenes from country and courtly life and fantastic drawings of grotesque animals). In these Hispano-Hebraic Bibles the text itself was rarely illumi-

nated, although one exception is the Book of Jonah, whose beginning often displays a ship next to the whale that is swallowing the prophet.

During the 15th century, new schools sprang up in towns where none had existed before, such as Corunna and Seville, the manuscripts from the latter clearly displaying Muslim influence. By the end of the 15th century, the Portuguese school, based in Lisbon, was the peninsula's most important. The margins of its Bibles were decorated with wide, extremely elaborate borders containing flowers, leaves, birds, grotesque elements, dragons, and vases of flowers. The Spanish and Portuguese styles and

Bible manuscript on parchment, copied by Samuel ben Abraham ibn Nathan and illuminated by Joseph Hasarfati, Cervera, Spain, 1300 (Biblioteca Nacional, Lisbon). In addition to the entire text of the Bible, the codex contains the grammatical treatise Sefer Mikhlol, *by the Provençal writer of Hispanic origin David Kimhi, as well as Masoretic lists of words. The decoration of the miniatures, the Masorah, the colophons, and also Kimhi's work, from which these* two pages are taken, are particularly beautiful and meticulous. The text is surrounded by geometrical designs; in the corners of one page (left) are two unicorns and two dragons with human heads; on the other (right) are two tritons and two panthers with bared teeth.

systems of illumination lived on even after the expulsions of the Jews from the peninsula and influenced the illuminated manuscripts of Italy, Turkey, Tunisia, and Yemen.

The Italian school seems to have been one of the oldest in Europe and certainly had the greatest variety as far as styles and types are concerned. A faithful reflection of the dynamism of the Italian Jewish culture, it produced illuminated manuscripts from the late 13th century until the early 16th century, its fashions varying considerably from marginal illustrations to paneled first letters to whole pages covered with decoration and miniatures. The most important schools were in Rome and central Italy in the 13th century, in Bologna (which produced a large number of texts on the law) in the mid 14th century, and, in the 15th century, in Mantua, Ferrara, Padua, Naples, and Florence—one of the most prolific in terms of 15th-century illuminated manuscripts.

One extraordinary type of illumination found all over Italy from the 15th century on accompanies wedding poems, documents of rabbinic ordination, and wedding contracts, or *ketubboth*. Common from the middle of the 16th century were illuminated manuscripts, generally in the form of scrolls, containing routes to the Holy Land and naive depictions of the tombs of the saints.

Very similar in style to that of the Latin-German school of the times, the southern German school was one of the most important and prolific in the Ashkenazic world in terms of manuscript illumination. Among its most characteristic features is the substitution of the human head with that of an animal or imaginary beast.

From the late 17th century, the schools of Bohemia and Moravia specialized in the illumination of the Haggadoth and other liturgical books. These were small in size and intended for use in the home, their production being favored by the desire of rich families to possess such expensive items. At the beginning, the artists limited themselves to reproducing the illustrations from the Haggadah, which appeared in the Amsterdam editions, but they soon achieved a higher degree of independence and originality.

168

הדיש אשד ולו הלך בעצת
רשעים ובדרך חטאים לו עמד
ובמושב לצים לו ישב ׃

 גומר ׃ אשר לו הלך בעצת רשעים פעיטות סער פרולה הדרק
הרפו ממו טריול גם סך סוד קדש ועשה טוב כי ולתחל
ולשוד האוקס כהגבירין רקך האוונה העולס היה לאיהל
ולוהות ׃ גלשדרח וכהם הגד גרל כמו שהגור גוגדר
סי ישגר לכ האודס רע כגומרין ולו יגד כמו שהגין האורו
כל השגתו ויגל להכיר הטוב והרע הזהיין שיסור
שדירק השעיגים לשגת הטוב וההיות לבם כעגרלט בהשישט הד
כיו הטיב והרע וגאגל וכגתג לרשגג בעבוד הטוכני יכהגו
ואגרב מרדהם כי עשן הרשעא הוגל הח מרה כמו ואקר
ישחגט וסרי וכריגא ובכל אשד יפגה ירשיע ולו
ומלטריטב מה כגלין ׃ דל הרשיעוא הכבה כשטגו זה
סמדך הלך עם רשעים וכאן עלוהס העשוה כל הד

אשרי ׃ סלה משרי היו לשעולה כלטון רכיס
ההטעם כי לו ישטרין התורם בטובה כל חט שיטגלד
שהמריסא כג וכהיסלוה מחה שההנון לו ויום כטוג בטוגוה
רבות שיהגשוג בן יומירי צלין ומטרין וכלל הגר כזה
הסדיקוד כוגל הוגם רמה שארה לו לשטוש בוד
עולם והגמול הטוב ליריקרס והעגנט ליטיצגס
והוצו ביהיוור גבוד מור ׃ לפיכך הכל כן כפדן

Opposite: First page of an illuminated manuscript of the Book of Psalms with David Kimhi's commentary, Italy, 15th century (Staatsbibliothek, Berlin). The first word Ashre *("Happy") is inscribed in a scroll held by two cherubim and surrounded by four illustrations of scenes from the life of King David. This is the work of a Christian illuminator, as can be seen from the figure of God, who appears in three of the vignettes.*

Such manuscripts were often wedding presents containing a portrait of the bride. One characteristic of the manuscripts of this time is that some title pages bear depictions of Moses or Aaron in imitation of printed books, while in others the first page contains vignettes illustrating the life of a biblical figure chosen by the patron. Some 17th- and 18th-century miniatures in which the authors have deliberately chosen to depict the clothing of the age have served as vivid and colorful sources of information regarding the clothes worn by the Jews of central Europe.

The Jews considered the printing press the "crown of science," and printing, like the copying of sacred books, was "divine work." This new invention had far-reaching effects on the cultural and religious life of the Jewish communities. Printed Bibles, whether complete or in the form of individual books, were now within reach of a larger reading public, and the widespread use of dictionaries and grammar books led to a fuller understanding of texts and a wider knowledge of the sacred tongue. This was also true of the Talmud and the codes of law, which

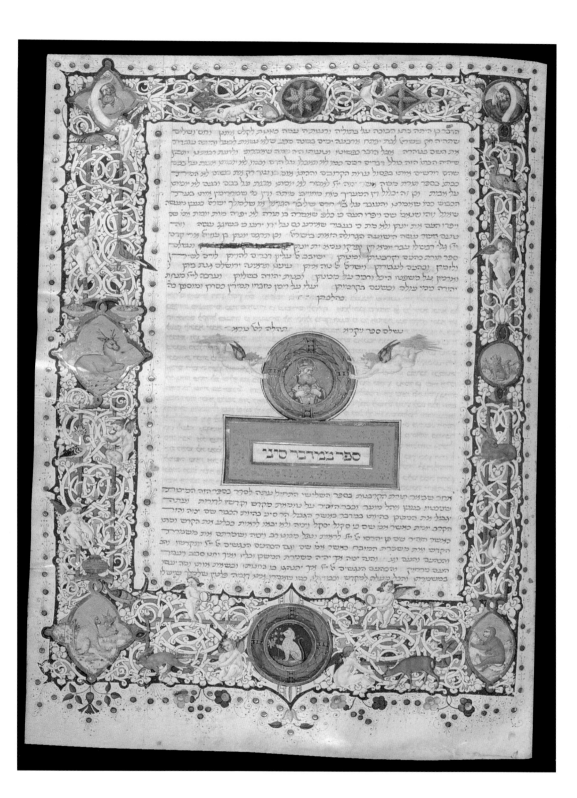

Above left: Judas the Maccabee in an illustration from the historical chronicle Sefer Josippon *included in the* Rothschild Miscellany, *northern Italy, c. 1470 (Israel Museum, Jerusalem). The illustration of Judas appears next to that of Judith (see page 164), the heroine associated in Jewish legend with the story of the Maccabees, the revolts against the Greeks, and the miracle of Hanukkah; this work is the first pictorial version of the legend. Above: Parchment manuscript with Nahmanides' commentary on the Pentateuch, illuminated by the Christian Mariano del Buono, Florence, 1470-80 (John Rylands Library, Manchester).*

Title page from the first volume of Bomberg's magnificent two-volume edition of the Yad ha-Hazakah *("Strong Hand"), the name given to Maimonides'* Mishne Torah *codex, Venice, 1524 (Biblioteca Nacional, Madrid). The pun in the title is based on the numerical value of the Hebrew word* yad, *whose consonants when added together come to fourteen—the same as the number of books that make up the code. Like so many other Hebrew books*

printed in Venice it is beautifully structured. It also features the oldest printed version of the famous Hebrew saying "From Moses to Moses there was no one like Moses," which links Moses ben Maimon (Maimonides) to the biblical Moses.

could now be studied by a much wider public. Additionally, printed versions of prayer books led to the disappearance of purely local versions of the liturgy, which until then had been passed on from one generation to the next in manuscript versions.

There are around one hundred and forty Hebrew incunabula. The first Jew mentioned in association with printing is Davin de Caderousse, from Avignon, who learned the new art around 1444, one year before the appearance of Gutenberg's first work. The first book in Hebrew was printed between 1469 and 1472 by Obadiah, Manasseh, and Benjamin of Rome, who had probably learned the art from the German master printers Conrad Sweynheym and Arnold Pannartz, who began working at the monastery of Subiaco near Rome in 1465. Soon after, Hebrew presses appeared in other Italian cities as well as in Castile, Aragon, Portugal, and

Constantinople. In Germany, however, Jews were banned from the new craft.

The primary aim of 15th-century printers was to produce versions of the Bible and the treatises of the Talmud, which led to the appearance of a large number of complete or partial editions of such books. Some of these Bibles included the classical commentaries on the text, although the commentaries also appeared as separate editions. Particular attention was paid to the codes of law of the great medieval rabbis, which accounts for the existence of incunabula of Jacob ben Asher's *Arba'ah Turim*, Maimonides' *Mishne Torah*, Alfasi's *Sefer ha-Halakhot*, and Moses de Coucy's *Sefer Mitzvot Gadol*. There are also incunabula editions on philosophy, morality, philology, medicine, history, astronomy, and literature, not to mention the liturgy.

Particularly important in Italian printing was the Soncino family, who worked for over half a century in various Italian cities, printing around fifty incunabula. Founded by Joshua Solomon Soncino in 1488, the Soncino press brought out the first complete edition of the Bible in Hebrew and was also a pioneer in the use of decorative elements; in 1483 Soncino used woodcuts to decorate first words, years later framing entire first pages of text in the same way. Although engravers were often Christian craftsmen, some Jews were also prominent in this field. Such was the case of Moses ben Isaac, who made the extremely beautiful woodcut used by Azriel Gunzenhauser (Naples, 1492) to surround the first page of Bahya ben Asher's biblical commentaries. The first known illustrated Hebrew incunabulum appeared in Brescia in 1491. This was the *Meshal ha-Kadmoni*, the book of *maqāmāt* by the Hispanic Jew Isaac ibn Sahula, some of whose stories are illustrated with woodcuts.

In the Iberian Peninsula, only a few years after the appearance of the first Latin incunabulum in Castile (Segovia), the workshops of Solomon ibn Alcabes in Guadalajara and Eleazar ibn Alantansi in Híjar (Aragon) among others printed the first books in Hebrew, the ornamentation and technical perfection of Alantansi's work being particularly noteworthy. The border print in his edition of the Pentateuch

in which zoophytic motifs surround the text on the Red Sea crossing is considered to be among the most outstanding of the times. The plate was engraved by the Valencian goldsmith Alfonso Fernández of Córdoba.

The history of Portuguese incunabula is linked directly to the Hebrew printing presses, for the Pentateuch edited in 1487 by Samuel Chacón in Faro was the first book ever printed in Portugal, appearing seven years before the first book in Latin. Furthermore, almost half the books printed in Portugal before 1500 were in Hebrew. Like their Italian counterparts, the Portuguese Jews printed books in other languages; for example, in 1496 Abraham de Ortas, who printed Hebrew books in Leiria, brought out versions of Abraham Zacuto's *Almanach Perpetuum* in Latin and Castilian in an abridged version by the Portuguese Jewish astronomer Joseph Vizinho.

Title page of the first edition of the Sefer ha-Zohar *("Book of Splendor"), printed in Mantua by Meir ben Ephraim and Jacob ben Naphtali Hakohen, 1558-60 (Jacob M. Lowy Collection, National Library of Canada, Ottawa). Best known as the* Zohar, *this is a fundamental work of cabalistic literature. Its most important sections were written c. 1270 by Moses de Léon (Léon, c. 1240-Arévalo, 1305), who claimed he had found a* commentary *on the Pentateuch written by*

Simon ben Yohai, a famous 2nd-century sage who, according to legend, had been instructed by angels who revealed divine meanings in the Bible. Redacted in Aramaic, it brings together a collection of short books with brief legendary tales, long homilies, and various discourses on a variety of subjects. This first version of the Zohar *was the cause of bitter controversy as many cabalists were opposed to its being printed.*

First page of Perush ha-Berakhot ve-ha-Tefilot, *a commentary on the synagogal liturgy written by David Abudarham in 1340, in an incunabulum printed by Eliezer Toledano in Lisbon on November 25, 1489, the second book printed in this capital city on the Tagus River (Jacob M. Lowy Collection, National Library of Canada, Ottawa). The extremely beautiful metal engraving that adorns the margin was made by the silversmith Alfonso Fernández of*

Córdoba and appeared in various other incunabula printed by Eleazar Alantansi in Híjar. This and other coincidences suggest that Eliezer of Lisbon and Eleazar of Híjar may well have been the same person. The same engraving was also used in Latin impressions by the printer as well as in Hebrew works that appeared in Constantinople at the beginning of the 16th century.

The expulsion of the Jews from Castile and Aragon in 1492 and the tragic end of Portuguese Jewry in 1497 put an end to the development of Hebrew typography in the Iberian Peninsula. The exiles took with them not only their art but also the presses, which were to print the first books to appear in the Ottoman Empire (Constantinople, 1493) and Africa (Fez, 1516).

Generally speaking, the first half of the 16th century is considered the golden age of Hebrew printing, from which time title pages decorated with prints became common. Particularly beautiful are the frontispieces and ornamental borders of architectural structures in many Italian editions; those produced later in Amsterdam are also outstanding. The most frequently used decorative elements were Moses and Aaron, scenes from the Bible, the columns of the Temple of Solomon, and motifs related to the contents of the book itself.

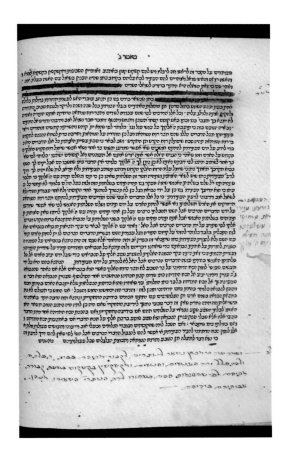

During this time Italy continued to be the main center of printing in Europe, due particularly to the Soncinos, who, until leaving Italy for the Ottoman Empire in 1526, concentrated mainly on the publication of the Bible, Bible commentaries, prayer books, and talmudic treatises. Shortly after their departure, the Christian printer Daniel Bomberg from Amsterdam set up his press in Venice and began systematically printing the fundamental works of Judaism. Particularly important among his books is the first complete edition of the Babylonian Talmud (1520-23), whose pagination and text layout with commentaries—Rashi's commentary in the inner margin and the tosafot in the outer, and the discussion of the *Gemara* following each Mishnah—became the model for all subsequent editions. Bomberg's typography was a great technical achievement for the period, with all the tiny marks of vowels, accents, and musical notation presented with dramatic clarity.

Other Christian families of printers in Venice were the Giustinianis, the Bragadinis, and the De Garas, who for a long period made the city the main center of Hebrew publishing in Europe; this period was interrupted during the reign of Pope Paul IV (1555-56), who ordered the Talmud to be burned and forbade the printing of Hebrew books in Venice. The Talmud was thus never printed there again, the next editions, whether complete or in part, appearing in Lublin (1559), Salonica (1563), and Basel (1578). From the middle of the 16th century, all books printed by Jews were required to obtain approval from the tribunal of the Inquisition, which frequently led to censorship.

From the 16th century on, other Italian cities became prominent in printing. These include Sabbioneta, Mantua, Riva di Trento, Ferrara, where the Portuguese convert Abraham Usque printed prayer books, literary works in Castilian and Portuguese, and the first edition in Spanish of the Bible (1553), Cremona, where the *Zohar* was printed for the first time (1559), and Leghorn, which was the leading publishing center of Hebrew books in Italy from 1740 until the Holocaust.

Second in importance to the presses of Italy during the early decades of the 16th century

were those founded by expelled Spanish Jews in Istanbul (from 1493) and in Salonica (from 1513). Around 1530, the Soncinos also established printing presses in these two cities. As time passed, typographic establishments sprang up in many other cities in the Ottoman Empire, and until the first half of the 20th century these produced a large number of both sacred and secular books in Hebrew and Judeo-Spanish.

From the 16th century, Hebrew books were printed for Jews and non-Jews alike in France, Germany, and other Western countries where Christian humanists and Bible experts had begun to take an interest in the study of the language.

The settlement in Holland of New Christians who returned to Judaism brought an important change as far as the main printing centers of Hebrew books in Europe are concerned. In Amsterdam and in many other northern European cities from the end of the 16th century

173

First edition of the Sefer ha-Ikkarim *("Book of Principles"), by Joseph Albo, 1425, printed in Soncino in 1485 by Joshua Solomon Soncino shortly before the Soncino family fled to Casalmaggiore in 1486 (Jacob M. Lowy Collection, National Library of Canada, Ottawa). Beautiful wood engravings were used to decorate the first words in a style characteristic of this family of printers. In the work, which was warmly welcomed by Jews, Albo reduced*

Jewish faith to three principles; the existence of God, the divine origin of the law, and retribution in the hereafter.

and until well after the beginning of the 18th century, Jews originally from the Iberian Peninsula published a large number of secular and sacred books in Spanish and Portuguese, particularly for the new arrivals who were unable to understand Hebrew. When, soon after, the new Jews needed books in Hebrew, these were imported from Venice. In 1626, Manasseh ben Israel founded the first Hebrew press in Holland, developing his own type and beginning to print in a new style that was soon taken up by Jewish printers all over Europe. In subsequent years, many other printing presses appeared, owned mainly by Sephardim and, to a lesser extent, by Ashkenazim and Christians. From this period until early in the 19th century, Amsterdam was one of the most important publishing centers of Hebrew books in Europe. Like the books printed in Italy, these reached Jews all over the world.

At the turn of the 16th century, the monopoly on Hebrew publishing, which by the whim of history had fallen to the Jews of southern Europe, came to an end. At first tentatively, due to the

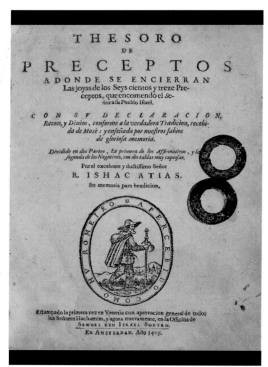

174

Portrait of Manasseh ben Israel, oil painting by Govert Flinck, Amsterdam, 1637 (Koninklij Kabinet van Schilderijen-Mauritshuis, The Hague). Born in 1604 into a family of converts on the Portuguese island of Madeira, Ben Israel was baptized with the name Manoel Dias Soeiro. When he was a child his family emigrated to Amsterdam, where they publicly returned to Judaism. Having studied at the Portuguese community's talmudic school, at the age

of eighteen he was appointed preacher to the Neve Shalom community. His wide secular education and knowledge of languages earned him a distinguished reputation with Christians, who considered him the greatest Jewish scholar of his generation. He wrote books in Spanish and Latin on philosophical and theological subjects and various other works in Hebrew.

Thesaurus of Precepts, by Ishaq Atias, second edition, Amsterdam, 1649 (Biblioteca Macías, Madrid). In 1626 Manasseh ben Israel founded the first Hebrew printing press in Holland and shortly after began to publish non-Hebrew books. Between 1646 and 1652 the press was run by his sons, Joseph and Samuel, the latter printing Atias' work (which bears Manasseh ben Israel's trademark—the coat of arms of the pilgrim—on its title page).

Below left: Copy of the Sefer ha-Berith *belonging to Moses David Gallichi, Siena, 1740, bound in Morocco leather with gilt iron and silver clasps. Below right: Filigree-silver binding with the menorah and the crown as central motifs, Venice, c. 1850. (Both from the William, L. Gross Collection, Ramat Aviv, Israel). With the invention of the printing press and the proliferation of printed books, the number of Jewish bookbinders in Europe increased. In 17th- and*

18th-century Italy it was common practice to give Bibles and prayer books as wedding presents. These were bound in silver engraved with the two families' coats of arms or with scenes of characters from the Bible after whom the bride and groom were named.

limitations placed on the Jews, printing began to spread throughout central and eastern Europe. The first Hebrew press in central Europe opened in Prague in 1512, one of its employees being Gershom Cohen, the first in a long line of printers, who used elaborate decoration based on angels, birds, lions, and so on in his works. In 1526, he printed the first illustrated version of the Passover Haggadah, some copies of which are still in existence. With its typography and lovely borders and illustrations, Cohen's version is considered one of the most noteworthy examples of 16th-century Hebrew printing.

The first presses in Poland appeared in the middle of the same century, the most important being those of Kraków and Lublin; these were, in fact, the only printing centers of importance in all of eastern Europe until the late 18th century, from which time the number of books printed in Hebrew in eastern Europe increased considerably, with cities such as Vilna, Warsaw, Zhitomir, and Berdichev becoming major printing centers. These supplied the Jewish communities of eastern Europe whose numerous rabbinic

academies were now being attended by thousands of students, leading to a considerable growth in demand for books in Hebrew.

Although Hebrew printing spread to a number of towns in Germany during the second half of the 17th century and more particularly during the 18th century, it was still extremely difficult for Jews to take an active part in the field of publishing. Determined to produce books in Hebrew, many had no alternative but to form partnerships with Christians, who appeared as the owners of the presses. From the 18th century on, the main printing centers were Berlin, Frankfurt am Main, Frankfurt an der Oder, Sulzbach, Fürth, and Hanau—one of the few towns in Germany to have a Jewish press in the early 17th century. Hebrew printing reached Austria somewhat later, presses being established toward the end of the 18th century, although those in Vienna soon rivaled the great publishing houses of Amsterdam and Italy.

As with so many other things, the Holocaust brought an end to the art of Hebrew printing in Europe.

Above: Prayer book bound in wood carved with a view of Jerusalem as its main theme, as was common in the second half of the 19th century; made by the Polish Jewish artist Moshe Stern, Galicia, 1879 (William L. Gross Collection, Ramat Aviv, Israel). The fame of the Jewish bookbinders of Poland was long-standing, and as early as the reign of Sigmund III (1587-1632) church and state made use of their services.

175

Painting

During the long Jewish Middle Ages—a period understood to have ended in the mid 18th century—few Jews dedicated themselves to the plastic and pictorial arts. While not precisely negative, the Jewish attitude toward art was ambivalent. The Bible's injunctions against "graven images" or "likenesses" (Exodus 20:4; Deuteronomy 5:8 and especially 4:16-18) cannot be construed as satisfactory explanations for this attitude, for these passages were always understood to refer to the use of such art for idolatrous purposes, and indeed the Jews often used representational art for religious and liturgical purposes. Even so, it is clear that at certain periods and in certain contexts the Jews exhibited iconoclastic tendencies quite similar to those of their Muslim and Christian neighbors, and in certain situations the widespread Catholic art dedicated to the adoration of icons served only to intensify the rejection of figurative art by the Jews. Attempting to explain the modest part played by Jews in the plastic arts during the Middle Ages, several critics have given as one of the main reasons the fact that, unlike the case of the Christians, a high percentage of Jews were literate and familiar with Bible history thanks to their educational system and therefore did not need pictorial representation to illustrate their history. Furthermore, whereas the cult of the saints made the plastic and pictorial arts essential to Christian churches, no such cult existed in Judaism.

Whatever the reason, the fact remains that with the exception of certain, isolated cases, Jews did not begin to make an appearance as artists in Europe until the 18th century; nor is it easy to explain why so many have appeared so suddenly in recent generations. In examining the arts, we shall deal only with Jews involved in the field of painting and leave aside the other arts, both major or minor, in which they have played exceptional parts—medal and seal engraving, silverwork, clockmaking, jewel-cutting, jewelry in general, sculpture, modern architecture, art magazine criticism and publishing, art history, museum management, and so on.

The first Jewish artists were miniaturists, the 18th-century masters in this field including Raphael Bachi in Paris, the convert Abraham Cooper in England, the Pinhas and Treus in Germany, and, particularly important in the early 19th century, David Alexander Fiorino in Dresden.

In the Ashkenazic world, and particularly in Germany, many families of 18th-century assimilated Jews shared the taste of their Christian contemporaries for family portraits as objects to adorn their drawing rooms. A gradual secularization of the subjects depicted brought about a change in the attitude toward European painting, making it easier for Jews to take part in the different activities connected with painting. These and other factors led to the appearance in the 18th century of a number of Jewish professional artists in the socially emancipated and semi-emancipated communities of western Europe whose clientele included non-Jews. However, in general it is true to say that until the age of emancipation, which is to say until the 19th century, it is not possible to cite any Jewish artist of great importance, as it cannot be confirmed, as has been claimed, that some exceptional artists of the times, such as the German historical painter Raphael Mengs and the English portraitist and landscape artist Johann Zoffany, were of Jewish origin. But from this time on Jewish artists were active in all the schools of painting, from the most conservative to those that were the most progressive.

176

The Old Rabbi, *painting by Solomon Kornik, a Dutch artist who belonged to Rembrandt's circle, 1678 (Galeria Sabauda, Turin). Portrait painting, which Jews had hitherto shunned, became popular with the Sephardim of northern Europe. Important personalities of the Amsterdam community, rabbis included, commissioned the most eminent Christian artists of the times to paint their portraits, as was the case of Rembrandt's paintings of Manasseh ben Israel and Dr. Bueno. In the 18th century, English artists as famous as Reynolds and Gainsborough painted the portraits of members of well-to-do Jewish families.*

The Harpist, *painting by Jozef Israëls (Rijksmuseum, Amsterdam). A Dutch Jew born in Gröningen, Israëls (1824-1911) studied first at the Amsterdam Academy and later at the Academy of Fine Arts in Paris. He began by painting portraits and historical scenes, among which are a number of pictures dedicated to Jewish life and history. From 1855 he specialized in scenes of fisher folk and peasantry, although he never abandoned Jewish themes completely. He belonged to the School of The Hague and is considered one of the major 19th-century Dutch painters.*

Painters

The first Jewish painter of renown was the German artist Moritz Daniel Oppenheim, famous for his sentimental depictions of Jewish home life. Oppenheim was followed by other artists (who were Jewish by birth, but Christian through conversion), such as Philipp Veit and Eduard Bendemann. The former was a member of the group that rebelled against contemporary classicism, while the latter specialized in compositions depicting great historical events. In England, too, a number of artists painted scenes from both history and everyday life; among these were Solomon Alexander Hart, teacher and librarian at the Royal Academy, the portrait painter Solomon Joseph Solomon, president of the Royal Society of British Artists, and Simeon Solomon.

In the course of the 19th century, Paris became the art center of the European world and gave birth to a new trend in painting inspired by Manet, Monet, Millet, and Renoir. One of the founders of the new school was the Jew Camille Pissarro, who strongly influenced the early work of Cézanne. Jews also played an important part in

the dissemination of this new spirit beyond the frontiers of France. In Italy, Serafino da Tivoli welcomed the new currents, rejecting neoclassicism. In Holland, influenced by the French realist school and above all by Rembrandt, Jozef Israëls became the most outstanding figure on the 17th-century art scene, drawing his inspiration from fishermen, peasants, craftsmen, and Jewish life; his son, Isaäc Israëls, led the Dutch impressionists, among them Josef Mendes da Costa. In Sweden, Ernst Josephson promoted new ideas. In Russia, the life of the humble served as the source of inspiration for the Jew Isaac Levitan, who painted life on the steppes and in the countryside, while among the paintings of the English impressionists, various interiors of Jewish synagogues by William Rothenstein are especially worthy of mention.

Of particular importance in Germany was Max Liebermann, one of the great figures of German art. Liebermann also drew his inspiration from scenes in the life of humble folk, finding some of the best subjects for his work in orphanages and asylums for the old and among

178

Above: The Rabbi and His Sons, *naif oil painting by Dora Holzhandler, contemporary English painter (private collection, London). Above right:* The Three Rabbis, *oil painting by Mané-Katz, 1935 (Christie's Gallery, London). Katz (1894-1962) was born in Kremenchug (Ukraine) and left in 1913 to study in Paris, returning to Russia during World War I. He returned to Paris in 1921 and was arrested when France was occupied by the Germans in 1940.*

He managed to escape and fled to the United States, returning yet again to Paris after the war. The subjects of his early paintings were exclusively Jewish—Hasidim, rabbis, talmudic students, fiddlers, and beggars from the Pale of Settlement. He died in Israel and bequeathed his collection to the city of Haifa.

Burning hamez *in the Portuguese synagogue of Amsterdam, oil painting by Martin Monnickendam, 1940 (Joods Historisch Museum, Amsterdam). Monnickendam (1874-1943) is ranked among the most outstanding pre-World War II Dutch Jewish artists.*

the peasants of the villages in the Dutch country-side; in 1919 he was elected president of the Berlin Academy, a position he held until the Nazis came to power. At the turn of this century, the Jewish critic Herrwarth Walden founded the Der Sturm group. The most distinguished Jewish artist of the period prior to World War II was probably the German Lesser Ury, a genius with color. Also worthy of mention are a number of painters from central and eastern Europe, such as Horovitz, Kaufmann, and Epstein, all of whom painted Jewish life in the small villages of the Austro-Hungarian Empire.

The 20th century saw the explosion of the pictorial talent of Jewish artists who have left their imprint on the development of painting in general. From the ghettos of eastern Europe, from the Balkans, Africa, Germany, England, and America emerged a new generation of painters, most of whom traveled to Paris. Artists such as Jules Pascin, Chaäm Soutine, the Ukrainian Mané-Katz (who in his early period drew his inspiration exclusively from Jewish motifs), Szyk, Kisling, and above all Modigliani

and Chagall (second only to Picasso in the 1950s and 1960s) became world famous.

Of particular importance in England were the landscape artist David Bomberg and other painters originally from central or eastern Europe, one example being Jankel Adler. In Russia, Nathan Altman reorganized art after the revolution with a certain cubist style, laying the foundations of constructivism. Another outstanding cubist painter was El Lissitzky, whose style was taken up throughout Germany. Lissitzky built constructions that, though outwardly realist in style, were full of surprises and optical illusions. In Germany, with the rise of Hitler, the careers of the Jewish painters practically came to an end, their work branded as degenerate. What has reached us from this period are the shocking pictorial documents of artists who, interned in the Nazi death camps and despite difficulties virtually impossible to overcome, succeeded in continuing with their work. By the end of the war, however, only a handful of artists who were later to paint their experiences had managed to survive the Holocaust.

179

The Passover in Russia, *oil painting by Norman Ubër, a Czech expressionist artist, 1949 (Max Berger Collection, Vienna). The prophet Elijah is eagerly awaited in all Jewish homes at the ritual supper on Passover night and, in accordance with custom, a cup of wine is placed on the table for him. In the picture, the wait is over and Elijah (right, foreground), startling both humans and animals, makes his appearance to drink the wine.*

Homage to Marc Chagall

Below: Poster of the exhibition held in Haifa on the occasion of Chagall's eightieth birthday, 1967. Right: *The Gates of the Jewish Cemetery*, 1917 (Mme. Meyer Collection). Opposite left: *I and the Village*, 1911 (Museum of Modern Art, New York). Opposite right: *The Red Jew* (Russian State Museum, St. Petersburg).

Born in Vitebsk in 1887, Chagall studied art in his hometown and in St. Petersburg. He then journeyed to Paris, where he lived from 1910 to 1914, finally returning to Vitebsk. He returned to Paris in 1923. In 1937 the Nazis confiscated fifty-seven of his paintings from German public collections, placing some on display in an exhibition of "Degenerate Art" held in Munich. When the Germans occupied France, the Chagall family moved to the United States, from where the painter returned to Paris in 1948. He died in 1985. His most important decorative works include the twelve stained-glass windows symbolizing the tribes of Israel in the Hadassah-Hebrew University Hospital in Jerusalem; the glass panels of the Secretariat of the United Nations in New York; the audience room at the Vatican; the ceiling of the Paris Opera; and

murals in New York's Metropolitan Opera House and the Israeli parliament building. Jewish themes are particularly important in Chagall's paintings, his main source of inspiration being the Jewish quarter of his hometown during his childhood and adolescence. Equally important is the influence of Hasidism, which surrounded him in family life. Chagall wrote of the Jewish quarter: "That little house near the Pestkowatik road [where he was born] . . . I saw it not so long ago. . . . The place reminds me of the bump on the head of the rabbi in green I painted, or of a potato tossed into a barrel of herring and soaked in pickling brine. Looking at this cottage from the height of my recent 'grandeur,' I winced and I asked myself: 'How could I possibly have been born here? How does one breathe?' However, when my grandfather with the long, black beard, died in all honor, my father, for a few rubles, bought another place. In that neighborhood . . . all about us, churches, fences, shops, synagogues—simple and eternal, like the buildings in the frescoes of Giotto. Around me come and go, turn and turn, or just trot along, all sorts of Jews, old and young, Javitches and Bejlines. A beggar runs toward his house, a rich man goes home. The Heder boy runs home. Papa goes home." (*My Life*, translation by Elisabeth Abbott.)

Music

As in the case of other Jewish artistic manifestations, Jewish music is largely the result of borrowing musical elements from other peoples and cultures and adapting them to Jewish artistic tastes and religious values. Just as Jewish music had been influenced by the music of Sumer, Egypt, and other countries in times before the destruction of the temple, so it was to be influenced by the music of Europe.

Jewish music is divided in three types: the liturgical or *hazzanut*, the art of the *hazzan*, or cantor; secular music of the folkloric kind; and artistic music, which, with a few exceptions, made its appearance after emancipation. Since few pieces of notated music remain from before the 19th century, any study of Jewish music must be based on indirect documentation.

Classical Jewish sources provide a wealth of information on temple and early synagogal music. Such sources relate that, among many other things, antiphonal chants (music sung in alternate parts or in response, as was common in the ancient East) already existed, that the Levites were charged with all matters pertaining to music, and that a long period of training was required in order to hold such a position. Music did not disappear with the destruction of the temple, but remained central to synagogal worship, although priority was always given to the passages chanted and the religious service itself.

Biblical texts and certain prayers were chanted during the service, as were the liturgical poems, or *piyyutim*, which were free in rhythm in their most ancient forms and, from the 6th century on, formed part of the prayer book. In the liturgy, the passages from the Bible are not read out but chanted—the same system is used in Mishnaic and talmudic study—and to make this task easier for the reader a system of musical accentuation was devised and introduced into the text in the period between the 6th and 10th centuries. Known as the *taamim* system, it does not indicate individual notes but melodic cadences connected to clauses and sentences in each passage. At the time of the Mishnah and probably due to Greek influence a certain degree of importance began to be attached to the skill of the interpreter, so that it was not long before the figure of the *hazzan*, or professional cantor, appeared. The *hazzan*'s role became particularly important in the rendering of the *piyyutim*, in which he was expected to display both creativity and skill in improvisation. Since the first Christian cantors were trained in Jewish prayer houses, the different forms of Jewish liturgical chant had a decisive influence on the earliest Western music. In this way the early Christian church adopted the antiphonal chant, the modal melody, the notation of music with symbols—neumes—which developed into complex forms, and various other features of Eastern music.

For a long period, Jewish secular and instrumental music met with the same opposition as music had encountered from the Muslim theologians and fathers of the Christian church. It must be assumed that in the case of Judaism nationalistic reasons underlay such opposition, for the songs sung at marriages and at other festivals, whether joyous or mournful, were not of Jewish origin, being taken from or at least influenced by the music of the enveloping culture and thus jeopardizing Jewish religious tradition itself.

The decline of the rabbinic academies in Mesopotamia and the Near East, which for centuries had determined the development of almost all aspects of Judaism, including music, caused the center of Jewish art and knowledge to shift to the West. One result of this was greater creative freedom within the different communities, leading to diversification in the musical traditions of the Jews of Europe.

In Al-Andalus, the Jews formed part of a flourishing civilization that was extremely fond of music. Islamic influence on synagogal music must have been considerable, for in the 11th century the voices of many rabbis were raised in protest at the excessive use of Arabic melodies in the synagogue. The adoption of Arabic quantitative meter into Hebrew poetry as opposed to the traditional free verse was decisive in the renovation of Andalusian Jewish music. From this point on poetic synagogal compositions strove for beauty, and new melodies were composed and adapted for the *piyyutim*, written according to the new meter system. The art of the *paytanim*, or poets of religious texts (who included Solomon ibn Gabirol and Judah ben Samuel

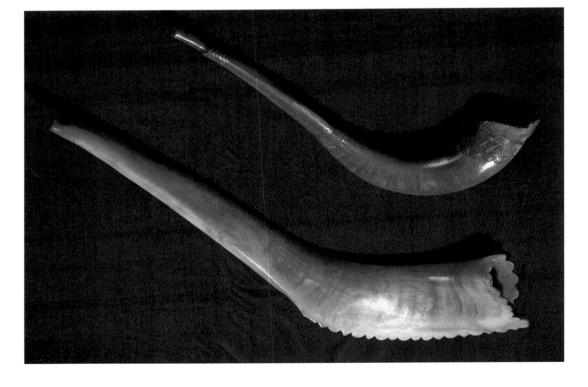

Shofroth (Old Cemetery Museum, Prague). The shofar (plural shofroth), the horn of a ram, kid, mountain goat, antelope, or gazelle, is a musical instrument capable of producing a variety of complex sounds. It is one of the oldest instruments still in use. In ancient Israel it was used to announce the jubilee year and was also sounded at the New Year's festival, during processions, and to rally men to war. In the Middle Ages, it was also sounded at times of fasting, at excommunications, and at funerals. On Friday evenings it was sounded at intervals as a signal to workers to leave their tasks, and on the third blast the candles were lit. Today it is used mainly on New Year's Day, when several series of notes are blown during the synagogal service. For ritual use the shofar may not be painted, although it may be carved.

Halevi, among many others), flourished until the 15th century.

The Andalusian and Hispanic Jews occupied themselves not only with synagogal but also with secular music, and Jewish court musicians are known to have existed as early as the 9th century; such was the case of Al-Mansur the Jew, a musician at the caliphal court in Córdoba. Indeed, until only a short time before the expulsion this was also the case at the courts of the Christian kingdoms, where Jewish minstrels, most of whom played a small type of guitar known as the *vihuella*, or Spanish lute, were held in high esteem.

For the Jews, music became a subject for study, the development of their musical theory being dependent on Arabic and, to a certain extent, Greek music. In addition to the works on the theory of music written in Arabic and Hebrew by men such as Abraham bar Hiyya (known as Savasorda) and Ibn Falaquera, one of the most important contributions to the theory of Jewish music was Levi ben Gershon's treatise *De numeris harmonicis* (Provence, 14th century).

After the expulsion of the Jews from Spain, the history of Jewish music continued for a further century in another Mediterranean country, Italy. There Jewish composers wrote the first artistic music of importance not only for the Jewish spiritual tradition but also for the development of music in general.

Toward the end of the 15th century, music became part of everyday life for both the aristocracy and the masses, the study of music and dance being gradually included in the general education of noble families. Secular music took on forms and styles of its own, and its slow ascent to more artistic levels can be seen to have been simultaneous in various countries. Even so, the invention of truly independent instrumental forms of original types of secular song can be attributed only to Renaissance Italy. Italy's privileged place in trade and industry had led to great social and economic prosperity in the cities, and it was here where the cause of music was furthered most. Thanks to Jewish exiles from Spain and groups of Levantine and Ashkenazic Jews, the Jewish communities of Italy became the

most cosmopolitan of all those in Europe, and this became evident not only in music but in other fields of art as well.

Italy was the country to which young cantors went to study, and by the end of the 16th century the Casale de Monferrato school had become the most famous. The first field of musical activity in which Jews excelled outside their own communities was dance, particularly in Ancona and at the Urbino court. In the second half of the 16th century, a considerable number of Jewish musicians distinguished themselves at the Italian courts, even at the papal court, and were particularly prominent in Mantua and Venice. In Mantua, the Gonzaga court orchestra was made up of Jewish musicians under Solomone de' Rossi, one of the greatest violinists and composers in the early history of music. Rossi distinguished himself not only in music in general but also in music written especially for the synagogue. The numerous editions of his madrigals and instrumental music reached courts all over Europe, and in 1606 he was exempted from wearing the yellow badge that was compul-

dering troubadours, minstrels, and minnesingers whose styles served as the basis for the various musical forms that took shape at the end of this period. Jews figured among these singers, and of those whose names are known were two 13th-century Provençal troubadours, Bonfils de Narbonne and Charlot le Juif, and the German minnesinger Hugo von Trimberg, whose portrait appears in an illuminated manuscript from around 1300. The poetry of these troubadours was written in the vernacular language, and their songs, in addition to themes taken from the Bible and the Midrash, swelled the repertories of medieval poetry. Another Jew famous for his music in these times was Wölflin of Lochheim, who around 1450 compiled the greater part of *Lochheim's Songbook*, which contains the first secular German songs in polyphony.

From the end of the 12th century, the effect of the music of the enveloping cultures became more and more evident in both sacred and secular Jewish music. Fearful that external influences might lead to the adoption of alien musical features and so contaminate traditional Jewish song,

sory for all Jews. As master of the first school for violinists in Mantua, he produced a generation of accomplished instrumentalists who made Italy famous the world over. In the synagogue, Rossi was the first composer to make major reforms in the musical style of the traditional liturgy; the music from his collection of religious songs entitled *Hash-shirim asher li-shelmo* (Venice, 1622) was written in the style of his madrigal period and reflects nothing of the Eastern nature of synagogal music. Indeed, this was the first step in the process of assimilation (ending in the 19th century) that Hebrew sacred music underwent within Europe.

There must also have been much musical activity in Venice during the same period. Indeed, the synagogal chants of Venice inspired the *Estro poetico-armonico*, an extensive volume of settings for the psalms that brought worldwide fame to Benedetto Marcello. It is also known that instrumental music was allowed in the city's Sephardic synagogue and that musical comedies, often attended by Christians, were performed in the ghetto. In 1629, Jews founded an academy of

music in Venice. Active for ten years, it performed concerts twice a week and was directed by the erudite and highly versatile Renaissance Jew Judah Aryeh of Modena (Leone Modena).

The situation for the Jews of central Europe was far from that of their Hispanic or Italian coreligionists. Living conditions did not encourage cultural development or the appearance of music and poetry. In the 11th and 12th centuries, music as an art form in Christian Europe reached its first peak with France as the home of music in Europe, the maestros of Notre Dame in Paris creating musical forms whose nature and purposes matched the design and style of Gothic architecture. Christian liturgical chant was enriched by polyphony, and the last bond between liturgical melodies and Hebrew chant was severed.

The 14th century saw the appearance of a new type of music, which having won its freedom from the domination of the church was taken up by the aristocracy, thus making it as inaccessible for Jews as clerical music had once been. In the Christian Middle Ages the representatives of secular music and song were the wan-

Jewish minstrels acted as go-betweens, taking the musical fashions of the ghetto to the outside world and vice versa. They also passed on the European instrumental traditional. By performing at weddings and other festive occasions, they brought part of the international musical repertory to the Jewish world. It is therefore not surprising that the dance melodies of Europe came to form part of the most popular sections of religious songs, even those sung in the

synagogue. In Germany until well after the turn of the 19th century, no Jewish wedding or festive occasion— even religious festivals such as Purim and Simhat Torah—was complete without a group of klezmerim, *or musicians, to sing, play, and improvise. The singers not only wrote their own songs but also adapted the melodies and lyrics of their times for Yiddish-speaking audiences. They became such an integral part of the community that when German*

Jews began to emigrate to Poland in the 13th century, the lezan, marsalik, *or* badhan, *as they were later to be known, came to occupy a permanent place in the Jewish life of eastern Europe.*

Jewish musicians playing at a wedding, watercolor by J. S. Dlayewski, Poland, 1850 (Israel Museum, Jerusalem). Ashkenazic musicians normally played popular music solo on the lute or else formed small string groups, usually made up of two violins and a viola da gamba, or, as in this case, a violin, a cello, cymbals, and a zither. Playing a wide variety of melodies, most were professionals who also performed for their Christian neighbors—for which

they sometimes won special privileges that helped them overcome the fierce opposition of their Gentile colleagues and their guilds.

the rabbis forbade the playing of Christian melodies and instruments in the synagogue. The playing of such melodies was also forbidden on the Sabbath, as was listening to female voices. But in spite of this the Jews could not break away from such strong external influences, and many popular songs of Provençal or German origin were sung in the synagogue; this was followed by a period of adaptation to the new situation. During this period, wandering Jewish musicians, known as *lezanim, badhanut,* and *klezmerim,* also wrote and transmitted folk music in a way similar to that of the old minstrels and troubadours. Like these they sang their lyrics in the vernacular language. On many occasions they performed before non-Jewish audiences—they were called "wanderers between two worlds" because of their involvement with both Jews and Gentiles—and they are known to have organized guilds in Frankfurt am Main and Prague in the 16th and 17th centuries. These musicians not only made a decisive contribution to Jewish folk music but also facilitated the process of Westernization that took place within Jewish popular music.

Salonique. Femmes israélites de Salonique dansan.

The German Jewish Pietist movement, spread throughout Germany in the 13th century by Judah the Hasid and his followers, developed a devotional, highly emotional way of life that sought its own kind of musical expression to aid concentration in prayer. Pietism's predilection for musical expression favored the adoption of a large number of non-Jewish melodies, the musical concepts developed by the school making a deep impression on the communities of central Europe until they were replaced in the 18th century due to the influence of the Hasidic movement of eastern Europe.

In the 16th century, the sometimes considerable differences among the various types of liturgical music in the European communities became more and more pronounced, giving rise to different systems of musical expression, some of which were used by large sectors of Judaism—Sephardic, Ashkenazic, Italian, Romanita, etc.—while other, smaller groups in Avignon, Mainz, and Prague developed their own musical styles. Such differences had much to do with the music of the enveloping culture.

During the period in which the Jewish population regrouped in the European Diaspora, the most significant population shifts from the musical point of view were those of the Jews of Spain to the Ottoman Empire and the Ashkenazic Jews to Poland and eastern Europe. Such shifts led to the formation of two branches in Jewish music, the eastern Sephardic and the Ashkenazic, the latter being subdivided into the eastern European (enriched through contact with the Slavonic world) and the central and western European, which was strongly influenced by Western music. Each of these branches developed its own particular characteristics.

The musical tradition of the Iberian Peninsula gradually faded in the memories of the Sephardim of the Ottoman Empire, with the result that both synagogal and secular music were deeply influenced by the Turkish *maqāmāt* system, made up of musical forms based on states of mind. Turkish musical instruments were also adopted. The 16th-century Palestinian poet Israel Najara, whose book of songs *Zemiroth Israel* ("Songs of Israel") was published in Safed

185

Salonica Jewesses dancing to a tambourine and violin, from an early 20th-century postcard, Salonica (William. L. Gross Collection, Ramat Aviv, Israel). The small musical group was also traditional in the Sephardic communities of the Ottoman Empire. Known as chalgis in imitation of the Turkish musicians, they were indispensable at any social celebration or festival until the arrival of the new musical trends from the West at the turn of this

century. The most usual instruments were the ut, or lute, the kieman, and the tambourine. As with the Ashkenazim, the Sephardic religious authorities did not approve of such groups, and in an 18th-century rabbinic ruling men were forbidden to play musical instruments at banquets in the presence of women—a prohibition rarely obeyed.

in 1587, compiled Arabic, Greek, Turkish, and Spanish melodies modified in the style of the synagogal hymns, to which many of his own melodies were added. He was the first to assign each text to a particular *maqāmāt*. As in the Ashkenazic world, the popular Sephardic musicians, who from the 18th century arranged themselves in the manner of the *chalgis,* or Turkish orchestras, greatly influenced the exchange of styles and tunes with the music of the enveloping culture.

Despite all efforts to keep synagogal music free from external influences, from the 17th century on an unstoppable process of Westernization took place in liturgical chant and its interpretation, more notably in the central European communities than in those in the east. This process was boosted decisively by emancipation. When synagogal melodies were written down for the first time, in the mid 18th century, the new collections for use by the cantors contained many new pieces. Nevertheless, enough features have survived that a distinction can be made between synagogal and general Western music.

classical and romantic harmony were applied to liturgical chant; songs from the enveloping culture entered the synagogue, and traditions were rewritten and adapted to the musical tastes of the age; the cantors gradually lost their interpretive freedom as they strove to follow musical styles that left no room for improvisation; and the congregation played an ever smaller part in the religious service. Arising in Germany at the turn of the 19th century and pioneered by Israel Jacobson, the Jewish Reform movement expressed its ideas in a form of liturgy based on European aesthetic ideas in the style of the Protestant service, introducing into the synagogal service both a choir that sang hymns in German and an organ. Due to the influence of the Reformers, the use of these two innovations gained a following among the members of the Orthodox synagogue, who finally succeeded in ensuring that they were accepted despite tumultuous debates. In general, only those musicians who were capable of reconciling traditional values and the classical-romantic style were fully accepted by their congregations. Such was the

The communities of eastern Europe were more resistant to external influences, and the prime requirements in chant continued to be expressiveness, emotional depth, and virtuosity. Strong ties with tradition served to inspire the Jewish musical renaissance movement, discussed further on. The emotional tendency of the Ashkenazic music of eastern Europe was reinforced by the influence of the Hasidic movement of the 18th century, a movement that, like the ancient Pietism of the 13th century, attached great importance to music and chant, from then on the focal point of the religious experience. The depth of emotion and marked sentimentality that characterizes Hasidism is reflected not only in popular songs but also in the melodies used by the cantors to chant their prayers in their quest for spiritual exaltation. Chant then combined with ancient mystical practices, such as concentration, fasting, a contemplative approach, and rhythmic movement of the body.

As opposed to this, assimilation in central Europe led to changes in synagogal music that left its Oriental origins almost unrecognizable:

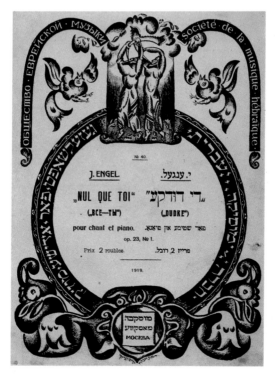

Title pages of scores by Yoel Engel published by the Moscow Society of Jewish Music (William L. Gross Collection, Ramat Aviv, Israel). Above: Jewish Songs for the School and Home, *illustrated by Leonid Pasternak, 1915. Above right:* Nul que toi *and* Di Dudque *for voice and piano, illustrated by El Lissitzky, 1919. A composer, critic, and music editor, Engel was born in Berdyansk (Russia) in 1868 and studied at the Kharkov and Moscow conservatories.*

Driven by the desire to create a form of Jewish national music, in 1900 he began to arrange traditional Jewish songs, organizing concerts for the Moscow Ethnographic Society. This attracted young Jewish musicians who in 1908 founded the Petrograd Society of Traditional Jewish Music. Engel was among the group of compilers under Ansky sent by the society to southern Russia between 1912 and 1914. There a large number of traditional songs passed

down orally over the generations by the Jewish populations of villages and hamlets were recorded with a phonograph. One of Engel's most famous compositions was the music for Ansky's The Dybbuk. *He settled in Palestine in 1924, devoting himself to compositions in Hebrew in the Holy Land.*

most significant from then on is that it was not Jewish music but music written by Jewish composers that was to play an important part in the history of European music, some of these composers severing all bonds with all things Jewish.

The beginning and end of the one hundred and fifty years of Jewish emancipation are marked by two outstanding composers, both of whom are prominent figures in the history of music. The period opened with Felix Mendelssohn, Christian grandson of the founder of the German Haskalah movement, who distanced himself from his Jewish background to concentrate on German music; and it closed with Arnold Schoenberg, originally from a fully assimilated Jewish family, who initially converted to Catholicism but returned to Judaism and found inspiration for many of his works in the Bible.

Mendelssohn was followed by many other 19th-century Jewish composers, the most important of whom include Giacomo Meyerbeer, a master virtuoso of opera in Germany, Italy, and France and composer of

case of Solomon Sulzer in Vienna, Samuel Naumbourg in Paris, and Louis Lewandowski in Berlin, whose liturgical music made a great impression even on non-Jewish musicians. Indeed, non-Jews frequently adopted Jewish religious melodies, one example being Max Bruch's *Kol Nidre* for cello and orchestra.

The position occupied by Jews in 18th-century central European society did not allow them to participate in the great stylistic changes that occurred in music during that century, when creative artists freed themselves from the bonds of church and court patronage and placed themselves at the service of the middle class. However, it must be pointed out that from the 16th century on the children, particularly girls, of well-to-do Jewish families often studied music, and that the trend toward musical integration became more pronounced during the 18th century. After the brief interlude at the Renaissance Mantua court, only emancipation in the 19th century was to open the doors to participation by Jews in the cultural activities that developed in the countries of Europe. What is

various pieces inspired by biblical themes; Jacques Offenbach, famous for his *Tales of Hoffmann*, who was the son of a Cologne cantor and wrote no fewer than ninety operettas in which he criticized the superficial and decadent French society of the Second Empire; and finally, at the end of the century, the strong personality of Gustav Mahler, of Bohemian Jewish origin, who marked the end of the romantic period. The tragedy of an age in which many Jews believed that they could form part of Christian society is deeply reflected in their work; work that despite being devoid of Jewish connotations, provoked the hostility of German musicians. Prominent among the Jewish instrumentalists of this period was the great Hungarian violinist and composer Joseph Joachim, who wrote *Hebrew Melodies* for viola and piano.

The 20th century saw the rise to fame of the convert Arnold Schoenberg. World War I demonstrated to him how absurd the idea of Jewish assimilation was and inspired him to write a prophetic drama on the theme of an independent Jewish state. Particularly important

187

among his works are the oratorio *Die Jakobsleiter*, the opera *Moses und Aron*, and his most Jewish composition, *Kol Nidre*. Upon returning to the faith of his fathers, Schoenberg brought an end to the cycle begun a century before by the Mendelssohn family and to an age of which Felix Mendelssohn had been one of the greatest representatives—romanticism.

Three currents have characterized the music of the 20th century. One followed the way paved by the national renaissance, the second revived the polyphony of preclassical music, while the third concentrated on revitalizing the purely melodic features that were stifled by the exuberance of romantic harmony. The first was reflected mainly in the Jewish music of the countries of eastern Europe, where the need to uphold a national way of life and culture was most vehemently felt, Jews doing their utmost to reinforce the idea of the Jewish nation. There were noteworthy exceptions in the communities, however, of Jewish musicians who turned their gaze not to their own level of society, nor to Russian national music, but rather to the West.

One example is Anton Rubinstein, who won worldwide fame as a pianist, composer, and teacher and founded the St. Petersburg Conservatory. The subjects of many of his operas and oratorios are Jewish. Thus, following a general trend, the Jewish communities of eastern Europe showed renewed interest in the richness of Jewish tradition and popular song. The pioneer in this field was Yoel Engel, whose merit lies principally in his determination to bring about a renaissance of Jewish music and whose circle of followers included the founders of the Petrograd Society of Traditional Jewish Music (1908); during its ten years of activity, which came to an end during the Russian Revolution, its members compiled thousands of songs from provinces all over Russia as well as from Latvia, Poland, and Galicia. Research into music thus received a boost and took shape mainly in the monumental work of Abraham Zevi Idelsohn, who compiled a collection of the ancient and medieval Jewish melodies of eastern Europe. Engel based his own works on Russian popular songs in Yiddish and, in addi-

tion to his piano arrangements for popular melodies, composed lyrical songs to poems by Bialik, Tchernihovsky, Peretz, and other contemporary Hebrew poets. His best-known work is the music for Ansky's *The Dybbuk*, a drama performed by the Habima Hebrew Theater group. The composers who came after Engel used traditional melodies for works of greater scope, and although they sought contact with new achievements in Western music, each one attempted in his own way to create a form of Jewish national music and to use Hebrew themes, thus enabling us to speak of the birth of a Jewish school of music.

In western Europe, Jewish composers played an extremely active part in the years after World War I, Vienna, Berlin, and Paris being the main cities where their music was performed. The central figure on the French music scene of this period was Darius Milhaud, who was a prolific composer. Milhaud used Jewish themes, including an ancient legend upon which his opera *Esther of Carpentras* is based, as well as the traditional prayers of the Jewish communi-

Scenes from the 1985 performance at the Paris Opera of Robert le Diable, *by Giacomo Meyerbeer (Jakob Liebmann Meyer Beer, 1791-1864), the German Jewish composer of spectacular operas and son of Jakob Herz Beer, a prominent Jewish Berlin banker. Impressed by his talent for music, his grandfather, Liebmann Meyer Wulf, named him sole heir to his estate on condition that he add "Meyer" to his surname. After a stay in Italy (where he changed his first name to Giacomo) in 1826 he traveled to Paris, where* Robert le Diable *(1831) was one of his successes. Always ready to help other musicians, he recommended Wagner's* Rienzi *for production in Dresden and as music director of the Berlin Opera (1842-47) staged* The Flying Dutchman. *Wagner, however, in his anti-Semitic fervor, severely criticized Meyerbeer both personally and as a musician.*

ties of southern France, which inspired some of his most beautiful religious songs, and the popular Jewish songs and Hebrew poems from his long list of lyrical songs. Important among the many Jewish composers who wrote music specifically for Jews are Paul Dessau, who wrote an oratorio for the Passover Haggadah with lyrics by Max Brod, and Karol Rathaus, who wrote the music for *Uriel Acosta*, another drama performed by the Habima Theater group. Italy's Mario Castelnuovo-Tedesco stands out among the by no means small number of western European Jews inspired by the idea of Jewish music who have contributed to the popularization of the traditional popular song.

A special case among the musicians for whom the national renaissance movement was a decisive experience was that of Ernest Bloch, from Switzerland. When the waves of this movement began to spread through western Europe shortly after World War I, Bloch produced the numerous Hebrew works that made him the creator of a musical language of his own in which the theory of the eastern European musicians on popular melodies was deliberately rejected. Among his works are two *Psalms* for soprano and orchestra, *Three Jewish Poems* for orchestra, a rhapsody, *Solomon*, and a symphony, *Israel*. Furthermore, a large number of works of contemporary Jewish music testify to Bloch's influence, the American Jew Leonard Bernstein's *Jeremiah* being just one example.

Other European Jews who have excelled in the field of music are the conductors Bruno Walter from Germany and Georg Solti from Hungary; the Poles Arthur Rubinstein, the pianist, and Bronislaw Huberman, the violinist and founder of the Palestine Orchestra (1936); and the Russian pianists Vladimir Ashkenazy and Vladimir Horowitz.

Scenes from the performance at the 1983 Salzburg Festival of the Tales of Hoffmann, *by Jacques Offenbach (1819-80), who composed comic operas and operettas. Born in Cologne, at the age of fourteen he was sent by his father, Isaac Offenbach, to study cello at the Paris Conservatory, where due to lack of funds he was obliged one year later to earn his living as a cellist with a theater orchestra. He was instructed in the art of composition by Jacques*

Halévy and after a number of years managed to establish a certain reputation for himself. The turning point in his career came at the Paris International Fair of 1855, when he managed a very successful small theater on the Champs-Elysées. In spite of his popularity, he was constantly in debt and never saw his great opera, the Tales of Hoffmann, *staged (it was first performed in 1881).*

Cinema

From the very beginning, Jews played an extremely important part in all fields of cinematography, as producers, directors, and actors, and not only in Hollywood, where many have worked, but also in the film industries of many European countries—in Germany until the rise of Nazism, in Russia until Stalin's purges in the 1930s, in Great Britain even now. Various reasons can be given for the presence of Jews in the world of cinema. Filmmaking was a new industry in which there were no vested interests to defend, and film production involved risks that Jews in search of ways of forming part of the economic and cultural life of their respective countries were prepared to take. Furthermore, in its beginnings, cinema was considered a low-class form of entertainment suitable only for immigrants and the uneducated masses. Few people imagined that with the passage of time such a lowly field would become an art capable of generating thousands and thousands of dollars.

The cinema was fostered in Germany by the Jewish owners of theater chains. In 1913, Paul Davidson and Hermann Fellner, who had shown films in their theaters since 1905, founded their own company, producing comedies and films based on themes from German legend and folklore. It was for this company that Ernst Lubitsch directed his first comedies before turning his attention to historical themes. Lubitsch's great success in Germany paved the way for his career in the United States, where he emigrated in 1923. His American period includes films such as *Ninotchka, To Be or Not to Be*, and *Cluny Brown*. In 1915, Erich Pommer founded the Decla film production company (absorbed by UFA in 1923) and went on to produce many of the major films of the 1920s and 1930s. Thanks to Pommer, the German cinema became one of the most advanced of the time, and this period is considered the golden age of German cinema. Among Pommer's many successes are *The Cabinet of Doctor Caligari*, written by Hans Janowitz and Karl Mayer, and *The Last Will of Doctor Mabuse*. The Austrian Fritz Lang, who became the most important director in German cinema, also worked with Pommer, his films perfectly capturing the society and cul-

tural atmosphere of the Germany of that time. Another great figure was Josef von Sternberg, who directed *The Blue Angel* in 1930, followed by a series of further films with Marlene Dietrich. When Hitler came to power, the Jews who worked in the German film industry were obliged to leave the country, most moving to Hollywood, others to London, Paris, and Prague. Among the directors and producers whose film careers began in Germany and who later emigrated to the United States are William Wyler, Hans Richter, and the Austrians Fred Zinnemann and Samuel Spiegel. In America they made such films as *The African Queen, The Bridge on the River Kwai, Lawrence of Arabia*, and *The Night of the Generals*. Other actors who continued their careers in the United States include the Viennese actress Louise Rainer; the Hungarian actor Peter Lorre, who as a young man worked with German theater groups and collaborated with the playwright Bertolt Brecht; and the Austrian Erich von Stroheim. In the United States, Von Stroheim became famous for his portrayal of cruel Prussian officers—he was

Top: Poster for The Cabinet of Doctor Caligari *(1919), the German film classic written by Hans Janowitz and Karl Mayer and produced by Erich Pommer. Above: Poster for the German silent film* The Golem *(1920), directed by Paul Wegener and Henrik Galeen and inspired by Gustav Meyrink's novel. The German Jewish film producer Erich Pommer (1889-1966) founded the Deutsches Eclair (Decla) film company in 1915, bringing together Fritz Lang and a team of*

designers and technicians previously involved with the Der Sturm avant-garde theater group. The films Pommer produced during that period include The Cabinet of Doctor Caligari *(1919),* The Last Will of Doctor Mabuse *(1922),* Die Niebelungen *(1924; produced after Decla merged with the great German cinema company UFA),* Variety *(1925), and* Metropolis *(1926). When Hitler came to power, Pommer went to Paris, where he produced* Liliom

(1934) and in the late 1930s worked independently in England and subsequently with 20th Century-Fox in the United States, where he produced Jamaica Inn *(1939) with Alfred Hitchcock and adapted Sidney Howard's play* They Knew What They Wanted *(1940) for the screen. After the war, he went to Germany to oversee restoration of the German film industry, returning to Hollywood in 1956.*

The Rabbi's Creature

Above: Rabbi Judah Löw ben Bezulel in a sculpture by L. Saloun from the New Town Hall in Prague's old quarter, 1908-11. Right: Scene from the first film version of *The Golem* (1920); the creature of clay is in the center. According to an old legend common to a number of countries, man is capable of creating semi-human beings by magic and the power of God's name (the word *golem* comes from a Yiddish word meaning "shapeless mass"). In the 12th century, the legend, which is mentioned in the Talmud, was reinforced in the Jewish world due to certain sectors of the Ashkenazic cabalists, one of the commonest versions being that which attributes the creation of the *Golem* to the Prague rabbi Judah Löw, who is said to have destroyed the creature when it became a threat to mankind. A literary theme that has inspired a number of works of literature and music by Jews and non-Jews alike, the story was finally brought to the screen. The first, silent version appeared in Germany in 1920 (right), and another version, directed by Julien Duvivier, was made in France in 1936. The script for the Czech version, made after World War II, was written by Arnost Lustig.

billed as "The Man You Love to Hate"—and although in reality the son of a Jewish hatter, he claimed to be a member of a Prussian noble family, a graduate of Heidelberg, and a former cavalry officer. He himself had added the "von" to his name.

Until the creation of the state of Israel, Poland was the only country where a Jewish film industry could develop. The first attempts were made before World War I, when Mark Tovbin and Nahum Lipowski adapted plays by Jacob Gordin for the cinema. These were performed by such famous Polish Jewish stage actors as the Kaminski family and Esther Lipowska. In 1924 Leah Farber and Henrik Baum began producing films on themes taken from Yiddish folk sources. The first sound film in Yiddish was made in 1932 by the Sektor company, founded by Itzhak and Shaul Goskind, who began to make documentaries on the Jewish communities of Warsaw, Lodz, Vilna, Lvov, and Kraków before going on to produce many other types of film. After the war, the Kinor cooperative of Lodz made films in Yiddish until 1951, when most of its members emigrated to Israel. Among the Polish Jewish directors of modern times is Roman Polanski, who was born in Paris but grew up in Kraków.

The Jews of the Soviet Union played an active part in the development of the film industry in that country, the list of outstanding figures led by Sergei Eisenstein, the great genius of Soviet cinema. Eisenstein's films include *Alexander Nevsky, Old and New, October, The Battleship Potemkin*, and *Ivan the Terrible*, all of which are considered masterpieces. Also outstanding are Dziga Vertov (Denis Kaufman), of Polish origin and considered the father of documentary cinema, and the producer and director Anatole Litvak, born in Kiev, who left Germany with the advent of the Nazis, came to Hollywood in 1937, and made commercially successful films for twenty years. Yiddish cinema also flourished in the Soviet Union thanks to the great actor Sholem Mikhoels, who died during Stalin's purges. His greatest productions include *King Lear* and *Menahem Mendel*.

The contribution made by Jews to British

192

Top: Paul Newman in a scene from Exodus *(1960), a film about the birth of the state of Israel and the difficulties the British authorities placed in the way of Jewish survivors of the Holocaust wishing to emigrate. Based on Leon Uris's novel, the film was produced in Israel by Otto Preminger. Above: Scene from the American film* Crossfire *(1947), directed by Edward Dmytryk, which deals with the problem of anti-Semitism in the United States at the end of World*

War II. European films on the subject of anti-Semitism are generally less superficial than their American counterparts. Among these are André Cayatte's Before the Flood *(1954) and Claude Berri's* The Two of Us *(1967), both made in France, and the Polish film* Bad Luck *(1960), directed by Andrej Munk, which tells the story of a Polish Gentile and his life of suffering due to his "Jewish nose."*

cinema is also significant. After World War I, Alexander Korda, one of the pioneers of Hungarian cinema, worked in Austria, Germany, France, and Hollywood, finally settling in 1930 in England, where he founded London Films and produced and directed some of the best films made in Great Britain in the 1930s and 1940s. Thanks to Korda, the British film industry was able to compete with America on the international market. His most successful films as a director include *The Private Life of Henry VIII, The Private Life of Don Juan*, and *Rembrandt*, and as a producer *The Scarlet Pimpernel, Catherine the Great*, and *The Third Man*. Other famous British directors are Michael Balcon, responsible for the famous comedies made by the Ealing Studios as well as many well-known films, and John Schlesinger, whose films include *Billy Liar, Darling,* and *Midnight Cowboy*. Among Britain's most famous Jewish actors are Herbert Lom (born in Prague), Leslie Howard, Elisabeth Bergner (who left Germany in 1933), Claire Bloom, Laurence Harvey (born in Lithuania), and Peter Sellers.

In France, between 1905 and 1916 the silent film actor Max Linder, who wrote and directed most of his own films, played an important part in the making of comedies in the style of Charlie Chaplin and was quite possibly the best-known screen comic on either side of the Atlantic during the years just before World War I. Among the modern-day French directors are Claude Lelouch, whose films include *A Man and a Woman*, and Claude Berri, who often dealt with Jewish themes. Famous actors and actresses include Harry Baur, Simone Signoret, and Anouk Aimée.

In other eastern European countries Jews became involved in the world of cinema after World War II. Such was the case of Czechoslovakia's Jan Kadar and Milos Forman. Mauritz Stiller, born in Helsinki to Russian-Polish parents, began his career in the Swedish cinema in 1912, becoming the greatest director of the "golden age" of silent Swedish cinema, famous for his own, particular form of aesthetics and peculiar sense of humor. And it was Stiller who introduced the world to Greta Garbo in his *Story of Gösta Berling* (1924).

193

Scene from the musical film Fiddler on the Roof *(1971), directed by Norman Jewison and based on the play that opened on Broadway in 1964. It is inspired by the stories of Shalom Aleichem, the main character being the Jewish milkman Tevye. The action takes place before the revolution in a small town in the Russian countryside and includes a veritable gallery of characters (among them a father of five unmarried girls) who suffer the trials and tribulations of life in a* humble Jewish community. Particulary effective are Tevye's long monologs to God in which unyielding faith—at times not without a certain sense of rebelliousness—is displayed.*

שני בשבת עשרים לחדש אדר
שנת חמשת אלפים ושבע מאות
שלוש ושלושים לבריאת עולם
למנין שאנו מונים פה בלונדון

אמר ר׳ יוחנן בן ר׳ אברהם הלוי
למרת יהודית בת ר׳ משה

הוי לי לאשה
כדת משה וישראל

ואני אוקיר ואכבד ואפרנס אותך כדרך
בני ישראל המוקירים ומכבדים
ומפרנסים את נשיהם באמונה.

והסכימה מרת יהודית בת ר׳ משה הכלה
ר׳ יוחנן בן ר׳ אברהם הלוי החתן

וקבלה עליה להיות לו לאשה
כדת משה וישראל ולהוקירו
ולכבדו כדרך בנות ישראל
על כן כרתו שניהם ברית אהבה
ואחוה ברית שלום ורעות
לבנות בית בישראל לכבוד
הקדוש ברוך הוא
המקדש עמו ישראל ע׳י הכלה
וקדושין. כן נעשה. בפנינו והכל
שריר וקים.

Languages
and
Literature

Opposite: Ketubbah *(marriage contract) in Hebrew,*
illustrated by Y. Boussidan, London, 1973 (West
London Synagogue). Above: Basin, Tarragona, 5th
century (Museo Sefardí, Toledo). With its inscriptions
in Hebrew (left), Latin, and Greek (right), this is a
magnificent example of Jewish linguistic symbiosis.
The first inscription reads "Peace be unto Israel and
unto us and unto our children, amen"; the second
reads "Pax fides"; the third, in Greek, is illegible.

European Jewish Languages

Over the centuries, the Jews of the European Diaspora have used a number of different languages for communication and literary expression. These can be arranged in three categories. First are the classical Jewish languages, Hebrew and Aramaic, which have been used in literature throughout the entire history of the Jews in Europe. Second are the languages of the enveloping cultures in each historical period: Greek in the Judeo-Hellenistic world; Latin in certain parts of the Roman Empire and, after its fall, wherever Latin was used as the language of culture in European intellectual circles; Arabic in Al-Andalus; the various Romance languages of the Christian kingdoms in the Iberian Peninsula, basically Castilian and Catalan; Spanish and Portuguese in the Diaspora of the Iberian converts; and in modern times the national tongues of all the European countries in which Jews have lived. Third are the Jewish languages that developed as the result of merging with other European languages: Judeo-French, Judeo-Provençal, Judeo-Italian, Judeo-German or Yiddish, and Judeo-Spanish, the last two being the most important in terms of literary creativity, length of time they have existed, and number of speakers.

Linguists classify the development of Hebrew into four stages: biblical, rabbinic or Mishnaic (from the Mishna, certain Midrashim, and other classical sources and Gaonic literature), medieval, and modern. The first, which is a constant point of reference and a source used by all Jewish writers, flourished with particular intensity during specific periods of European Jewish literary production, as in the poetry of the Spanish Hebraic school and that of the central European authors of the earliest Haskalah period. Medieval Hebrew reached its greatest heights in Europe. Finally, the rebirth of Hebrew as a live, modern tongue may also be attributed to European Jews.

After the destruction of the first temple of Jerusalem and particularly after the Babylonian Exile, biblical Hebrew gradually ceased to be spoken and was replaced in everyday communication by Aramaic. Likewise, rabbinic Hebrew ceased to be spoken at the end of the 2nd century A.D. However, Hebrew continued to be the language of prayer and the liturgy and was always taught in the Diaspora schools. It was also the language of literature and science and, as from time to time it was brought up to date, in each age it became a useful instrument for communi-

Greek inscription on a Jerusalem synagogue, dating from the reign of Herod (Collection of the Israel Antiquities Authorities, Israel Museum, Jerusalem). The inscription reads: "Theodotus ... priest and leader of the synagogue ... built it to recite the law and study the Commandments, and the hospice... and the water system to accommodate strangers." This is only one of the many examples that demonstrate the deep influence of Greek on classical Judaism long before the end of the Second Temple era. The Jews of the Greek world accepted the Greek koine in the Balkans, Cyprus, southern Italy, Magna Graecia, Egypt, and certain areas around the Black Sea. In addition to the large amount of Judeo-Greek literature, many funeral and public inscriptions are also to be found in Greek. Furthermore, the ancient rabbinic texts (the Talmud and Midrash) contain around 3,000 Greek words.

cation. At the same time it was influenced by the non-Semitic languages with which it came into contact. It also became the lingua franca among Jews scattered all over Europe who also used it as a secret language in their private correspondence and in their trade dealings. To a much lesser degree Aramaic also appears in European Jewish literature, one example being the *Zohar*, the fundamental book of the cabala.

Grammatical studies of biblical Hebrew reached their greatest heights in Al-Andalus in the 10th century with the Arabic and Hebrew works of the poets Menahem ibn Saruq of Tortosa and Dunash ben Labrat and their pupils, and, in the next century, with Judah ben David Hayyuj and Jonah ibn Janah. The 12th and 13th centuries saw the appearance of the grammatical works of Abraham ibn Ezra of Tudela and those of the Provençal writer of Hispanic origin David Kimhi, whose Hebrew grammar has served as the basis for all those written since. The works written between the 6th and 10th centuries in Palestine and Babylonia on biblical philology—the group of works of the Masorah, which sets out the rules for reading the Bible, defining vowels, accents, and other reading guides—were compiled by the Italian scholar Jacob ben Hayyim and published together with Daniel Bomberg's edition of the Bible (Venice, 1525). Also outstanding in this field was Elijah Levita (1468-1549), who wrote an explanation on how to read and use the Masorah.

The most important medieval work on rabbinic Hebrew is the *Arukh*. Written by Nathan ben Jehiel (1035-c. 1110), who lived in Rome, it is a kind of encyclopedic dictionary of the Talmud and is essential for any modern study of talmudic lexicography, for Ben Jehiel gives not only the meanings but also the etymology of the words of the Talmud. The work also describes Jewish customs and explains subjects in the Talmud. Except for the occasional work written in Italy in the 16th and 17th centuries, Hebrew grammar was not studied again in Europe until the time of the Jewish scholars of central Europe and after emancipation.

Yiddish has been spoken by Ashkenazic Jews for the last thousand years. Arising from an intricate fusion of elements based on various

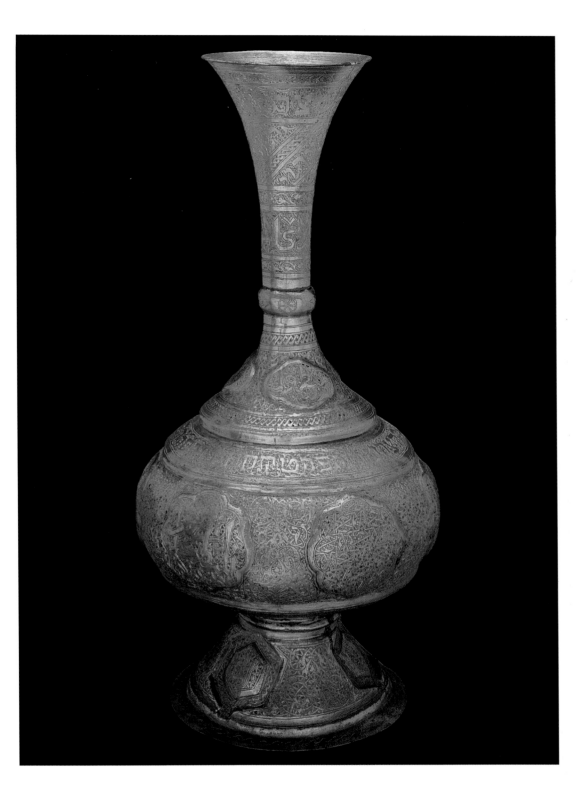

197

Brass water jug with inscriptions in Hebrew and Arabic and elaborately decorated with geometric and plant motifs, Turkey, 19th century (Judah L. Magnes Museum, Berkeley, California). For the Hebrew world of the Middle Ages, contact with Arabic was long and fruitful. In Europe, Arabic was above all the language of culture, the Hispanic Jews of Al-Andalus writing most of their works on Hebrew grammar, philosophy, morality, astronomy, and medicine in the language. As one example, Maimonides wrote his entire work on medicine, his philosophical The Guide of the Perplexed, *and his synthesis of the legal content of the Mishnah (*The Luminary, *in Hebrew Sefer ha-Maor) in Arabic. In the Christian kingdoms of Castile and Aragon, the Hispanic Jews' knowledge of Arabic enabled them to collaborate with efficiency in the task of translating a wide variety of classical and Arabic works.*

medieval German dialects to which must be added a number of Hebrew-Aramaic and Slavonic components, it gradually took shape and adapted itself to the needs of communication. From its origins in the 10th century and until the end of the 18th century, Yiddish became diversified into regional varieties and was the only means of oral communication between the Jews of central Europe from Holland to the Ukraine and from Lithuania to the Ashkenazic communities in Italy.

Its history is usually divided into four periods: early (until 1250), old (1250-1500), middle (1500-1700), and modern (after 1700). In the first period and prior to contact with the language of the Slavonic world, Jews from the north of France and northern Italy who spoke different varieties of Romance languages established their first settlements on German-speaking soil and with the passage of time a merging of

the multiple linguistic components took place. In the second period, Yiddish speakers came into contact with the Slavonic and Judeo-Slavonic world, first in southeast Germany and later in Bohemia, Poland, and beyond. From this point a relatively standard literary language developed, always written in the Hebrew alphabet and understood by speakers who lived in both western and eastern Europe, the latter by now having begun to drift away from spoken Yiddish. In the third period, the Ashkenazic world expanded considerably toward eastern Europe, and the dialects multiplied, although a standard written form of the language continued to exist. After 1700, the use of Yiddish declined in western Europe, leading to the disappearance of old literary Yiddish. After emancipation, the Judeo-German authors and intellectuals of the Haskalah made a determined effort to stamp out the use of Yiddish in the Ashkenazic world and replace it with German and Hebrew, succeeding in the countries of German influence and in Holland, but not in eastern Europe. Here, from 1820 a new literary form of Yiddish, based on the eastern dialect and officially recognized at the Czernowitz Language Conference of 1908, took shape. In Russia, the teaching of Yiddish in schools and the work of researchers led to the enrichment of Yiddish vocabulary and its stabilization as a language.

The number of Yiddish speakers in western Europe decreased drastically after the Nazi Holocaust; the same happened in the Soviet Union after schools were closed in 1930 and Yiddish books and newspapers were banned in 1949. Yiddish continues to be spoken in Israel and survives, albeit uncertainly, on the American continent, mainly in the United States and Argentina.

Judeo-Spanish (also known as Ladino or Spanioli), the language of the Sephardic Jews who settled in the Ottoman Empire, has served them as a means of communication and literary creation since the 16th century. The isolation of these Jews, who left the Iberian Peninsula to settle in the Balkans, was broken occasionally throughout the 16th and 17th centuries by the arrival of crypto-Jews from Spain and Portugal, so that with the passage of time the language

Title page of a play by Abraham Goldfaden, 1922 (Biblioteca Arias Montano, CSIC, Madrid). Author of 400 plays, Goldfaden (1840-1908) is considered the founder of Yiddish theater. When Russian authorities banned Yiddish theater in 1883, Goldfaden and his followers founded troupes in Paris, London, and New York City. Goldfaden settled in New York in 1903 and opened a drama school.

199

The Rabbi in His Study, *painting by Alois Priechenfried, 19th century (Christie's Gallery, London). Joseph Delmedigo (Candia, 1591-Prague, 1655) wrote of the contemporary passion for printing: "In times past... only good... and useful books were bought, the useless ones disappearing by themselves. But that is not the case nowadays, when the ignorant set themselves up as sages and though immersed in the darkness of ignorance... seek the position of* luminaries for the generations who have never heard of them. And all those who have... greater wealth than intelligence contrive to publish books in which they are arbitrarily cited as important men of great worth, although they have no more authority than a carpenter's apprentice." *(From* Noveloth Hokhma, *in* Ideario Judío, *ed. Eduardo Weinfeld, Mexico, 1958.)*

evolved independently of the Spanish spoken in Spain and gave rise to another language. Judeo-Spanish was used in written form, mainly in the Hebrew alphabet, until just before World War II.

Judeo-Spanish was based on certain forms of the Hispanic languages of the late 15th century, particularly Castilian, although it contained a large number of Hebrew words and numerous borrowings from the languages with which, over the centuries, it came into contact—Italian as the lingua franca of the Mediterranean ports, Turkish, Bulgarian, Greek, Serbo-Croat, etc.—giving rise to a large number of dialects. Works dating from the 16th century contain what may be considered a form of pre-Judeo-Spanish close to the Castilian of the times, but certain features later found to have developed fully in the Sephardic language were already evident. By the 18th century it had become a literary language in its own right, from which time and with the normal development and changes that any living language undergoes, it remained more or less stable until the late 19th century, when a form of Neo-Judeo-Spanish began to take shape. This contained a large number of lexical, morphological, and syntactic Gallicisms that drastically reshaped both literary and spoken Judeo-Spanish.

The 20th century has seen the inexorable decline of Judeo-Spanish, now relegated to the position of a passive language spoken primarily in the home. Its creative strength lasted as long as historical and social conditions allowed, as long as extremely stable, close-knit communities with their own vehicle of communication existed—a situation that came to an end with the waves of emigration and the slaughter of Sephardim during World War II.

Rabbis of Morocco during a study session, painting by J. A. Lecomte de Novy, France, 19th century (Guildhall Art Gallery, London). One of the main destinations of the exiles from Sepharad was neighboring North Africa. Like the emigrés who settled in the Ottoman Empire, these Sephardim maintained their peninsular customs and their language, which is still spoken today. Known as Haquetia, it is based on Castilian-Andalusian, contains Hebrew words, and is strongly influenced by the Arabic spoken in the region. As they had no printing presses until more recent times, the Sephardim of Morocco read works printed in Hebrew and Judeo-Spanish in the large publishing centers of the Ottoman Empire and, above all, in Leghorn, Italy. Local production is preserved in manuscript form.

Ancient Literature

Below: Page from the tractate Bava Mezia of the Babylonian Talmud with an English translation and commentary (edited by Adin Steinsaltz), New York, 1989 (Biblioteca Macías, Madrid). Other, individual treatises from the Babylonian Talmud have been translated into Latin (by Blasio Ugolino in the 18th century) and the majority of the languages spoken in modern cultures (German, Spanish, French, and English). The first complete translation into German was by L.

Goldschmidt (1897-1935) and into English by a group of scholars led by Isidore Epstein (Soncino Press, 1935-52). At the present time, two more ambitious projects that include an English translation are underway; these are Steinsaltz's bilingual edition with a complete criticism and the Talmud with English Translation and Commentary, published in fascicles (El Am, 1965-), which contains the original text vocalized, a large number of commentaries, biographies of rabbis, etc.

In many of its genres Jewish literature is a "continuum" that spans 3,000 years. As a point of reference with the Jewish literature of Europe, and in brief summary, what follows is a discussion of Jewish works written before the dispersion of the Jews through Europe.

Ancient Judaism's greatest book is the Hebrew (and Aramaic) Bible, which constitutes the "Written Law" and whose twenty-four volumes are divided into three groups: first, the five books of the Pentateuch (Genesis, Exodus, Leviticus, Numbers, and Deuteronomy); second, Prophets, divided into the Former Prophets (Joshua, Judges, Samuel, and Kings), the Latter Prophets (Isaiah, Jeremiah, and Ezekiel), and the twelve Minor Prophets; and third, the "Writings" or Hagiographa, which are divided into three books of poetry (Psalms, Proverbs, and Job), the Five Scrolls (Hebrew: *megilloth*, consisting of the Song of Solomon, Ruth, Lamentations, Ecclesiastes, and Esther), and three historical books (Daniel, Esdras-Nehemiah, and Chronicles). From the 3rd century B.C. until the end of the 1st century A.D., Jewish creativity took on form in

the Apocrypha and in the so-called apocalyptic literature or pseudepigrapha. The first of these are canonical to the Christian but not to the Jewish Bible and are varied in content, being: moralistic fiction (Tobit); didactic (Son of Sirach and Ecclesiasticus); historical allegories (Judith); and truly historical and apologetic (Maccabees). As regards apocalyptic literature (Jubilees, Enoch, etc.), also rejected by Jewish tradition yet maintained by Christianity, the main themes are eschatological in content—the coming of the Messiah, the Day of Judgment, the vision of the new world, etc.

Another corpus of ancient Jewish writings, most of which are now lost, corresponds to the cultural production, from the 3rd century B.C. to the 1st century A.D., of the various millions of Jews who lived beyond Israel in Greek-controlled territories. One such work was the translation of the Bible into Greek (known as the Septuagint) in Alexandria in the 3rd century B.C., which, as the first translation of its kind, was highly influential and became a model for all subsequent translations. The versions of the

Bible translated in Palestine into Aramaic are known as Targums; among the best-known surviving Targums are the *Targum Onkelos* and the *Targum Jonathan*.

Other examples of the flourishing and rich Judeo-Hellenistic culture are the development of biblical exegesis and the birth of philosophy, the most important writer in both these fields being Philo Judaeus of Alexandria (c. 30 B.C.-A.D. 42). The most outstanding Jewish historian at the beginning of the Common Era was Flavius Josephus, some of whose works, such as *History of the Jewish War* and *Antiquities of the Jews*, were highly influential for centuries after his death.

According to Jewish tradition, Moses not only received the Written Law on Sinai but also the Oral Law, which for generations was passed on from teacher to pupil. As regards its content, this traditional work of wisdom is divided into two large groups—*Halakah*, or legal material used to determine the "norms" (ritual, moral, civil, etc.) that must rule each action in Jewish life, and *Haggadah* or "narrative," composed of

Druck u. Verlag v. A. J.Menkes & S.Sprecher in Lemberg 1865

Title page (above) and text page (above right) of the tractate Nidah from the Babylonian Talmud, edited by A. J. Menkes and S. Sprecher, Lemberg, 1865 (Biblioteca Macías, Madrid). Publishers began printing the Talmud shortly after the invention of the press, some isolated treatises appearing toward the end of the 15th century, particularly in Portugal. The best known are the volumes printed by Joshua Solomon and his nephew, Gershom of Soncino (Italy),

between 1484 and 1519. The first complete edition of the Talmud was printed by the Christian Daniel Bomberg in Venice (1520-23), its external form determining that of all later editions, which followed the original in pagination, the inclusion of Rashi's commentary on the inside margin, and the tosafot on the outside margin. The first edition was followed by that of Giustiniani, also in Venice (1546-51), the most famous subsequent versions being those of Lublin

(1559-76 and 1617-39), Basel (1578-81), and Kraków (1602-5 and 1616-20). Other editions appeared in Amsterdam, Frankfurt an der Oder, and Sulzbach.

historical and legendary and ethical and religious literary texts in which Jewish ethics are reflected and expounded. When historical events threatened the continuity of the rabbinic schools around the 2nd century, the Halakah, or religious regulations, were compiled in a precise written form in Hebrew to constitute a broad legal corpus (*Mishnah*) arranged in a series of treatises grouped in six "orders." In subsequent centuries, the process of study, commentary, explanation, and development of the laws established in the *Mishnah* was continued in the academies of Palestine and Babylonia. Redacted in Aramaic and set out in the same orders and treatises as the *Mishnah*, the commentary received the name of *Gemara*, and together with the *Mishnah* made up the Talmud in its two versions: the Jerusalem, or Palestinian, version, on which work ended around 365 in unsettled historical circumstances that led to the closure of the rabbinic academies and the emigration of many scholars to Babylonia; and the version known as the Babylonian Talmud, redacted in the Babylonian academies of Nehardea, Sura,

Pumbedita, Mahoza, Naresh, and Mata Mehasya and completed in the year 499.

While there are thus two Talmuds, the Babylonian is generally accepted as the authoritative version and indeed has been since its completion. This authority had never been stated formally but grew over the course of time; scholars came to accept it as "the Talmud," and it was studied in all Jewish communities, while the Jerusalem version was neglected. In part, this is because the Jerusalem version is only one third the length of the Babylonian: it was completed a century and a half before the Babylonian, so the editors of the Babylonian had access to it. The Babylonia is also more interesting intellectually, its discussions sharper and more sophisticated, its style more lively. Furthermore the text of the Jerusalem version is not well preserved; when Daniel Bomberg set about printing an edition of it (1523-24) he could find only one extant manuscript, known as the Leyden manuscript, which included a note from the original copyist about the number of errors in the work.

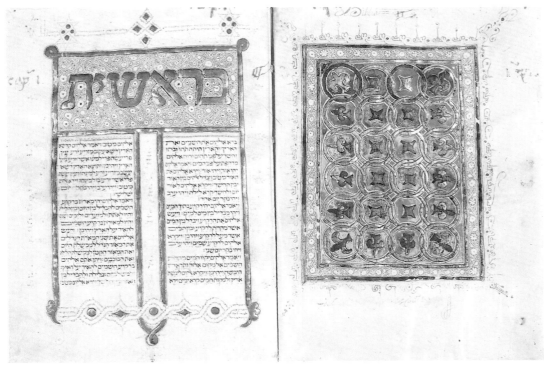

Above left and top: From an illuminated Hebrew Bible, the end of Genesis and beginning of Exodus, Spain, 15th century (Biblioteca Nacional, Madrid). Above: From another illuminated Hebrew Bible, the beginning of Genesis, 15th century (Biblioteca de El Escorial, Madrid). Both contain the notes of the magna *and* parva Masorah *usually found in Hebrew Bibles. This is a traditional system of marginal notation on text, spelling, and grammar written in*

small print in the blank spaces, its main purpose being to fix the text and ensure that it is correctly copied. The parva Masorah, *found between columns and in the margins, is in the form of very short notes, whereas the* magna *contains longer notes found both above and below the text and, in later codices, often as long ornamental lines.*

Medieval Literature

Entrance to a Venice Synagogue in a contemporary photograph. For centuries the city was an important Hebrew publishing center. In addition to the press run by Daniel Bomberg (assisted by the convert Frelice da Prato), which operated for over thirty years, there were those of Marc'Antonio Giustiniani, which was founded in 1545 and produced 85 works; Alvise Bragadini, which began publishing in 1550 with Maimonides' Mishne Torah *and continued in operation for another 150 years; Bomberg's heir, Giovanni di Gara, who acquired most of Bomberg's type and published around 100 works between 1565 and 1609; Giovanni Vendramin, who in 1631 succeeded in breaking the virtual monopoly of the Bragadini press (with which his company merged in the 18th century); and that of the Foa family, in operation in the 18th century.*

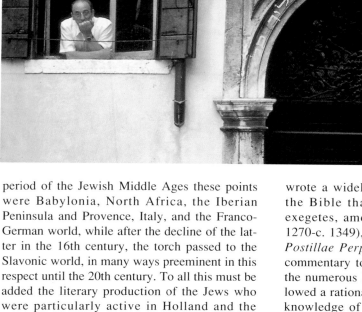

During the Jewish world's own particular Middle Ages—a period that continued until the second half of the 18th century—literature written by Jews for Jews in Europe on Jewish themes appeared in many different languages. This was due to the dispersion of the Jewish people in a number of countries. To use any one language as an example, therefore, would not be representative, as in the majority of its genres Jewish literature is no more than an ongoing continuation stemming from the same traditional and religious base, where the language used for expression is of no special significance and in each case would only be the tongue that historical circumstances had obliged the author to use.

When deprived of the conditions necessary for scientific and literary development, the Jews of Europe were forced to look elsewhere for peace and prosperity. Thus there was always at least one focal point, and at times even two or three simultaneously, where Jewish creativity was able to develop. In the twelve-hundred-year period of the Jewish Middle Ages these points were Babylonia, North Africa, the Iberian Peninsula and Provence, Italy, and the Franco-German world, while after the decline of the latter in the 16th century, the torch passed to the Slavonic world, in many ways preeminent in this respect until the 20th century. To all this must be added the literary production of the Jews who were particularly active in Holland and the Ottoman Empire after the expulsion from Spain. Furthermore, there was always considerable contact between the Jewish communities of the various European countries, so that what one produced had a more or less immediate effect on the literature of the others.

The fundamental texts of Judaism, the Bible and the Talmud, formed the basis of medieval Jewish literature, which focused mainly on the interpretation of the Bible and the oral law through grammar, exegesis, commentary, philosophy, mysticism, liturgy, didactic poetry, historiography, and polemic writing.

In the field of biblical exegesis, the great figure of the medieval period was the French rabbi Solomon ben Isaac (1040-1105), known as Rashi, an abbreviation of his name. Rashi wrote a widely disseminated commentary on the Bible that influenced many Christian exegetes, among them Nicholas de Lyre (c. 1270-c. 1349), a Franciscan who composed the *Postillae Perpetuae*, the first Christian Bible commentary to be printed. Outstanding among the numerous Hispanic commentators who followed a rationalist method based on a scientific knowledge of Hebrew, logic, and philosophy were Abraham ibn Ezra (c. 1089-c. 1164), a "troubled spirit" and wandering scholar who wrote poetry as well as works on the structure of the Hebrew language; Judah ben Barzillai (12th century), a rabbi of Barcelona who wrote works on the Jewish calender and Sabbath festivals and on aspects of Jewish law; Moses ben Nahman (1194-1270), known as Nahmanides, who included mystical considerations in his commentaries; and Levi ben Gershon (1288-1344), known as both Gersonides and Ralbag, a mathematician, astronomer, philosopher, and biblical commentator who employed a philosophical form of hermeneutics. The last great exegete of the Hispano-Jewish school was Isaac Abrabanel (15th century), whose commentaries on the entire Bible include philosophical, theo-

Street in the Jewish quarter of Gerona. Among the many Jewish scholars and rabbis who were born and lived there, particularly important was Moses ben Nahman (Nahmanides, 1194- c. 1270), the biblical and talmudic commentator and leader of the city's cabalistic circle. In spite of his opposition to Maimonidean rationalism, he took up a conciliatory position between the supporters and critics of the Cordovan sage's philosophical theories. From 1264 he was chief rabbi of Catalonia, representing the Jewish communities before the king of Aragon, and was obliged in 1263 to take part in the public disputation of Barcelona conducted by the convert Pablo Christiani. In 1267, he left Spain for the Holy Land and died in Acre in around 1268. It was probably in Acre that he completed his Bible commentary (first edition, Rome, c. 1480).

Fountain of the Lions in the Alhambra (Granada). Some experts believe that the Hispanic Jewish poet Solomon ibn Gabirol (12th century) described both the Alhambra and the fountain in The Palace and the Garden*, from which the following verses are taken:*
Let us wander in the shade of the vines,
allowing ourselves to be overcome by the desire
to gaze upon radiant images
in a palace that towers above its surroundings.

made of rich stones...
beds of narcissus adorn its courts;
its chambers, which have been built
and decorated with reliefs in open and closed work
are paved with marble and porphyry
and I cannot count its portals...
There is a large pool which resembles
the Sea of Solomon
but it does not rest on bulls;

such is the aspect of the lions,
on the curb, it is as if the cubs
were roaring for the prey;
and like springs they spill out their entrails
pouring forth from their mouths jets like rivers.

logical, historical, and on occasion mystical considerations.

Arabic influence and the rebirth of the Hebrew language led to a blossoming of poetry in the Middle Ages. Since the earliest times the Jews had composed *piyyutim*, religious poetry for the liturgy, but in medieval Al-Andalus they also began to write secular poetry in Hebrew for the first time. In contrast, the Franco-Germanic poets cultivated religious genres only, and the quality never equaled that of Al-Andalus.

Thanks to the fertile fusion of Arabic and Hebrew culture that occurred in Al-Andalus, the work of the Hispano-Hebrew school was revolutionary from the very beginning. Innovation lay not only in the subjects dealt with, in the genres themselves, or in the poetic styles and forms, but also in the language used as the means of expression. There was a return to biblical Hebrew, and post-biblical language—the language of the ancient *piyyutim*—was scorned. The Jews also adopted the Arabic systems of rhyme, both the classical Arabic of the mono-rhyme *qasida* (used in traditional songs) and those of Al-Andalus— the *zejel* and the *moaxia*, the latter being a composition sometimes ending in a stanza in vulgar Arabic or in the Romance language of the Mozarabs. These compositions were the famous *kharjahs*, the first poetic manifestations in proto-Castilian, a large number of which have reached us in poems by Jewish writers. With these formal schemes a type of secular poetry was developed that was full of nuances and whose genres include the panegyric, the elegy, the love song, the bacchanal, the song to nature, the philosophical and sapiential poem, the satire, and the lament.

The birthplace of Hebrew secular poetry was 10th-century Córdoba, a city that under the caliphs Abd ar-Rahman III (reigned 912-961) and al-Hakam II (reigned 961-976) became the most important center of culture in the West and a meeting-place for intellectuals, scientists, and artists from far-off lands. A significant contribution to this rebirth of Hebrew culture in Córdoba was made by Hisdai ibn Shaprut (c. 915-970), whose protégés included the first Hispano-Hebrew poets, Dunash ben Labrat of Fez, who introduced the quantitative meter of Arabic poet-

ry into Hebrew poetry, and Menahem ibn Saruq of Tortosa, a bitter opponent of Labrat. However, it was during the *taifa* kingdoms, which appeared after the fall of the caliphate, that Hebrew poetry reached its greatest heights. The golden age of Hebrew poetry, which lasted for over a hundred years, began with Samuel ibn Nagrela (993-1055), known as Samuel ha-Nagid, who marked the highest achievement of a Jew in

medieval Muslim Spain. A poet and scholar, he was also vizier to the minor king of the *taifa* of Granada and commander of Granada's army, which he led in almost constant warfare, particularly against Seville. Indeed, he died while on campaign. His greatest poetry is his songs of war, which recount his victories.

Solomon ibn Gabirol (c.1020-c. 1057), sometimes considered the foremost Spanish

Jewish poet, displayed a deeply critical view of his fellow men and a constant search for wisdom and perfection. Both his parents died when he was young, his life was troubled by poverty and sickness, and his work reflects his bitterness and disappointment. In addition to poetry, he wrote a philosophical work and a book on ethics.

The works of Moses ibn Ezra (c. 1055-c. 1135) are divided in two parts, that of his happy

youth as the son of a rich Granada family and— when the Almoravids brought his lost paradise of Granada to an end—the years of exile in the arid lands of the north, which seemed like a cultural desert to him.

In his youth, Judah ben Samuel Halevi (c. 1075-1141) rejoiced in life, love, and friendship; in later years he turned to themes of philosophy and ethics. He wrote 800 known poems—secu-

Jerusalem in a map by Bernard van Breydenbach, Mainz, 1486 (Biblioteca Nacional, Madrid). Benjamin of Tudela visited Jerusalem on his travels in the Near East (1159-73) and described the city in his diary: "It is a small city fortified by three walls. A large number of people live there... as well as more who speak many other languages. There is a dyer's shop that the Jews rent annually from the king so that none but they shall make dyes in Jerusalem. Some two hundred Jews live

at the foot of the Tower of David on one side of the city... There are two buildings: one, the Hospital... and the second, [which] they call the Temple of Solomon, is the palace made by this king... There is also a great church, which they call the Sepulcher, where the man to whom all the pilgrims go is buried. The city has four gates: that of Abraham, that of David, that of Zion, and that of Josaphat... before the Temple which existed in former times; ...upon this

lar, religious, and nationalist—as well as several hundred *piyyutim* and books on philosophy. His works are marked by great beauty and a lofty spirit. Among his best known works is *Shirei Ziyyon* ("Poems of Zion," or "Zionides"), which includes thirty-five odes to Zion. These poems express his yearning to return to the land of his fathers.

A host of brilliant poets gathered around

these four great figures, among them Abraham ibn Ezra (c. 1089-c. 1164), considered the last of the great writers of Al-Andalus. All these poets wrote religious poems, many of which now form part of the Hebrew prayer book.

In the middle of the 12th century and after the disappearance of Jewish Al-Andalus, the Hebrew poets continued to uphold the tradition of their lost homeland in the Christian kingdoms—a tradi-

tion now modified by the new environment and their own inner development. Of importance during this period are four poets, two from the 13th century—Todros Abulafia of Toledo, who was linked to the court of Alfonso X, and Meshullam ben Solomon da Piera (Gerona), whose work reflects the influence of troubadour poetry—and two 14th-15th century poets—Solomon ben Meshullam da Piera, a relative of the earlier poet,

and Solomon ben Reuben Bonafed. The Hispano-Hebrew school ended with the expulsion of 1492, but its influence lived on all over the Jewish world until the 18th century.

Hispanic Jews wrote poetry not only in Hebrew but also in the Romance languages. Two particularly outstanding 14th-century works in Castilian are *Proverbios Morales,* by Shem Tov Ardutiel, known as Santob de Carrión and a dis-

tinguished author of *maqāmāt* in Hebrew, and the anonymous *Poema de Yoçef,* which tells the Bible story of Joseph and his brethren with an abundance of legendary material.

Much Hebrew religious poetry was written in Italy and the Ashkenazic world in the Middle Ages. Particularly important, too, are various works in vernacular languages, such as the *Complainte de Troyes,* composed in old French by Jacob ben Judah in remembrance of the Jewish victims of a massacre of 1288, and, in the field of secular poetry, the works in French of the troubadours of 13th-century Provence Bonfils de Narbonne and Charlot le Juif and those in German of the minnesinger Hugo von Trimberg.

The torch of Hispano-Hebrew poetry was borne in 14th-century Italy by Immanuel of Rome, who also wrote sonnets and other poems in Italian based on the aesthetic principles of the *dolce stil novo.* An important Renaissance writer was Judah Leone ben Isaac Sommo (1527-92), known as Leone De Sommi Portaleone, who wrote the first treatise in Italian on theatrical productions, a work that influenced the history of Renaissance theater in general. He also wrote several dramas that were performed at the court of the duke of Mantua in the 16th century, the company of local Jewish actors gaining a great reputation, and the oldest Hebrew drama extant, *Zahut Bedihuta de-Kiddushin* ("An Eloquent Marriage Farce").

Among the 17th-century Italian poets who wrote in Hebrew and Italian was Judah Aryeh (1571-1648), known as Leone Modena, who wrote plays in Hebrew and the treatise *Historia de' Riti Ebraici,* written at the request of the English ambassador in Venice for presentation to King James I and a fine example of the erudite literary style of Italian baroque. Also important were the brothers Jacob and Immanuel Frances, while another poet of the period, Moses Zacuto (c. 1620-1697) is famous as the first writer of plays in Hebrew verse in the manner of the Spanish comedy. He also wrote a dramatic poem, *Tofteh Arukh,* inspired by Dante's *Divine Comedy.* The age of Hebrew theater in Italy ends with the works of Moses Hayyim Luzzatto (1707-47), who was influenced by cabalistic

207

temple Umar ibn al-Khattab built a huge and beautiful dome... Opposite this place is the Western Wall, [which] is one of those that existed in the Holy of Holies and they call it the Gate of Mercy. To this wall go all the Jews to pray... [and] they write their names on the wall."

studies and claimed divine revelation for his own works of mysticism.

Consisting of codes and talmudic commentaries, by far the largest proportion of medieval Jewish literature is rabbinic and refers to the law. From the 11th century, the Jews of Europe returned to the commentary, a form developed long before in Babylonia and North Africa, its greatest exponent being the rabbinic academy of Lucena in Al-Andalus, where such great rabbis as Isaac Alfasi and Joseph ibn Migash both studied and taught. The illustrious Cordovan doctor Maimonides (12th century) also turned his attention to talmudic commentary in his *The Luminary*, a complete commentary in Arabic on the Mishnah in which he presented the laws in an orderly and systematic manner through the use of logic. The most important 13th-century Hispano-Hebrew commentators were Nahmanides, who adopted the method of the French school, and his pupil Solomon ben Adret. Among the principal talmudists of the 14th century were Meir Halevi Abulafia of Toledo, Nissim Gerondi of Gerona, and Asher ben Jehiel of Germany.

Talmudic commentary was developed in France and Germany, too, but it was based less on logic and rationalism than that of the Hispanic school. Religious feeling in central Europe was characterized by simplicity, deep piety, strict observance of the precepts, and contempt for the secular sciences. Of particular importance was the rabbinic academy of Mainz, led by Gershom ben Judah, to which hundreds of disciples flocked. Among these disciples was the famous Rashi, who wrote a complete commentary on the Talmud that, due to its lucidity, brevity, and depth, became a much referred-to model. The work of Rashi was continued by the so-called Tosafists with their "additions" of explanations to the Talmud; the most important of the various generations of Franco-Germanic scholars were Jacob ben Meir Tam (also known as Rabbenu Tam), Isaac ben Samuel of Dampierre, and Meir ben Baruch of Rothenburg.

Considerable talmudic activity also took place in Italy, where in the 11th century Nathan ben Jehiel of Rome wrote his dictionary of the Talmud, the *Arukh*, and in the 16th century

Obadiah ben Abraham Yare of Bertinoro wrote a detailed commentary on the Mishnah. Halfway between the Hispano- and Franco-Germanic Hebrew commentators, the academies of Provence, whose rabbis included Abraham ben David of Posquières (12th century), a bitter opponent of Maimonides, employed the methods

of both schools. From the 16th century, Polish Jewry took the lead in commentary under the rabbis and scholars who had left Germany.

From the time of the Talmud's completion, Jews scattered throughout a large number of countries felt the need for a clear, concise code that would enable them to lead those who, often

Beginning of the second book of the Mishne Torah *by Maimonides in a manuscript copied in Spain, c. 1350, and illuminated in Perugia, c. 1400 (Jewish National and University Library, Jerusalem). The* Mishne Torah *(known in English as the* Strong Hand*), Maimonides' most important rabbinic work, was the most widely circulated among the Jews both of his age and after. Maimonides finished it in 1180, having worked on it for ten years. Consisting of fourteen books, it comprehensively and exhaustively catalogs the subjects of all the religious and legal regulations of talmudic literature in the form of a systematic exposition never before achieved. During Maimonides' lifetime this work was criticized by sectors of Judaism who accused him of wishing to abolish talmudic study. The controversy raged until many years after his death.*

lacking competent rabbinic authority, could not find their way in seeking specific regulations among the thicket of legal texts. In Babylonia some rabbis had already made attempts at codification, but the task of drawing up legal summaries fell to the Jews of Europe, particularly to those of Al-Andalus and the Hispanic kingdoms.

The first attempt at codification was made in the 11th century by Isaac Alfasi (1013-1103) in his *Sefer ha-Halakhot*, but the giant step was taken in the next century by Maimonides in his *Mishne Torah* ("The Torah Reviewed"), a systematic summary of Jewish law and ritual. Although his work gained widespread acceptance and became a milestone in Jewish literature, at first it met with opposition from those who saw it as a threat that could supplant the study of the Talmud.

Worthy of mention among the various, more or less complete, codifications written in the 12th century by the Franco-Germanic and Italian schools was the *Mahzor Vitry* by Samuel of Vitry, who in dealing with the liturgy and the yearly religious cycle quoted numerous laws. The *Mahzor Vitry* is a fundamental work in the history of the Jewish liturgy.

The Hispano-Hebrew school took up the task of codification once again in the 13th century, its work being more systematized, less strict in its decisions, and less determined by its use of customs than that of its Franco-Germanic counterpart. The most significant work of this period was written by Asher ben Jehiel and served as the basis for the complete work, *Arba'ah Turim* ("Four Rows"), written by Asher's son Jacob and accepted at the time by a wide sector of the Jewish population. But the definitive work was to be that of Joseph Caro, who was expelled from Spain as a child, moving with his family to Bulgaria and finally to Safed in Palestine. Following the arrangement of *Arba'ah Turim*, he wrote *Beit Yosef* ("House of Joseph") and also a kind of manual of much shorter formulations, the *Shulhan Arukh* ("The Table Set"), which was to become—and remains—the definitive code of the entire Jewish world.

For the work to be accepted by Franco-Germanic and Polish Jewry, the intervention of Moses Isserles was necessary, the much more

inflexible Ashkenazic viewpoints being included and, wherever there was discrepancy, the rulings of the central European school being applied.

In the 11th century, the main centers of Jewish philosophy lay in the al-Andalusian and Christian Hispanic kingdoms. The first major philosopher was the poet Solomon ibn Gabirol,

whose major philosophical work, showing the influence of Neoplatonism, was written originally in Arabic and later translated into Hebrew and Latin with the titles *Mekor Hayyim* and *Fons Vitae* ("The Well of Life"). The Latin version exercised much influence on Christian thought in the Middle Ages and was attributed to

209

St. Dominic and the Albigenses, oil painting by Pedro Berruguete, 15th century (Museo del Prado, Madrid). The first public burning of the Talmud was preceded by the appearance of sectarian movements (Cathari and Albigenses) in the bosom of Christianity that were violently suppressed by the church (Pope Innocent III sent Dominic to preach to the Albigenses in southern France). Concern about rationalistic tendencies led to the burning of Maimonides' Guide of the Perplexed (Montpellier, 1233), which served as a precedent for the burning of the Talmud, ordered by Pope Gregory IX and executed by the Dominicans and Franciscans in Paris in 1242. The public burning of Hebrew books had the most far-reaching consequences in Italy. Due to a dispute between two of the Christian printers of the Talmud in Venice, the work was condemned in 1553, thousands of Hebrew books being burned in Rome and the Papal States (particularly in Bologna and Ravenna), in Ferrara, Mantua, Urbino, Florence, and Venice, and in Cremona in 1559. The Jewish printers of Poland and the Ottoman Empire then took up the task of producing texts for study, the Talmud being published in Lublin in 1559 and shortly after in Salonica. The Talmud was publicly burned for the last time in Poland in 1757 as the result of differences between the rabbis and the adherents of the Frankist movement.

Philosophy and Morality

Avicebron, a transformation of Ibn Gabirol's name. Ibn Gabirol also wrote a work on ethics, *Tikkun Middot ha-Nefesh* ("Improvement of the Moral Qualities"), originally in Arabic. During the same period, Bahya ibn Paquda wrote *Hovot ha-Levavot* ("Duties of the Heart"), a work in Arabic on morality greatly influenced by Muslim mysticism.

Important 12th-century philosophers include the scientist Abraham bar Hiyya (known as Savasorda) of Barcelona, who was the first to write philosophical works in Hebrew; many terms coined by him passed into accepted Hebrew usage. There were also Joseph ben Zaddik of Córdoba, who elaborated the theory of man as microcosm (man is a microcosm and can know the world by knowing himself); the poet

Judah Halevi, who wrote *Kuzari*, a vindication of Judaism in which he attempted to demonstrate that the truths of revealed religion are superior to those of reason; Abraham ibn Ezra, also a poet, whose philosophical considerations contain an almost pantheistic notion of God; and the historian Abraham ibn Daud, who paid special attention to the problems of freedom and providence and introduced Aristotelianism into Jewish thought.

However, the great master of the Jewish philosophy of that age was Maimonides whose *Moreh Nevukhim* ("Guide of the Perplexed"), originally written in Arabic, was studied by both Christians and Muslims and deeply affected scholasticism. The book is aimed at those who are confused by the contradictions existing

between philosophy and religion.

Maimonides' philosophical writings led to bitter controversy among his supporters and critics, the majority of the latter being rabbis from northern France. However, in France, too, Maimonides won followers, one being Levi ben Gershon, who wrote *Milhamot Adonai* ("The Wars of the Lord") and who, like Maimonides, dealt with a wide variety of subjects, including psychology, the immortality of the soul, free will, divine providence, and cosmology as seen from an Aristotelian point of view.

Among the host of Hispano-Jewish philosophers and moralists of the 14th and 15th centuries, three stand out: Hasdai Crescas of Barcelona, who wrote *Or Adonai* ("The Light of the Lord"), Joseph Albo, whose book *Sefer ha-Ikkarim* ("Book of Principles") investigated the theory of Jewish religious dogmas, and Isaac Aboab of Toledo, whose extremely popular book *Menorat-ha-Ma'or* ("Candelabrum of Light") contains a large number of legends and allegories taken from the Haggadah.

In sapiential literature there is the compilation of maxims from Arabic and Hebrew sources, *Llibre de paraules e dits de savis e filosofs*, written in Catalan by Jafuda Bonsenyor of Barcelona (died 1331) and dedicated to James II of Aragon. The last of the Hispano-Hebrew philosophers was Isaac Abrabanel, whose many works on specific subjects display a deep knowledge not only of Jewish but also of Arabic and Christian philosophy. In Italy, his son Judah Abrabanel, known as Leone Ebreo, wrote *Dialoghi di Amore* ("Dialogs of Love"), a Renaissance-style philosophical work in Italian.

The work of the translators of Provence was extremely important in the diffusion of philosophy among the Jews of Europe. In this field, the Ibn Tibbon family, originally from Al-Andalus, was particularly important in the 12th and 13th centuries, while in the 14th century Kalonymus ben Kalonymus is the most famous. These men translated the majority of the Jewish and Muslim philosophical works and the commentaries on classical Greek philosophy into Hebrew for Jews who did not understand Arabic.

Ashkenazic works on morality are somewhat more abundant than those on philosophy.

Detail from The Crucifixion, *by Luis Borassá, Gerona, 14th-15th centuries (Museo de Arte de Cataluña, Barcelona) showing Jews in a public debate. Literary polemics appeared in the Iberian Peninsula with Joseph Kimhi, an Andalusian who took refuge in Provence (c. 1150). The arguments of his* Sefer ha-Berith *("Book of the Covenant") were taken up by his son David in* Vicuah *("Dispute"). Other authors in this field include Solomon ben Adret* *of Barcelona (1235-1308); Isaac Profiat Duran, whose work* Kelimat ha-Goyim *("Shame of the Gentiles," 1397), spurred on other polemicists; Hasdai Crescas, who wrote the* Refutation of the Principles of the Christians; *Simeon ben Zemah Duran, who wrote* Magen Avot *("The Shield of the Fathers"); and his son Solomon ben Zemah Duran, whose work* Milhemet Mishva *("Preceptive Battle," 1438), which defended the Talmud, was attacked by* *Jerónimo de Santa Fe (formerly Joshua Lorki) in the disputation of Tortosa in 1413.*

The most ancient work is the *Sefer Hasidim* ("Book of the Pious"), attributed to Judah the Hasid of Regensburg (c. 1200). It contains detailed instructions for everyday life, from matters concerning the liturgy to the family, all profusely illustrated with stories and narratives. Also worthy of mention are Elijah Moses de Vidas' *Reshit Hokhmah* ("The Beginning of Wisdom"), with its mystical elements, and, in much more modern times, *Cab Hayasar* ("The Measure of the Just"), written in both Hebrew and Yiddish by Zevi Hirsch Koidonover (18th century), which reflects the mystical spirit of Polish Judaism.

The origins of the cabala, or Jewish mysticism—an esoteric system of interpretation of the Scriptures—are to be found in the Apocrypha, the Talmud, and the Haggadic commentaries on the appearance of God to man as described in the first chapter of the Book of Ezekiel.

Its first, great development began in Provence with Moses of Narbonne (12th century), whose school produced the *Sefer Ha-bahir* ("Book of Brightness"); it then developed further in Catalonia, one of the greatest representatives of that period being Azriel of Gerona—who is associated with Isaac the Blind of Provence—and later spread through Castile, the birthplace of the cabala's greatest work, the *Zohar* ("Splendor"), written in Aramaic largely by Moses de León (13th century).

In the 16th century, work on the cabala continued in Safed, where it was developed by a group of Sephardic and Ashkenazic mystics, including Solomon Alkabez, Moses Cordovero, Isaac Luria, and Hayyim Vital. Among the most important cabalists of the next two centuries were Joseph Solomon Delmedigo and Isaiah Halevi Horowitz, while later work on the cabala is reflected in the writings of the Italian Moses Hayyim Luzzatto and especially in the writings of the Polish Hasidim of the 18th century.

One of the first historical works to be written by a European Jew was the *Sefer Ahima'az* ("Scroll of Ahimaaz"), the family chronicle of Ahimaaz ben Paltiel (1017-c. 1060). It discusses Jewish life in southern Italy and testifies to the legal autonomy of the Jews of Italy and their close links with the Jews of Palestine. The Jewish

211

Moreh Nevukhim ("Guide of the Perplexed") by Maimonides, Barcelona, 1347-48 (Det Kongelige Bibliotek, Copenhagen): astronomers discussing Maimonides' opinions on astrology and astronomy: "Know... that all those matters decided by the stars, in which they say that such a thing will take place and such a thing not take place and that a man's birth sign determines that he will be so and that this and that will happen to him, all these things are not scientific at all but nonsense... Science that is true science is the knowledge of the shape of the spheres, their number, their measurements, and their movement, the time of revolution of each one, their inclination to the north or to the south, their rotation to the east or to the west, and the orbits of the heavenly bodies and whither they go." (From a letter to the rabbis of Marseilles.)

History and Fiction

chronicles of France and Germany deal mainly with the Crusades, as do those of Ephraim of Bonn, and of Solomon ben Simeon and Eliezar ben Nathan, both of Mainz. The first historiographic work of importance written in the Iberian Peninsula was the *Sefer ha-Kabbalah* ("Book of Tradition"), by Abraham ibn Daud of Al-Andalus (12th century). A kind of world history, it attempts to demonstrate that over the centuries the chain of oral tradition and the authority of the rabbis have never been broken.

Although they continued to mix fact and fiction, the later medieval works display a greater critical approach and attempt to place Jewish history within a general context. Many such works serve as chronicles for individual families, entire communities, and even specific events, one example being that of Menahem Meiri of Provence (1249-1316), which is a source of information on Provençal and Franco-Germanic intellectual circles. The most interesting historical works of the 15th and 16th centuries are those written in the Iberian Peninsula by Joseph ben Zaddik of Arévalo and Abraham ben Solomon of Torrutiel (Valencia) who in his *Sefer ha-Kabbalah* ("Book of Tradition") described the period of expulsion from Spain. One particular type of literature deals with the persecutions, of which two 16th-century works, the *Shevet Yehudah,* by Solomon ibn Verga of Seville, and *Emek ha-Bakha* ("The Valley of Tears"), written in Italian by the Sephardic Jew Joseph ha-Kohen, are particularly important.

Following in the footsteps of Ibn Daud, a significant number of authors dealt with the history of Jewish tradition since its origins, the

Above and center: Two of the eighty woodcuts from Meshal ha-Kadmoni *("Example of the Ancient"), by Isaac ben Solomon ibn Sahula, 1281, in the Meir ben Jacob Parenzo edition, Venice, 1546-50 (Jacob M. Lowy Collection, National Library of Canada, Ottawa). Ibn Sahula wrote this* maqāma *to demonstrate that Hebrew was as suitable as Arabic for rhyming prose. Among his overlapping stories are a number of fables with animals.*

majority of their works being a combination of chronology and biography. Those written by Sephardic authors include Abraham Zacuto's (15th century) *Sefer Yuhasin* ("Book of Genealogies"), which deals with its subjects rigorously, and Gedaliah ibn Yahya's (16th century) *Shalshelet ha-Kabbalah* ("Chain of Tradition"), while among those by Ashkenazic Jews are *Zemah David* by David Gans (16th century), which contains interesting information on the history of Polish and German Jewry, and *Kore ha-Dorot* by David Conforte (17th century), of primary interest for the information it contains on the Tosafists of eastern Europe in the 16th and 17th centuries. The most important 18th-century work was the *Seder ha-Dorot* ("Order of the Generations"), by Jehiel Heilprin.

One of the oldest works on literary history and bibliography is Moses ibn Ezra's 12th-century *Poetics*, written in Arabic. Much more modern are the works of Joseph Delmedigo (17th century), which deal with certain aspects of medieval Jewish literary history, and those of Hayyim David Azulai (18th century), which contain 3,000 short biographies. The writer who best combined far-ranging knowledge, a critical approach, and a sense of history was the Italian Azariah dei Rossi (c. 1511-c. 1578), who in his *Meor Enayim* ("Light of the Eyes") critically analyzes aspects of Jewish institutions, history, and literature.

Finally, certain Jewish authors dedicated their work to history in general, making only isolated references to Jewish history. Such was the case of Elijah Capsali of Crete (c. 1483-1555), whose *Seder Eliyahu Zuta* (1523) is a history of the Ottoman Empire and contains

important information on the Sephardic Jews who settled there.

The leading book on travel during the Middle Ages was written by Benjamin of Tudela, who between 1159 and 1173 journeyed through southern Europe, Africa, and the East—he is considered the first European to have reached China—to gather information for merchants. His account of these journeys, *Massaoth*

Schel Rabbi Benjamin (published in English in 1840 as *The Itinerary of Rabbi Benjamin of Tudela*), describes the life of the Jews in the cities he visited and sheds light on the history of the times. There was also the work of Pethahiah of Regensburg, who wrote of his travels between 1175 and 1185 through the Slavic countries, Babylonia, and Palestine. From the 13th century on, Jews wrote a considerable amount of literature dedicated mainly to descriptions of journeys to Palestine. These contain information on the communities visited along the way. Although many of these works consist of compilations of legends and mere descriptions of holy places, others contain information of greater interest.

In Al-Andalus, the contact between Jews and Arabic culture affected not only poetry but also prose fiction, giving rise to the appearance of tales, fables, and didactic booklets in which ethics merged with satire, humor, and proverbs. Such literature was aimed at entertainment and the creation of aesthetic pleasure, and many of these works adopted the formal style of rhyming prose typical of the Arabic *maqāmāt*. Other writers took their inspiration from the Bible, the Apocrypha, and the broad field of the Haggadah. At first most of this literature was written by Hispanic Jews, but Provençal and Italian authors also later turned to this style of writing. Without doubt, the most outstanding work in this genre is the Catalan Judah ben Solomon al-Harizi's (12th-13th century) *Tahkemoni* ("The Pedant"), which contains fifty *maqāmāt*. This was followed by other works, such as *Yehuda Sone ha-Nashim* ("Judah the Misogynist") by al-Harizi's contemporary Judah ibn Shabbetai and, from the 13th century, the anonymous *Ezrat Hanasim* ("The Women's Help") and *Ohev Nasim* ("The Lover of Women") by Jedaiah Hapenini of Beziers. Translated directly from the Arabic was the *Iggeret Ba'alei Hayyim* ("The Animals' Collection") by the Provençal (Arles) writer Kalonymus ben Kalonymus.

The Jews of medieval times continued to write traditional narratives directly related to the classical Haggadah. In this respect must be mentioned *Yalkut Shimoni* ("The Collection of Simeon"), an anthology from the ancient Midrash that is rich in the legends referred to by preachers to illustrate their sermons and is attributed to the German Jew Simeon Kara of Frankfurt (13th century); and the numerous legends that interlace the discourse of works such as *Kad Hakemah* ("Flour Basket") by Bahya ben Asher of Saragossa (13th century), and the previously mentioned *Menorat-ha-Ma'or*. Talmudic legends were also compiled and printed outside Spain by Jacob ibn Habib of Zamora (15th century) in his book *Ein Ya'akov* ("The Springs of Jacob").

Calendar from the Catalan Atlas (1375-77), illuminated by Abraham Cresques and his son Jafuda (facsimile edition; Museo Marítimo, Barcelona). Particularly outstanding among medieval astronomers was the versatile Levi ben Gershon (1288-1344), known as Gersonides and also as Ralbag, from the initials of his Hebrew name. Mathematician, philosopher, and Bible commentator, he was probably born in Bagnols-sur-Cèze (Languedoc). His chief work, Milhamot Adonai ("The Wars of the Lord"), contains a treatise on astronomy one hundred and thirty-six chapters in length that was translated into Latin. Various inventions are popularly attributed to Gersonides, including the camera obscura and the Jacob's staff, the device used to measure the angular distance between celestial bodies.

Judeo-Spanish Literature

For centuries the abundant literature written in Judeo-Spanish by the Sephardim of the Ottoman Empire coexisted with the extremely rich literature written in Hebrew. In modern times, other languages have been used, such as French and the Balkan tongues. The leading publishing centers were Constantinople, Salonica, Smyrna, Jerusalem, Sofia, Belgrade, Alexandria, Vienna, and, due to the importance of their printing presses, certain Italian cities, such as Pisa and Venice during the early period and, at all times, Leghorn, where a large number of works published in the East were reprinted for distribution to Sephardic readers in Morocco.

In addition to literature, the Sephardim passed down a diverse oral form comprised of lyrical songs, tales, and proverbs. A prominent place is occupied by the songs known as *romanceros*, most of which derive from the Hispanic tradition prior to the expulsion. To these must be added the *romanceros* brought to the East by the converts who left the peninsula in subsequent centuries.

The 16th century was a period of settlement and consolidation for the new communities formed by the exiles from Spain, and writings in Judeo-Spanish were mainly limited to translations from Hebrew. Only two pieces from this period survive: *Extremos y Grandezas de Constantinopla* and *Regimiento de la vida*, both by Moses Almosnino (c. 1515-c. 1580).

The most important works in translation were those of the literature necessary for the synagogal service—the Bible, prayers, and the liturgical poems included in the prayer books for daily use and at festivals, as well as other works of special significance for worship, such as the Mishnaic treatise *Pirkei Avot* and the Passover Haggadah. The translations of the Bible that date from the 16th century are worthy of mention. The complete text of the Pentateuch was first published in a trilingual version (Hebrew, Neo-Greek, and Judeo-Spanish) in Constantinople in 1547; the remaining books of the Bible were translated in Salonica between 1568 and 1600. In the 18th century, when a new version of the Bible was required, Abraham Asa made a new translation. Printed between 1739 and 1745 in Constantinople, it appeared first in Hebrew script

Sulayman the Magnificent during the siege of Belgrade, 1621 (Topkapi Palace Museum, Istanbul). Particularly important among the various industries developed by the Sephardim in the Ottoman Empire was that of arms manufacturing. This was described by the Frenchman Nicolas de Nicolay, who journeyed through Turkey in 1551 (Les quatres premiers livres de navigations et pérégrinations orientales faicts en Turquie, Lyons, 1568): "To the detriment of Christianity, these people are familiarizing the Turks with recent discoveries in weapons of war, the manufacture of projectiles, harquebuses, ammunition, and other things of the kind."

Title page of the fourth edition of Me'am Lo'ez; *first part, Leghorn, 1823 (Biblioteca de Estudios Sefardíes, CSIC, Madrid). Jacob Culi, pioneer of the* Me'am Lo'ez, *wrote one commentary on Genesis and began another on Exodus. The work was then continued by Isaac Magriso (1746-47), who also wrote a commentary on Leviticus (1753) and Numbers (1764). Magriso was succeeded by Isaac Arweti, who wrote the commentary on Deuteronomy (1773).*

and served as the basis for all editions printed in the East from then until this century. In the early 19th century (1813-15), Israel B. Hayyim's complete version of the Bible, commonly known as the *Minhat Shai* after the commentary that accompanied it, was printed in Vienna.

In addition to liturgical texts, works of varied content were translated. These included manuals of religious ritual, such as *Hilkhot Shehitah*, concerning the regulations of ritual slaughter, prayer books, and books of biblical interpretation and ethics, such as Joseph Caro's *Shulhan Arukh*, Bahya's *ha-Levavot*, Aboab's *Menorat-ha-Ma'or*, and Elijah Benjamin ha-Levi's *Shevet Musar*. Most of these versions were literal translations, the most characteristic feature of the language used in them being that it keeps strictly to the original in accordance with ancient rules on translation that developed before the expulsion.

After the silence of the 17th century, a period from which little Judeo-Spanish literature survives, literary creativity blossomed. This was the result of several historical factors.

After the bitter failure of Shabbetai Zevi's movement and the decline in the late 17th century of rabbinic studies in Hebrew, a group of writers appeared whose goal was to provide Jews with traditional religious education in a language understood by all—Judeo-Spanish. This literary renaissance was furthered by two other factors: the existence of Sephardic families that, having become prosperous through trade, served as patrons to publishing; and the perfecting of the printing techniques developed in the East in the 1730s by central European Jews who had fled the persecutions in Poland and other countries. One such case in this respect was Jonah Ashkenazi and his sons, thanks to whom Constantinople became the capital of Hebrew publishing in the entire Mediterranean area. All the literature produced at the time of this cultural renaissance had religious connotations.

Throughout the 18th century Sephardim published numerous works on religious regulations, morality, and other rabbinic wisdom, both originals and translations. Of these, two of the most representative genres are the *Me'am Lo'ez* and the *coplas*.

The *Me'am Lo'ez*, one of the literary milestones of this period, confers upon Sephardic the category of a language appropriate for free literary creation (or it is, at least, the best example of it). It was begun by Jacob Culi (c. 1685-1732), a highly educated rabbi and editor who conceived of the work as a vast commentary on the Bible to include all religious, juridic, legendary, historical, moralistic, mystical, anecdotal, and folkloric matter developed in previous rabbinic commentaries. Furthermore, he wished to include illustrations of passages and even individual verses from the Bible. Although Culi's aim was both to teach and entertain, his main intention was to transmit knowledge of the Halakah, or religious law. More than a book, the *Me'am Lo'ez* is a series of commentaries on which a dozen different authors worked for over a century and a half, the result being a kind of encyclopedia of traditional Sephardic knowledge. The common feature linking Culi with his immediate successors is that of a firmly based

El emperador Jusepo el segundo y la hermosa Rahel, a novel in Judeo-Spanish published in episodes in the Güerta de Historia, *Vienna, 1864 (Biblioteca de Estudios Sefardíes, CSIC, Madrid). The* Güerta, *one of the first versions of a serialized novel, flourished in 19th-century Constantinople (*Güerta de Romanzos, Güerta de Historias, Buqueto de Romanzos*),* Smyrna *(*Buquieto de Historias*), and other cities.*

Front page of the Judeo-Spanish newspaper La Epoca *(Salonica 1875-1912), a "political, trade and literary magazine," for June 29, 1900 (Biblioteca de Estudios Sefardíes, CSIC, Madrid). Founded in 1875 by the ballad writer Saadi Haleví, it was one Salonica's most important and longest-lived Judeo-Spanish periodicals. After Haleví's death and until 1912 it was edited by his son, Sam Levi. Its literary supplement was called* La Epoca Literaria.

rabbinic education that made use of a system intimately related to the spirit and form of traditional rabbinic commentary.

The genre known as the *coplas* contains the most genuine and typically Sephardic poetry as rooted in the medieval Hispanic *copla* tradition and represented by the *Poema de Yoçef*, Santob de Carrión's *Proverbios Morales*, and other poems. These are texts that are strophic in form and follow a thematic connection throughout. However, in only a few cases are the names of authors known or is it possible to speculate on who wrote them. Although they were transmitted mainly in written form, oral forms of a large number do exist. The revitalization of the genre

in the East at the beginning of the 18th century came about for the same reason as the return of the great *Me'am Lo'ez*—a wish by certain writers to broaden popular knowledge of traditional Jewish culture. Which explains why the themes of the oldest *coplas* to have reached us are mainly "religious" in the broadest sense of the word—hagiographic, legal, moralistic, paraliturgical, etc.—and to a large extent drew from the narratives of Midrashic legend. Throughout the 18th century and the first half of the 19th century, the genre developed profusely, so that when, in the last third of the 19th century, a radical change came about in Sephardic language and literature, the genre did not die out. There

were noteworthy changes in style and theme, but its vitality did not flag, and old *coplas* were reedited and new ones written.

After the 1850s, the Sephardic world underwent a process that could be called a cultural revolution, in this case a movement contrary to that of the early 18th century. The change was profound, taking the form of a break with the old in order to open up to Western culture. There are various reasons for such a transformation, some of which affected the Jewish world as a whole, while others affected the Sephardic community in particular. After the Balkan Wars and the breakdown of the political authority of the Ottoman Empire, nationalistic movements

216

Above left: Portrait of Rabbi Jacob Sasportas (Oran, 1610-Amsterdam, 1698), in a late 17th-century Dutch engraving (William L. Gross Collection, Ramat Aviv, Israel). Above right: Portrait of the pseudo-messiah Shabbetai Zevi (1626-76) from a contemporary German engraving (William L. Gross Collection, Ramat Aviv, Israel). The engraving shows two scenes from Zevi's life: at upper left, the ship that took him from Smyrna to Constantinople; at upper right, Zevi

imprisoned by the sultan. The Shabbetean movement appeared with unusual force within the Jewish community of Amsterdam, becoming a focus for the dissemination of the ideas of the false messiah, whose large masses of followers were headed by rabbis and community leaders. The various editions of the writings of Zevi's prophet, Nathan of Gaza, were published in Amsterdam by Joseph Athias and David de Castro Tartas and distributed throughout Jewish

communities all over Europe. Zevi's fiercest opponent was Rabbi Jacob Sasportas, who at the time of the controversy lived in Hamburg. In his book Sisat novel Tzevi, *he contested various Shabbetaianistic letters and pamphlets, in many cases including the origin texts, with the result that his book has become an important source of Shabbetaianistic study. It covers the years 1648 and 1676, from the proclamation of Zevi as the Messiah until his conversion.*

became a general phenomenon, the various peoples embarking on a search for national identity and the recovery of their own, unique cultures. Foremost among the factors of change that directly affected the Sephardic world were the echoes of the central European Haskalah movement, but the decisive factor in the transformation was the establishment in the last three decades of the 19th century of the group of French Alliance Israélite Universelle schools through which French literary production and culture were channeled to the Sephardim. Through French culture the Sephardic world thus opened to the West, the French language and indeed all things French in general having a decisive influence on Sephardic literature and an irreversible influence on the language.

Traditional religious literature continued to exist, but now lived alongside such recently adopted "secular" genres as journalism (which developed so vigorously that over three hundred very different publications were soon in circulation), narrative literature and theater, poetry, historiography (both general and on specific periods or events), biographies, autobiographies, and educational books on such subjects as science, grammar, and hygiene.

Here the theater is worthy of special mention, particularly the Sephardic plays of manners and history. Many plays were inspired by the Bible and the classical history of the Jewish people, some described Jewish life in the Diaspora and dealt with the problems of assimilation and anti-Semitism (to which the Zionist solution was proposed), while others described non-Sephardic Jews and their environments through the adaptation of the major works of the Ashkenazic theater, such as Ansky's *The Dybbuk* and literature of manners, such as that of Shalom Aleichem, into Judeo-Spanish. To these must be added the adaptations of the major works of world theater, the French theater being the most familiar to Sephardic audiences and Molière their favorite playwright.

217

Top: Istanbul street in a lithograph by Antoine I. Melling, France, 1829 (private collection, Madrid). Above: Jewish trader from Istanbul, 19th century (I. Einhorn Collection, Museum of the Jewish Diaspora, Tel Aviv). From the 16th to the 18th century, Istanbul was one of the main centers of Hebrew book publishing. In the 16th century, it was a rendezvous for Sephardim who were not only experts in the art of printing but also owned priceless manuscripts, which

could be published and circulated in the Ottoman Empire with complete freedom. The first Hebrew printing press in the empire (the first book in Turkish was not published until 1728) was founded in Istanbul by the Spaniards David and Samuel ibn Nahmias and operated between 1493 and 1518. By 1530, over one hundred important works had been printed, and from that time on the number of printing presses in Istanbul grew. Of these, particularly important were the

presses of the Italian Gershom Soncino and his son Eliezer (operating from 1530 to 1547), from 1548 to 1553 run by an employee; and above all that of the Spaniards Solomon and Joseph Yabez (1559-93). Among the most important printers of the 18th century were Jonah ben Jacob Ashkenazi and his son, who printed 188 works between 1710 and 1778 and employed fifty workers.

Yiddish Literature

There are two, clearly distinguishable stages in the development of Yiddish literature: that of Old Yiddish, which ended in the late 18th century and consisted primarily of a type of popular literature; and Modern Yiddish, which is still used today.

Yiddish literature seems to have made its appearance around the 12th century and at the beginning served to bring the traditional genres of popular German literature (tales, songs, etc.) to the Jews of central Europe. Sometime later, works based on Jewish themes appeared. These were intended mainly for those with little or no knowledge of Hebrew.

The oldest existing texts consist of notes on the Bible that include Haggadic commentary. In the 16th century, various translations of the Pentateuch and other biblical books, some in the form of poetry, were printed. At the beginning of the 17th century, Isaac ha-Kohen of Prague began publishing a series of versions of the Pentateuch (which continued to appear until the 18th century) in which biblical text was mixed with interpretation of legends. The most widely diffused reworded version of the Pentateuch was *Ze'enah u-Re'enah* ("Come and See"), by Jacob ben Isaac Ashkenazi of Janow Lubelski (16th century), in which exegesis, mysticism, and passages from the Bible, the Haggadah, and the Midrash are all skillfully intermixed in an intentionally moralistic and didactic form. This book became particularly popular with women, for its arrangement allowed them to follow the readings in the synagogue every Saturday; for many generations, it was the most popular book among eastern European Jewish women, and the linguistic differences in the many editions made it a veritable laboratory of Yiddish. Literal translations of the Bible were also made according to a system similar to the versions mentioned above and were used by the Sephardim.

The 14th century marked the beginning of a number of poetic adaptations of Bible stories based on legendary material from the Haggadah and the Midrash. In this respect, the most important example is the *Shmuel Bukh*, an epic poem on King David that gave rise to a number of imitations that continued to appear until the 17th century. The prayer book and other books of a liturgical nature, such as the Passover Haggadah, were also translated into Yiddish at an early stage and in a number of versions. The 16th century saw the appearance of the *Tkhine*, private prayers of supplication in a simple, sentimental, and romantic style. Generally considered prayers for women, many were in fact written by women, a phenomenon by no means common in medieval Hebrew literature.

This creative process in Yiddish also gave rise to the development of lexicographical works, among which the *Mirkevet ha-Mishnah—Sefer*, also known as the *Sefer Rabbi Anshell*, is of great importance. Compiled by a Rabbi Anshell and published in Kraków in 1534, it is a dictionary and concordance of the entire Bible and is also the first book known to have been printed in Yiddish. Other important works are Elijah Levita's *Shemot Devarim* (16th century), the first known Yiddish-Hebrew dictionary, which lists 985 Yiddish words with Hebrew, Latin, and German translations (in Hebrew and German characters); and in the next century, Nathan Hannover's *Safah Berurah* ("Clear Language"), an Italian, Hebrew, Yiddish, and Latin dictionary.

A great deal of moralistic literature translated from Hebrew, such as *Hovot ha-Levavot* by Bahya ibn Paquda, was also produced in Yiddish, although original works also appeared, many of these being compilations and adaptations of tales, parables, and legends. The best example of this genre is *Mayse Bikhlekh*, a chapbook full of the Yiddish sayings of rabbis along with nearly hundred stories taken from the Talmud, the Midrash, and even contemporary oral tradition. Books were also written or compiled on the religious obligations of women, one example being the very popular *Frauen Buchlein* (16th century), written in verse. Another group

218

Jewish quarter of Kazimierz (Kraków, Poland) in an anonymous drawing on paper from the early 19th century (Max Berger Collection, Vienna). The first printing press in Kraków was the Hebrew press founded in 1534 by the brothers Samuel, Asher, and Eliakim Halicz, all of whom converted to Christianity in 1537. This was followed by the press of Isaac ben Aaron of Prossnitz, founded in 1569. Over the next sixty years Ben Aaron and his successors produced some 200 books, of which 73 were printed in Yiddish. Between 1630 and 1670, the most active press in Kraków was that of Menahem Nahum Meisels, and in the 19th century (there were no Hebrew presses in Kraków in the 18th century) another was founded by Naphtali Herz Shapiro and his son, operating from 1802 to 1822. Finally, between 1878 and 1914, Joseph Fisher printed a large number of works by authors belonging to the Haskalah movement.

of works were the guides to customs, such as *Der Brant Spiegel* (1602) by Moses Hanoch of Prague, which dealt with subjects like educating children and the treatment of servants, and *Simhat ha-Nefesh* ("The Joy of the Soul") by Elhanan Hendel Kirchan (18th century), a treatise on etiquette in German Jewish society that includes traditional songs for different occasions with musical notation.

In addition to this religious type of literature secular genres also appeared in Yiddish. These included the narrative, both as new versions of chivalric legend and Germanic stories, and original works of poetry, didactic prose, and drama. Drama did not appear as a genre until the 17th century, its main source of inspiration being Bible stories and an abundance of material from the Midrash. One aspect of Yiddish theater to develop considerably was the *Purim-shpil* (Yiddish for "Purim Play"). These were originally monologs or short group performances given during the festive family meal held on Purim, but they gradually grew, becoming plays with a certain conventional form, usually satirical and burlesque in content. In time, they were even performed by large casts in public places for an admission price (although they maintained their connection with Purim and were performed at the time of the festival).

A large number of poems of very different kinds—satirical, historical, ethical, amorous, as well as others for singing on the Jewish holidays—were also written. Particularly interesting are the historical poems on the vicissitudes of the Jewish communities and their individual members published in small books written at a time close to the events described. Among historical works in prose, unique are the memoirs of a woman, Glueckel of Hamelin (17th-18th century), whose book is an interesting description of a woman's life in the German Jewish society of the time.

In the late 15th century and throughout the 16th century, secular Yiddish literature blossomed in northern Italy in the communities of the emigrés of German origin. The main centers of publishing for this were Venice, Cremona, Mantua, and Verona. Particularly active in this field was Elijah Levita, the most prominent fig-

219

The Talmudists, *oil painting by Max Weber, 1934 (Jewish Museum, New York). The system known as* pilpul *has often been used as a teaching method in the rabbinic academies. It takes the form of discussion based on conceptual and casuistic differentiation in which the teacher encourages the student to develop his sense of perception and imagination through group discussion of legal cases and problems (*pilpul *means "pepper"—the exercises are designed to* sharpen the students' thinking). Such problems, at times couched in the most abstruse casuistry, must be solved through the interpretation of rabbinical sources. In 16th- and 17th-century yeshivas, or rabbinic schools, a student was judged by his ability in *pilpulistic discussion, intuition in such matters being considered a form of divine inspiration. At the same time,* pilpul *served the purpose of training future rabbis to make decisions regarding the many new* legal problems that arose as the result of social and political change. Certain eminent rabbis severely criticized the extremes to which "pilpulmania" at times drove teachers and academies.

Hasidic Literature

ure in all of Yiddish literature until the 18th century. Not only was he a translator of Bible texts, an exegete, a grammarian, and a linguist, but he was also a versatile poet. Emulating the poetic form (*ottava rima*) of the original, in his *Bovo d'Antona* or *Bove-Bukh* and *Paris un Viene*, he translated and freely adapted two Italian works.

In the 18th century, two forces converged on Western Yiddish to cause its disappearance as a form of literary expression. On the one hand, the Haskalah looked upon Yiddish as the greatest hindrance to the Jewish world in becoming part of Western culture, and, on the other, emancipation drove Jews to adopt the languages of western Europe as a means of expression. Nevertheless, Yiddish literature continued to develop in eastern Europe, becoming a useful medium for giving expression to all intellectual and artistic aspects of Jewish life, and thus from popular literature it made its way solidly into modern literature. Yiddish also received a special boost from the workers' movement, which regarded it as the most effective language through which to diffuse its ideology. This stim-

Ze'enah u-Re'enah (*"Come and See"*), 16th century, by Jacob ben Isaac Ashkenazi of Janow Lubelski, Sulzbach, 1785 (Jacob M. Lowy Collection, National Library of Canada, Ottawa). This edition with wood engravings is one of the more than two hundred printed over the centuries. It is an exegetic commentary on the Pentateuch, the haftarot, and the Five Scrolls and is read mainly by women on the Sabbath. The first edition is lost, and the oldest existing edition (1622) is from Basel but was actually printed in Hanau. Its frontispiece claims it was preceded by at least three other editions, one from Lublin and the other two from Kraków, and that these earlier editions were already out of print.

ulus also proved important for the language in non-Zionist circles.

In spite of this, the first steps taken by Yiddish literature in the 18th century still belonged to the field of popular literature. In Yiddish, Hasidism, which at that time attempted to renew Jewish society and religion through mysticism and emotion, created a literature of its own; a literature with limited forms of expression and intention and constantly under attack from the Haskalah authors. Its great importance, however, lies in its long-lasting influence as the direct source of all the genres of modern Yiddish literature. Hasidism produced two types of tale: the hagiographic, which tells of the wonders of its main figures, gave rise to a series of oral and written stories and influenced Yiddish prose until the time of the Holocaust; and mystical stories, such as those of Rabbi Nahman of Bratslav, which, with the advent of modern symbolism in Yiddish literature in around 1890, became a source for the works of writers such as Isaac Loeb Peretz and Der Nister.

The greatest author of the period before

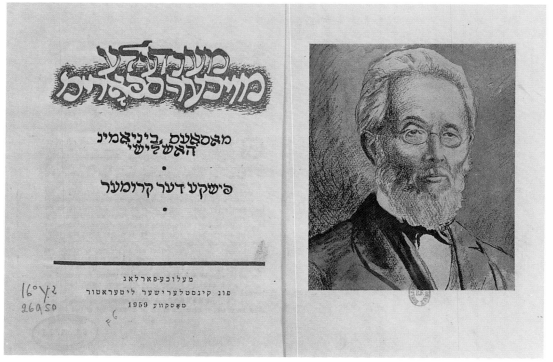

Title page of an edition of the Masaot Binyamin ha-selisi (*"The Travels of Benjamin the Third,"* first edition, 1878) and Fishke der Krumer (*"Fishke the Lame,"* first edition, 1869), novels written in Yiddish by Mendele Mocher Sforim, pseudonym of Sholem Yakob Abramovich (1836-1917), and a portrait of the author, Moscow, 1959 (Bibliothèque Nationale, Paris). Abramovich began his writing career during the Haskalah period in Russia and reached artistic maturity during the age of national renaissance (after 1881). One of the creators of modern literary Yiddish and new realism in Hebrew literature, he left his stamp on the style and themes of both. Orphaned at fourteen, he wandered through Lithuania, Volhynia, Ukraine, and Podolia, taking in details of Jewish life that he would reproduce in his books. Both Fishke and the Journeys (whose title is reminiscent of the medieval travel book of Benjamin of Tudela and was inspired by Cervantes' Don Quixote), reflect the Russian satirical tradition of Gogol and Saltykov-Shchedrin as well as the techniques of the picaresque novel.

World War I was Mendele Mocher Sforim (1836-1917), the first of the Haskalah writers to stop attacking Hasidism and concern himself with the movement and its troubles. In his works, Mendele realistically reflected a way of life that was beginning to disintegrate and succeeded in turning the course of Yiddish literature toward modernization and integration with general literary currents. Together with Mendele, two other authors—Shalom Aleichem and Isaac Loeb Peretz—are considered essential to Yiddish literature. The former, who wrote novels, tales, and plays, left behind a veritable gallery of characters who tell us of their trivial, everyday experiences in the first person, the sublime and the comic being reflected in Tevye the milkman (whose stories served as the basis for the play *Fiddler on the Roof*), Menahem Mendel, and others. Peretz' works include poetry, plays, tales, and essays in Hebrew and Yiddish, his poetic dramas and above all his tales being of particular importance. For these he turned to popular tradition and Hasidic tales, so giving rise to the Neo-Hasidic aspect of Yiddish and Hebrew literature that

exists even today. Yiddish theater in the 19th century appeared as a continuation of the *Purim-shpil* mentioned earlier. This type of play is typical of the early career of Abraham Goldfaden (1840-1908), the Ukrainian playwright considered the first important Yiddish playwright and the founder of Yiddish theater. In time, Yiddish theater matured and gave birth to such dramas as *Got fun Nekomeh* ("The God of Vengeance") by Sholem Asch, *Der Oitzer* ("The Treasure") and *The Eternal Jew* by David Pinski, and above all *The Dybbuk* by Ansky. Yiddish theater reached its peak in 1930 in Poland, when almost twenty theater companies existed simultaneously.

Of great importance in the development of Yiddish literature was the 1908 Czernowitz Conference, which served to boost the confidence and self-respect of readers and writers of Yiddish and make them more keenly aware of the standing of modern Yiddish literature. Another important event was the foundation of two Yiddish literary magazines—the Vilna *Literarishe Monatshriften* and *Di Yugend*, the organ of the New York *Di Yunge* group, whose aim was to

Title pages of children's books in Yiddish—In Vald (top) and Voigelen *(bottom)—written by Leib Kvitko (1890-1952) and illustrated by Issachar Ryback, Berlin, 1922 (William L. Gross Collection, Ramat Aviv, Israel). Children's literature in Yiddish developed with the establishment of secular schools in eastern Europe and the United States in the first decade of this century. Among the distinguished authors who wrote stories for children were Sholem Asch and Shalom*

Aleichem. Mendele Mocher Sforim's tales were also adapted to this genre. The most productive period was between the two world wars, especially in Poland, the former Soviet Union, Rumania, the United States, Canada, and Argentina (where specialized publishers of children's books and magazines appeared). Prominent among the Jewish authors in this field in the Soviet Union was the poet Leib Kvitko, who also wrote stories for and collaborated in the edition of five

children's newspapers published in Russia with the support of the Communist party. His books were translated into several of the languages spoken within the former Soviet Union, almost 11 million copies being printed. Arrested during Stalin's purges in 1949, Kvitko was executed along with another thirty Yiddish writers in 1952.

educate the masses and provide material for reading and entertainment. The Yiddish Scientific Institute (YIVO) was founded in Vilna in 1925 to serve as an academy to oversee the development of the language. Its headquarters were later moved to New York City.

The period following World War I was one of complications and changes in modern Yiddish literature resulting from the war itself, the Russian Revolution and the pogroms, the emigrations, World War II, and above all the Holocaust, which brought Judaism in eastern Europe—the only potential source of Yiddish writers—to the verge of extinction.

In the former Soviet Union, the desire for a solution to the situation of Russian Jews led many poets to believe that the revolution could solve the problems of societies and nations the world over. Thanks to government support, faith in the development of a secular culture expressed in a language of its own grew in the 1920s with the appearance of a group of schools in which lessons were held in Yiddish. Yiddish was also used in the theater and in a variety of activities aimed at bringing the language to the attention of the general public. These hopes and expectations crumbled within the next decade as a result of the ideological pressure that the Communist party brought to bear on anything that suggested nationalism. By the end of 1948, what was left of Yiddish culture in the Soviet Union had died out, and the vast majority of its most outstanding writers had been arrested and executed.

Until it was wiped out, the main center of Yiddish production, which included a variety of ideologies and political and literary currents, was the dynamic Polish community. The poets, novelists, and short-story writers of the prewar generation were joined by a large number of young writers, among them the Nobel Prize winner Isaac Bashevis Singer, Joshua Perle, Itzik Manger, and Aaron Zeitlin. Many of these writers were to die in concentration camps, their work denied the chance to reach maturity. In the period between the two world wars an important center of production of Yiddish literature formed in the United States, particularly in New York. Nor did Yiddish die out in Israel, although it declined as a language, in part due to the nationalistic boost given Hebrew.

222

Paintings by Marc Chagall. Above: Country Life, *1925 (Albright-Knox Art Gallery, Buffalo). Opposite:* The Newspaper Seller, *1914 (Ida Meyer Chagall Collection, Basel). The Jewish village, or shtetl, which has served as a source of inspiration for a large number of artists and writers, originated in Poland and Lithuania, where, under the protection of the nobles, Jews settled in villages and soon became the largest local population group. The lives of these Jews* *revolved around the synagogue, the home, and the market. The first served as a place for prayer, study, and assembly and extended into the home, the basic unit in the life of the shtetl, whose patriarchal system was based on traditional principles. Nothing that took place within the shtetl escaped the judgment of the group, whose control over the individual was one of the strongest forces by which life in the village was dictated; consequently this form of community* *survived for centuries without the need for a police force to ensure that law and order was enforced. The market was both a source of food supplies and a place where Jews and Gentiles came into contact, but Jews did not often go there as the vast majority of the Jewish population were poor, their main concern being to earn enough money during the week to be able to buy fish or meat for the Sabbath or to save enough for unleavened bread for the Passover.*

Modern Hebrew Literature

Hebrew literature in the modern age of Jewish history is basically secular and belongs exclusively to Ashkenazic Jewry. With time it became the vehicle of expression of the Zionist movement as opposed to Yiddish, which was seen as the language of the Jewish movements in the Diaspora.

This literature is usually divided into several periods, but primary interest goes to its beginnings in the Haskalah movement (1781-1881) and to the modern Hebrew literature of Russia and Poland (1881-1920).

The first center of production of modern Hebrew literature was Prussia, where it appeared in the cities of Berlin and Königsberg thanks to the influence of the German Enlightenment with its special interest in reason, refined taste, and the rights of man. Since the primary aim of the *Haskalah* ("Enlightenment") and its *Maskilim* ("The Enlightened"—intellectuals) was to educate readers in the Jewish communities of Germany and eastern Europe in social and aesthetic matters, the literature was essentially didactic and propagandis-

tic. Scorning Yiddish as a vulgar corruption of German, its authors chose Hebrew as their vehicle of expression, it being a language understood by the greatest number of Jews. The Haskalah's most important literary undertaking was the *Biur*, a translation of the Bible into German in Hebrew characters accompanied by a modern commentary, also in Hebrew. The project was begun by Moses Mendelssohn, who also encouraged the foundation of the first Hebrew language periodical, *Ha-Me'assef* ("The Gatherer"; 1783-1829), whose contributors included the main figures of the original Haskalah movement. Among these were Mendelssohn himself, Naphtali Wessely, David Franco-Mendes, and Isaac Satanow, their work consisting mainly of epic poetry written in a moralistic and didactic style and based on biblical stories and heroes. The best poetry of this period was written by the Italian Ephraim Luzzatto. With the rapid Germanization of the German Jews at the beginning of the 19th century, the production of Hebrew literature shifted to other countries, especially to Galicia in Poland, where *Maskilim* established centers in Brody, Tarnopol, Lemberg, and Kraków, their main contribution being in the field of Jewish studies rather than in literature. Among the most prominent of these writers were the poet Shalom Cohen, the philosopher Nachman Krochmal and his pupil Solomon J. Rapoport, the grammarian and exegete Samuel David Luzzatto (an Italian who maintained close contact with the Polish *Maskilim*), and the satirical writers Isaac Erter and Joseph Perl.

The *Maskilim* of Russia and, in particular, Lithuania were conspicuous for their poetry and prose fiction, one of their most important poets being Micah Joseph Lebensohn (Mikhal), author of epic poems and one of the first writers of love poetry. The truly great figure in this respect, however, was Judah Leib Gordon, a poet, story writer, and journalist who dominated the literary scene until 1880. The first novelist in modern Hebrew literature was the Lithuanian Abraham Mapu (1808-67), in whose historical novels inspired by biblical themes, *Ahavat Ziyyon* ("The Love of Zion") and *Ashmat Shomron* ("Guilt of Samaria"), the influence of Eugène Sue and

Dumas Père can be clearly observed. The most important Hebrew novelist in the generation after Mapu was the Russian Perez Smolenskin (c. 1840-1885), founder of the monthly journal *Ha-Shahar* (1869-84), who in time became a champion of Zionism. His *Ha-To'eh be-Darkhei ha-Hayyim* ("The Wanderer in the Paths of Life"), the greatest novel written by his generation, displays a complete panorama of the Jewish life of the times.

Around 1880, a number of literary and social factors prepared the way for a new period in Hebrew literature. By this time literature in Hebrew was abundant, its authors having coped with the task of transforming an ancient tongue into a modern language. Hebrew literature was now ready to try for true artistic achievement. Romanticism had given way to naturalism and realism, literary movements that viewed the universe from a more materialistic point of view. At the same time, Russian literary criticism, which called for a more realistic form of writing and themes of social criticism, left its mark on many young Jewish writers who, scorning the artificial

Hanna Rovina as the young mother of the Messiah in The Eternal Jew, *by David Pinski. Born in 1892 in Berezino, Minsk, she was one of the founding members of the Hebrew Habima Theater troupe. She was a great success both in* The Eternal Jew *and as Leah in Ansky's* The Dybbuk. *She performed with the troupe in Leningrad in 1925 and Riga in 1926 and took part in Habima's tour of cities in Poland, Austria, Germany, France, and the United States later that year. In 1928 the Habima troupe visited Palestine and permanently established itself in Tel Aviv.*

Spanish edition of Leonid Andreyev's Anathema, *Jacob Gordin's* Mirele Efros, *and Ansky's drama* The Dybbuk, *Madrid, 1930 (Biblioteca Arias Montano, CSIC, Madrid). For* The Dybbuk, *a cabalistic legend of a soul in torment reincarnated in two bodies, Ansky (born Solomon Seinwil Rapoport, Chashnik, 1863-1920) drew inspiration from his knowledge of eastern European Jewish folklore. The play was performed for the first time in 1920 in Yiddish by the Vilna theater group and subsequently in Bialik's Hebrew version by the Habima group in Moscow. It was made into an opera by Lodovico Rocca (1934) and by David and Alex Tankin (1949); a modern version, adapted by Paddy Chayefsky, appeared in New York City in 1960.*

attachment to biblical themes that had predominated until then, preferred motifs and themes more in keeping with the reality of everyday life. The new viewpoints were reinforced by certain political and social events, such as the pogroms of 1880, which led to the disenchantment of the majority of the *Maskilim*, and a new interest in people, their aspirations and ways of life, all of which supplanted the previous sarcasm of the Haskalah and its prejudice against the old, traditional ways of life.

The most outstanding figure of this period was Asher Ginsberg (1856-1927), who wrote under the Hebrew name Ahad Ha-am, a brilliant essayist and indeed the father of the modern Hebrew essay. He developed a philosophy for the new nationalist movement and was the editor of *Ha-Shilo'ah* (1897-1903), the most important periodical of the time. Another great man of this generation was Mendele Mocher Sforim, mentioned above, who was not only the father of the new Hebrew literary style but also the first author to write seriously in Yiddish. He was soon to abandon the biblical style for the simpler

styles of Mishnaic and talmudic literature, thus forging a language more appropriate for realism and typical of the new Odessa school. In contrast with this school, a neo-romantic and impressionist circle appeared in Warsaw whose authors were concerned above all with the aesthetic side of their writings; these included David Frischmann, Micha Josef Berdyczewski, and Isaac Loeb Peretz, mentioned earlier, who wrote mainly in Yiddish.

The greatest poet of Hebrew literature during this period was Hayyim Nahman Bialik (1873-1934), who also belonged to Odessa school. Most of his works were written between 1892 and 1917, turbulent years prior to the Russian Revolution and the decline of the Jewish communities of eastern Europe. With his genius Bialik set up a delicate balance between the traditional old culture, whose source lay in the sacred books and medieval religiosity, and the new European culture. The desperate quest for a link between past and present lies at the center of Bialik's poetry, and although he was committed to the ideas of nationalism, which earned him the name of "national poet," he was also a great lyrical poet who wrote on a variety of themes—songs of love and in praise of nature, folk poetry, children's poems, etc. One of the few poets of this generation not overshadowed by Bialik was Saul Chernikhovski, who introduced a number of unusual rhyming systems and poetic structures into Hebrew poetry.

Hebrew theater had already appeared in Italy, and playwriting was taken up by various authors of the Haskalah and Jewish national renaissance movements at the end of the 19th century. These writers preferred dramas based on historical subjects. In 1917 Hebrew theater received a boost with the Habima Theater company, the first established Hebrew-language theater, founded in Moscow and directed by Nahum Zemach, considered the father of Hebrew theater. The company also worked with the great director Constantin Stanislavsky and his Armenian pupil Yevgeni Vakhtangov.

After the Russian Revolution, attempts were made to create a Communist form of Hebrew literature, but the language was soon declared counterrevolutionary, publications in

Hebrew were banned, and many writers were sent to prison, among them Bialik, who was released on Lenin's orders and thanks to the intervention of Maxim Gorky. Forced to emigrate, Hebrew writers sought refuge in other parts of Europe, the United States, and particularly in Palestine, where from the beginning of this century a large number of authors born in eastern Europe had settled. These faced a new social and political reality that was to make a deep impression on their literary expression. To mention but a few names, among the prose writers were Y. H. Brenner, Hayyim Hazaz, and above all the Nobel Prize winner Shmuel Yosef Agnon, whose most forceful works were written before World War I in a style based mainly on the Hasidic prose of the period immediately before the development of modern Hebrew literature and whose writings mark the peak of Hebrew literature in Galicia, Poland. Among the poets of the period between the European Diaspora and the creation of the, as yet unborn, homeland were Abraham Shlonsky, Nathan Alterman, U. Z. Greenberg, and Leah Goldberg.

At the Gates of Jerusalem, oil painting by M. Ardon, 1967 (Israel Museum, Jerusalem). The following is from the poem On the Threshold of Bet-Hamidras, *from Hayyim Nahman Bialik's book* In the City of Slaughter:

You shall not perish, oh tent of Shem! I have still to rebuild you,
and you shall rise up among the rubble of your ruin. I shall give life to your walls.

Yet shall you see the haughty castles fall, just as you fell
on the day of the great destruction, when your towers tumbled down.
When I restore the devastated Temple of the Lord,
I shall widen its veils and enlarge its windows
so that the light will drive away the darkness,
and as night advances the glory of the Lord will descend upon it.

Then shall all flesh see, from the smallest land to the greatest,
how the grass withers, the flower wilts but the Lord abides forever.

Modern Literature in Other Languages

Below: Grace Aguilar (1816-47) from an engraving in her book The Women of Israel, *London, 1876 (Biblioteca Macías, Madrid).* The Vale of Cedars *(1850), her most famous Jewish novel, deals with the converts of Spain and has been translated into German and Hebrew. She also wrote short stories about Jewish life and family traditions;* The Women of Israel *(1845) is a compilation of biographies of biblical characters.*

Since emancipation, Jews in Europe have written in virtually all the languages spoken on the continent. Emphasis here is put on the important writers in English, French, Italian, and German, but mention should be made of the major contributions made to the literature of the Slavic languages by such Jews as Isaac Babel, Boris Pasternak, Osip Mandelstam, and Ilya Ehrenburg in Russia, Bruno Schulz in Poland, and Lustig Arnost in the former Czechoslovakia. There are also the works of Georg Brandes in Danish and those of Max Aub in Spanish.

Of particular importance among the large number of English Jewish writers of the last century is Israel Zangwill, the novelist and playwright who wrote *Children of the Ghetto* (1892) and several other novels describing life in the London Jewish community. Also important is Grace Aguilar, of Sephardic origin, whose novels and short stories often deal with Jewish subjects. In the middle of this century, the new Jewish world after the Holocaust and the creation of the state of Israel have influenced many Anglo-Jewish authors, but none has achieved

the importance of the American writers (Saul Bellow, Bernard Malamud, Philip Roth, Henry Roth). Also of great importance in English are the works of the Hungarian-born Jew Arthur Koestler, novelist, essayist, and author of books on philosophy and politics. Prominent among the postwar playwrights are Harold Pinter and Peter Shaffer. In the 1950s, in an attempt to reject the legacy of the previous generation, a new wave of English Jewish writers chose to criticize Jewish family life and its social forms. Outstanding among these are Brian Lester Glanville and his novel *The Bankrupts*, Dan Jacobson, Bernard Kops, and the humorist Chaim Bermant.

Few of the acclaimed French Jewish authors of the 19th century took an interest in Jewish themes. The rare exceptions include the poet and playwright Eugène Manuel, founder of the Alliance Israélite Universelle, and the comedy and libretto writers Ludovic Halévy and Tristan Bernard. Certain actresses, such as Rachel (Élisa Félix) and Sarah Bernhardt, who took pride in her Jewish origins, are also well known. By the

beginning of this century, the number of Jewish playwrights had grown considerably and included André Pascal, the Belgian Henry Kistemaeckers, and above all Henry Bernstein. Prominent in other genres are the essayists André Suarès and Benjamin Crémieux, the novelist and biographer André Maurois, and particularly the poet convert Max Jacob, who died in a concentration camp. The Dreyfus Affair led many assimilated writers to recall their own Jewish origins; these included the publicists Victor Basch and Bernard Lazare and even the half-Jewish Marcel Proust, who urged Anatole France to intervene on Dreyfus's behalf. Also worthy of mention are Edmond Fleg, poet, playwright, and anthologist, whose return to Judaism led him to seek a form of symbiosis between French and Jewish traditions, and, in the 20th century, the identity crisis that became the main preoccupation of writers such as the novelists Jean-Richard Bloch and Albert Cohen, the latter originally from Corfu and strongly influenced by his Mediterranean background. Together with all these are a large number of writers whose works

Above: Los hijos del ghetto, *Spanish edition of* Children of the Ghetto, *by Israel Zangwill, Madrid, 1921 (Biblioteca Macías, Madrid). Born in London into a poor family of Russian immigrants, Zangwill (1864-1926) wrote plays and novels, including* Children of the Ghetto *(1892),* Ghetto Tragedies *(1893), and* Ghetto Comedies *(1907), about the conflict between love for the values of Judaism as preserved in ghetto life and the urge to flee from the*

restrictions of that way of life. Children of the Ghetto *is a reflection of Zangwill's own life, with the author himself as the main character. He took various characters in* Dreamers of the Ghetto *(1898) from his own life and from Jewish history (his father, Moses; Benjamin Disraeli; Heinrich Heine; Ferdinand Lassalle; Shabbetai Zevi; and Baruch Spinoza), all of whom had to face the tragic dilemma of choosing between a Jewish heritage and the outside world.*

Above: First Spanish edition of Laudin y los suyos, *by Jakob Wassermann, Madrid, 1933 (Biblioteca Macías, Madrid). A typical example of the assimilated Jew, Wassermann (1873-1934) believed he had achieved the synthesis of being both a German and a Jew and was a foe of Jewish nationalism. The rise of Nazism and the burning of his books obliged him to return to the spiritual ghetto from which he had escaped.*

A Un Ami: Correspondence inédite, by Marcel Proust, Paris 1948 (Biblioteca de Cataluña, Barcelona). Proust's father was a Gentile and his mother, Jeanne Weil, came from an Alsatian Jewish family. His wealth and personal qualities gained him acceptance into the circles of high society which served as the background to his novels. His masterpiece, Remembrance of Things Past, *is not strictly autobiographical, but it does contain a great deal of material based on personal experience and includes three Jewish characters: the actress Rachel, the intellectual Albert Bloch, and the assimilated Jew Charles Swann, considered by some as Proust's alter ego. Educated as a Catholic, he nevertheless made reference to his Jewish ancestors in his books, describing his mother and his maternal grandparents. During the Dreyfus Affair Proust persuaded Anatole France to intercede on Dreyfus' behalf.*

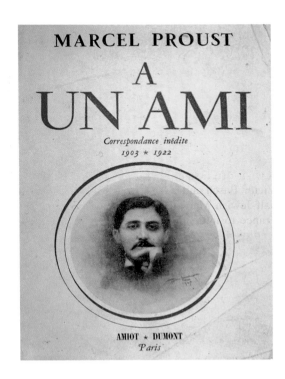

revolve solely around Jewish themes. A number of Rumanian-born authors also wrote in French, the greatest example being Eugène Ionesco, who was half-Jewish. Prominent writers after the Holocaust include the novelists Anna Langfus, who wrote semiautobiographical works, André Schwarz-Bart, who wrote the famous *Le dernier des justes*, and the Nobel Prize winner Élie Wiesel. Other writers, such as André Gorz (a pupil of Sartre's), the Tunisian Albert Memmi, and Emmanuel Eydoux, have turned their attention to the problems of contemporary Jews in a non-Jewish world. Nevertheless, in spite of this literary blossoming of postwar Jewish French literature, assimilation continues, and a whole generation of writers, some of them major literary figures, are Jews in name only.

The Italian Jewish literature of the 19th century is also marked by a tendency by authors to gradually forsake their Jewish identity in order to become fully integrated with the world of their surrounding culture. Examples of this tendency are the eminent philologists Salomone Morpurgo and Adolfo Mussafia. The unification

227

Sarah Bernhardt (1844-1923), painting by Bernard Buffet (Museum of Modern Religious Art, the Vatican). Daughter of a Jewish music teacher from Holland, she was adopted by the Frenchman Édouard Bernard. At the age of ten she was sent to a convent in Versailles, and although baptized a Christian, she always took pride in her Jewish origins. Having worked with the Comédie Française, where she won fame for her interpretation of Racine heroines, in 1879 she embarked on a series of tours, winning acclaim wherever she performed. In 1882 she formed her own troupe, and in 1899 she leased a theater in Paris, renamed the Sarah Bernhardt Theater, which she directed until her death. When one of her legs was amputated in 1915, she resigned herself to playing parts in which she could remain seated. The "divine Sarah," as she was dubbed by Oscar Wilde, died while making a film in Paris.

Italian and German

of Italy saw the appearance of the novelist in a genre in which Italian Jews had hitherto not been involved. Outstanding among these writers were Enrico Castelnuovo and Alberto Cantoni, whom Pirandello considered his master. The most important playwright at the end of the 19th century was Sabatino Lopez, author of almost seventy plays, who for many years dominated the Italian theatrical scene. Before and immediately after World War I, a number of Jewish authors, among them Giuseppe Morpurgo and Guglielmo Lattes, wrote novels describing Jewish life from a folkloric and impressionistic point of view. In the years prior to World War II, a group of writers and poets from Trieste (whose influence finally extended beyond Italy) made their own, major contribution to Italian literature; among these were Italo Svevo, the poet Umberto Saba, and the poet and philosopher Carlo Michelstaedter, who put forward the main theses of existentialism. In the wake of World War II and the Holocaust, a complete change came about in the attitude of Jewish Italian writers, things Jewish now reappearing not as a

Il giardino dei Finzi-Contini, by Giorgio Bassani, first edition, Turin, 1962. Born in Bologna in 1916, Bassani later lived in Ferrara. Because of anti-Semitic laws, he published his first work, Città di pianura *(1940), under the pseudonym Giacomo Marchi. His collection of short stories* Cinque storie ferraresi *(1956) deals with his own experience of persecution as a Jew, events during World War II, and his fight against fascism. Widely translated, his novel* Il giardino dei Finzi-Contini *deals with his youth in Ferrara and tells the story of an aristocratic Jewish family incapable of adapting to the outside world or of facing up to the cataclysm of fascism and war. The story was made into a film,* The Garden of the Finzi-Continis, *by Vittorio De Sica in 1971.*

problem for which to seek a solution but as an experience remembered from childhood or the time of Nazi persecution. In this respect, three authors estranged from Judaism—Giorgio Bassani, Natalia Ginzburg, and Primo Levi—combined family memories with the problems of assimilation in a Gentile world. This was not the case of Alberto Moravia and Carlo Levi, however, for their work displays no trace of their Jewish origins, and indeed they show a deliberate lack of interest on the subject.

Until the 18th century, few Jewish writers used German as a form of literary expression. The most important figure in the Germany of the Enlightenment and indeed of Jewish emancipation was Moses Mendelssohn, the first Jewish author to use the German language with all its subtleties and the founder of *Koheleth Mussar*, the Jewish German-language periodical. During the age of romanticism, Jewish and non-Jewish statesmen, philosophers, and artists met in the Berlin salons of such Jewish ladies as Henriette Hertz and Rahel Varnhagen von Ense. However, the constant struggle for full civil rights and the

lure of emancipation led many Jewish writers to seek a solution to the constant dichotomy of their lives through assimilation or conversion to Christianity. Such was the case of the most important Jewish German-language poet, Heinrich Heine, and indeed of many other writers. The impact of World War I led many Germans to feel a temporary revulsion for war and brutality, the expressionist literary movement committing itself to a fervent struggle in favor of peace and the dignity of man, and many Jews joined this cause. At the same time there was a reassessment of the Jew within society led by the philosophers Martin Buber and Franz Rosenzweig, whose large following of poets and novelists included Arnold Zweig, Jacob Picard, Else Lasker-Schüler (considered by some as one of the major poetesses of the German language), Jakob Wassermann, Alfred Döblin, Joseph Roth, and the Nobel Prize winners Nelly Sachs and Elias Canetti. From different points of view, these dealt with Jewish subjects.

Jews were also important in the German theater. In addition to the large number of actors

228

Above: Born into a Sephardic family in Bulgaria in 1905, Elias Canetti moved with his family to Vienna in 1913. During World War I he traveled to England, but later settled in Zurich. Despite his Jewish Spanish-speaking background, Canetti is considered a representative of German literature. Among his main works are the autobiographical The Tongue Set Free *and* The Torch in My Ear. *In 1981 he was awarded both the Kafka Prize and the Nobel Prize.*

Above right: Max Aub (1903-72), novelist, poet, and playwright, born in Paris to a German father and French mother. In 1914 the family moved to Valencia, Spain, where they were granted Spanish nationality. When Franco came to power, Aub fled to France, but was arrested in 1940 and deported to Algeria, where he was interned in jails and concentration camps for three years. In 1942 he escaped to Mexico, where he lived out the rest of his life, writing the majority of his

vast collection of works and becoming one of the most prolific and creative members of the Spanish "Generation of '27." The Spanish civil war and its consequences is the theme of his most important work, a trilogy of novels. Both his three-act tragedy San Juan *(1943), about a group of refugees that no country will admit, and* Imposible Sinaí, *a diary of his experiences on a journey to Israel, deal with Jewish themes.*

who appeared on the German scene at the beginning of the 19th century, there were various outstanding directors. These included Ludwig Chronegk, director of the theater company belonging to Duke George II of Saxony; Otto Brahm, pioneer of naturalist theater and founder of the Freie Bühne theater, whose thirty years of activity in the Deutsches Theater organization left an indelible mark on the history of German theater; Max Reinhardt, who gave free rein to fantasy and revolutionized the theatrical art of his time, directing a large number of Jewish actors; and finally Leopold Jessner, director of the Berlin Staatstheater, pioneer of expressionism in the theater and the last Jewish renovator on the German scene before the rise of Hitler. By the time Hitler came to power, around 2,500 Jewish actors and directors were working in German theater.

With Nazism the dream of a German-Jewish cultural symbiosis was shattered, and the history of Jewish German literature was brought to an end. Among the Jews who left Germany after 1933 and Austria after 1938 were some of the two countries' most important writers. There were also many who chose to stay or who were unable to escape, and these ended their lives in concentration camps. Incapable of accepting that their hopes and dreams were shattered, many others, like Stefan Zweig and the philosopher and historian Walter Benjamin, committed suicide.

In post-revolutionary Russia, the Jewish heritage was either forgotten or treated with indifference by the first generation of writers (Osip Mandelstam, the Nobel Prize winner Boris Pasternak, etc.). Other authors, such as Ilya Ehrenburg and Isaac Babel (who wrote the most comprehensive description of Russian Jewry from the end of tsarism to the early years of the Soviet regime), made efforts to reconcile their Jewish identity with loyalty to the system, although Babel and a large number of other writers were eventually annihilated by that same system. Oppression in the Soviet Union did not end with Stalin, however, and due to anti-Semitism in the 1970s the works of such writers as Yuly Daniel and Joseph Brodsky could be published only clandestinely.

229

Die Geschichten des Rabbi Nachman, *by Martin Buber, first edition, Frankfurt am Main, 1906 (Biblioteca del Instituto d'Estudis Catalans, Barcelona). A philosopher, theologian, and prominent Jewish thinker, Buber (1878-1965) was deeply involved in Jewish education and culture and founded the Jüdischer Verlag German book company in Berlin. At the age of twenty-six he became interested in Hasidism, freely translating and adapting into German* the tales of Rabbi Nahman of Bratslav and *subsequently those of Ba'al Shem Tov. From a simple interest in the aesthetics of Hasidism, contact with its literature led him to a genuine interest in its religious message, which he considered his duty to impart to the world. He wrote* Gog u-Magog *(1941, translated in English as* For the Sake of Heaven*) and* Or ha-Ganuz *(1943) and* Pardes ha-Hasidut *(1945; published as* Hasidism and Modern Man*).*

Glossary

Most of these special terms are from Hebrew (Hb.) and Aramaic (Ar.); Yiddish, Judeo-Spanish, Spanish, and Turkish words are indicated by the abbreviations Yd., JSp., Sp., and Tk. Cross-references are given in *italics*.

abel: period of mourning.

adafina (Sp., *dafina*): type of stew of medieval Hispano-Jewish origin served at lunch on the Sabbath; a traditional meal of the Sephardim in the area around the Strait of Gibraltar.

Adar: sixth month of the Jewish calendar; it usually lasts twenty-nine days and begins between February 1 and March 2. Purim falls in this month. In embolismic, or leap, years one day is added, and there is a second Adar (Veadar) of twenty-nine days.

aljama (Sp.): in Sepharad, a legal institution, similar to the Christian town council, governing the Jews of a given area.

amidah ("standing"): a prayer composed of seven, nine, or eighteen (actually nineteen) *berakhot* that is said while standing and is central to the three daily religious services.

Amoraim: scholars of the oral law whose opinions and doctrines are collected in the *Gemara*.

Aron Kodesh ("Holy Ark"): another name for the *heikhal*.

Ashkenazi(c): belonging to the Yiddish-speaking branch of European Jewry whose origin lies in the countries of northern Europe.

Av: eleventh month of the Jewish calendar; it lasts thirty days and begins between July 9 and August 7. As its name indicates, the Tishah be-Av ("Ninth of Av") festival falls in this month.

azara: area in the synagogue for women, often an upper gallery.

badhan (pl. *badhanut*): strolling players and wandering musicians who entertained at weddings and festivals with popular songs and comic tales.

Bar Mitzvah ("son of the Commandment"): name given a Jewish male of thirteen years of age; by extension, the ceremony at which he comes of religious age. Thereafter he is considered responsible for his actions, his duties being to observe the precepts of Judaism and to don the *tefillin*.

bedika ("examination"): careful scrutiny made by the *shohet* to ensure that the slaughtered animal has no defects that would make it *terefah*.

berakhot: benedictions and prayers of thanks to God. These prayers are said on fulfilling a ritual regulation, when taking enjoyment from the senses, and at times of joy and grief.

berit: covenant or pact.

berit milah ("pact of circumcision"): sign of the Jewish people's covenant with God.

bet din ("house of judgment"): rabbinic court made up of at least three *dayanim*.

bet kenisa ("house of assembly"): synagogue.

bimah. See *tevah*.

cholent (Yd.): Ashkenazic meal served at lunchtime on the Sabbath.

dayan (pl. *dayanim*): judge who is an expert of rabbinic law.

Donmeh (Tk.): belonging to the crypto-Jewish sect of the adherents of Shabbetai Zevi who followed his example and converted to Islam.

Elul: twelfth and final month of the Jewish calendar; it lasts twenty-nine days and begins between August 8 and September 6. Because it precedes the solemn celebrations held in the month of Tishri, it is a time of rejoicing and devotion.

Eretz Israel ("the Land of Israel"): the land promised by God to Abraham and his descendants.

etrog: bitter orange: citrus fruit for use during the *Sukkot* festival service that is waved together with the *lulav* in processions in the synagogue.

gaon ("eminence"): honorific title given certain rabbis and particularly to the leaders of the rabbinic academies of Babylonia and Egypt during the post-talmudic age. It occasionally forms part of a name (Gaon Saadia or Saadia Gaon).

Gemara: study, discussion, commentary, and interpretation of the Mishnah, which constitutes the most extensive part of the Talmud and brings together the oral law formulated by various generations of Amoraim at the rabbinic academies of Palestine (Israel) and Babylonia (Mesopotamia).

genizah: storehouse in a synagogue or adjacent room or outbuilding of a synagogue where sacred books and liturgical objects (and in general Hebrew written material of any kind, however fragmentary) no longer in use are kept to avoid profaning the synagogue before they are taken to the cemetery to be buried. The genizah discovered in a Cairo synagogue in 1896 is particularly famous because of the valuable works found stored there.

golem: a creature of human form brought to life by magical means through the use of God's name.

Habdalah ("separation, differentiation"): ceremony observed at the conclusion of a Sabbath or a festival that divides the end of the holy day from the beginning of the normal day.

Haftarah (pl. *Haftaroth*): chapter of portion of the Prophets chanted or read in the synagogue on the Sabbath, holy days, and certain days of fasting. It comes immediately after the *parashah*, with which it has some connection in content or form.

Haggadah ("narration"; pl. *Haggadoth*): a part or aspect of the oral law that is of varied content—ideological, historical, anecdotal, folkloric, legendary—and expresses the ethics or lore of Judaism. It does not deal directly with religious and legal regulations or prescriptions. Also, the narrative of the Exodus from Egypt composed of passages from the Bible, the Midrash, and other rabbinic sources together with prayers, hymns, and songs. It is read at the seder service on the Passover festival in compliance with the precept "And thou shalt shew thy son" (Exodus 13:8). The book in which it is contained is also known by this name.

Halakah: part or aspect of the oral law that deals with the determination of certain religious and legal rules and precepts; each of the rules and Jewish law in general.

hamez ("leavened"): used for any food or drink in which the fermentation of certain cereals (wheat, barley, rye, oats, etc.) takes place or which contain a leavening agent.

hamin: dish typical of the Sephardim of the Balkans and eastern Mediterranean that is served on the Sabbath.

Hanukkah: festival held in commemoration of the rededication of the temple after the victory of the Maccabees over the Seleucids in 165 B.C. Beginning on the twenty-fifth day of Kislev, it lasts eight days, during which time the *Hanukkah lamp* is lit.

Hanukkah lamp: lamp of eight candles arranged in a straight line with an additional ninth candle. It is lit at Hanukkah.

haroset: type of paste made with ground fruit, spices, and wine in which certain of the symbolic foods eaten at the seder meal at Passover are dipped.

Hasid ("pious man"): in the Middle Ages, a member of the *Hasid Ashkenaz*; in modern times, a follower of Hasidism.

Hasid Ashkenaz ("the pious of Ashkenaz"): ascetic, pietist movement that began in Germany in the Middle Ages. Its followers advocated humility and preferred ethical principles to the strict application of talmudic norms.

Hasidism (Hb. *Hasid*): mystical religious movement founded by Ba'al Shem Tov (Poland, 1700-60).

Haskalah ("Enlightenment"): intellectual and literary movement that began in Germany at the end of the 18th century and spread to Poland and Russia. It advocated breaking with traditional life and integration with the non-Jewish world.

Hatan Bereshit ("Bridegroom of the Genesis"): name given to the person who reads the beginning of the first passage from Genesis at the *Simhat Torah* festival.

Hatan Torah ("Bridegroom of the Law"): name given to the person who reads the last passage from the Torah at the *Simhat Torah* festival.

hazzan: cantor of a synagogue.

hazzanut: art and profession of the *hazzan*.

heikhal ("pavilion, palace"): arch, cupboard, or recess in the east wall of the synagogue where the scrolls are kept.

Heshvan: second month of the Jewish calendar; it lasts twenty-nine or thirty days and begins between October 6 and November 4.

Hevra Kaddisha ("Holy Brotherhood"): name given to the volunteer societies that arrange funeral rites and burial.

hosanna: prayer said during the *Sukkot* processions.

Hoshana Rabba: name given the seventh day of the Sukkot festival. It differs from the other days in that it is celebrated with a special liturgy containing a series of invocations to God for forgiveness and salvation.

huppah: canopy under which the bride and groom stand at weddings.

Iyyar: eighth month of the Jewish calendar; it lasts twenty-nine days and begins between April 12 and May 11.

Jaquetia (JSp.): name give the Sephardic language of southwestern Spain, spoken by the Sephardim who live in the area around the Strait of Gibraltar.

Kabbalat Shabbat ("Reception of the Sabbath"): ceremonies held in the synagogue and the home at the start of a holy day.

kaddish: prayer in Aramaic praising and glorifying the Lord and expressing hope for the establishment of the kingdom of God on earth. It is said daily between prayer sessions in the synagogue and by Jews in mourning.

kappel: skullcap or yarmulke.

keter: crownlike adornment affixed to the top end of the spindles that hold the Sefer Torah.

ketubbah (pl. *ketubboth*): marriage contract.

kibbutz (pl. *kibbutzim*): Israeli community, chiefly agricultural, usually organized as a collective.

kiddush: prayer of sanctification recited over a cup of wine. It is said at the beginning of meals on the Sabbath and festivals.

Kislev: third month of the Jewish calendar; it lasts twenty-nine or thirty days and begins between November 5 and December 3. Hanukkah falls in this month.

klesmorim (Yd.): popular musicians of eastern Europe.

kohen ("priest"): name given the descendants of Aaron, the first high priest. Since the destruction of the temple, the kohen's most important task has been to give the blessing that bears his name.

Kol Nidre ("All the Vows"): initial words whose name is given to the prayer said at the beginning of the Yom Kippur service asking that all unfulfilled vows be nullified.

kosher: suitable, permitted by Jewish law.

lezan: (pl. *lezanim*): popular musician.

lulav: palm leaf with myrtle and willow used in the *Sukkot* festival service. It is waved together with the *etrog* during the processions in the synagogue.

mahzor: prayer book used especially on solemn days and at high festivals.

mappah: (pl. *mappoth*): mantle, normally of richly embroidered material, that covers the Sefer Torah.

maror: bitter herbs; one of the symbolic foods present at the Passover seder.

Marrano (Sp. "swine"): Jewish convert to Christianity.

marsalik: professional actor who entertained at weddings with comic songs and described the gifts received by the bride and groom in improvised verse.

Maskilim (pl. of *maskil*, "enlightened"): advocate or supporter of the Haskalah movement.

Masorah: traditional system in the Hebrew Bible of marginal notation on text, spelling, and grammar written in small print in the blank spaces of codices. It remains faithful to the spirit of the original text, ensuring that it may be correctly transmitted. The *parva Masorah*, found between columns and in the side margins, is in the form of very short notes, whereas the *magna Masorah* contains longer notes in the upper and lower margins.

matzo (pl. *matzoth*): unleavened bread in the form of large crackers that are eaten instead of leavened bread at Passover.

megillah (pl. *megilloth*): the five scrolls, or books, of the Song of Solomon, Ruth, Lamentations, Ecclesiastes, and Esther, particularly the last, read at Purim from a parchment scroll smaller than the Sefer Torah and rolled around a single spindle.

menorah: candelabrum with nine branches for use during the Hanukkah festival; also a candelabrum with seven branches, as used in the biblical tabernacle in Jerusalem.

mezuzah: case containing a piece of parchment inscribed by a *sofer* with two passages from the Shema (Deuteronomy 6:4-9 and 11:13-21). In the home, it is attached to the upper, right-hand side of the doorpost.

midrash (pl. *midrashim*): system of commentary on a biblical text that contains analogic, parabolic, and allegoric interpretations as well as other Haggadic material expounded homiletically or exegetically; or each of the compilations of oral law contained in this type of interpretation; with a capital letter, the literary genre.

mikveh: public bathing establishment for ritual purification.

minyan: a group of at least ten males of age to don the *tefillin*. The minyan forms the necessary quorum for the saying of public prayer.

Mishnah ("teaching," "repetition"): canonic collection of the oral law formulated by various generations of Tannaim and compiled at the end of the 2nd century. It brings together and specifies the rules of the Torah and the written law and is divided into six "orders," in turn made up of a total of sixty-three tractates.

mitzvah (pl. *mitzvot*): the 613 legal and religious precepts—248 of which are "positive," or commands, and 365 "negative," or prohibitions—that govern the conduct of the observant Jew.

mohel: the person who performs the circumcision.

nasi: president; the honorific title given during the period of the Second Temple to the president of the Sanhedrin and in the Middle Ages to eminent rabbi leaders of the community.

Nisan: seventh month of the Jewish calendar; it lasts thirty days and begins between the March 13 and April 11. Passover falls in this month.

nissu'in: marriage ceremony.

omer: an ancient Hebrew unit of dry capacity. The expression "omer count" refers to the calculation of the 49 days between the second day of Passover, when the omer offering was made in the temple, and the Shavuot festival, when the new produce was offered to the temple.

parashah: sections into which the Torah or Pentateuch is divided for reading in the liturgy during the successive weeks of the year.

parokhet: richly decorated velvet, silk, or brocade curtain hung before the heikhal.

Passover (Pesah): one of the three Jewish holy festivals (in biblical times of pilgrimage) during which freedom from slavery and the Exodus from Egypt are commemorated. It begins on the fifteenth day of Nisan and lasts eight days, during which *matzo* is eaten and all traces of *hamez* must be eliminated. In the home, the celebration begins with the seder ceremony.

paytanim (pl. of *paytan*): authors and interpreters of piyyutim.

pilpul: method of study and interpretation of the talmudic and rabbinic texts based on dialectical reasoning consisting of conceptual and casuistic discussion of legal cases and problems.

piyyut (pl. *piyyutim*): religious poetry that often forms part of liturgical ritual.

Purim: minor festival commemorating the miraculous deliverance of the Jews of Persia under King Ahasuerus, according to the Book of Esther. It is celebrated on the fourteenth day of Adar and has a certain carnival air.

Purim-shpil (Yd.): plays, sometimes satirical and burlesque, staged during Purim and usually inspired by the Bible story of Esther.

Rabban: title of respect as a superlative form of rabbi, given to some rabbis during the period of the Second Temple.

rimmonim. See *tappuhim*.

Rosh Hoshana ("New Year"): solemn new year's festival commemorating the creation of the world and the sacrifice of Isaac. It is celebrated on the first and second days of Tishri and marks the beginning of the ten days of repentance that culminate in Yom Kippur. Its most distinctive observance is the sounding of the *shofar* during the morning service.

Sabbath: Saturday, observed chiefly as a day of rest. Kindling fire or doing any kind of work is forbidden on this day. In the home, the beginning of the Sabbath is marked by the ceremony of lighting candles or lamps.

sandak: godfather; the male who holds the child during the circumcision ceremony, having received him from the *sandakit.*

sandakit (fem. of *sandak*): woman who delivers the child to the *sandak.*

seder ("order or service"): name given to the ritual Passover supper ceremony, during which prayers and blessings are recited or sung, matzo and maror are dipped in haroset and eaten, wine is drunk, and the Haggadah is recited.

sefer (pl. *sefarim*): book; an abbreviated form of the Sefer Torah.

Sefer Torah: long roll of parchment inscribed by a *sofer* and used for liturgical purposes. It is held at both ends by spindles and contains the Torah.

Sepharad: biblical place-name identified since the Middle Ages with the Iberian Peninsula. In Hebrew the name is an ambiguous reference to each and all of the medieval Hispanic kingdoms and subsequently to Spain as a whole.

Sephardi: Jew from Sepharad; also the Hispanic language spoken by the Sephardim, now also called Judeo-Spanish or Ladino.

Shavuot: Pentecost; one of the three Jewish high holy days, in biblical times of pilgrimage, commemorating the giving of the law to Moses on Mt. Sinai. It lasts two days and begins on the sixth day of Sivan, at the end of the Omer, seven weeks after the second day of Passover.

Shebat: fifth month of the Jewish calendar; it lasts thirty days and begins between January 2 and 31.

shehitah: slaughtering of animals for food by a *shohet* in the manner prescribed by Jewish law.

Shema: main liturgical prayer, considered the Jewish profession of faith. It consists of three passages from the Old Testament: Deuteronomy 6:4-9 and 11:13-21 and Numbers 15:37-40.

Shemoneh Esreh ("Eighteen Benedictions"): the same as *amidah.*

Shivah ("seven"): traditional period of mourning observed by close relatives of the deceased during the seven days subsequent to the burial.

Shivviti ("I have set"): picture or wall decoration in houses and synagogues so-called after the initial word of Psalm 16:8 ("I have set the Lord always before me"), which appears in its ornamentation.

shnorrer (Yd.): beggar.

shofar (pl. *shofroth*): trumpet made from a hollowed ram's horn, it is sounded on Rosh Hoshana and other solemn religious occasions.

shohet: person certified to slaughter animals for food in the manner prescribed by the laws of *shehitah.*

shtetl (Yd.): Jewish village in eastern Europe.

siddur: prayer book used on days other than festivals and holy days.

Simhat Torah ("Rejoicing of the Law"): festival that marks the annual completion of the reading of the Torah in the synagogue and the beginning of the annual repetition. It is celebrated on the twenty-third day of Tishri, after the beginning of Sukkot, with the Sefarim paraded in procession.

Sivan: the ninth month of the Jewish calendar; it lasts thirty days and begins between May 11 and June 9. Shavuot falls in this month.

sofer (pl. *soferim*): scribe who writes out Hebrew legal documents and liturgical passages.

streimel (Yd.): type of fur-trimmed hat with a wide brim typical of Polish communities. It is still worn by some Hasidic groups.

sukkah (pl. *sukkot*; "booth): booth erected for the Sukkot festival.

Sukkot: Feast of the Booths or Tabernacles. One of the three main Jewish festivals and in biblical times a time of pilgrimage. It commemorates the forty years of wandering in the wilderness, when the Israelites lived in tents or tabernacles until they reached the Promised Land. Beginning on the fifteenth day of Tishri, it lasts for one week, during which Jews live or eat their meals in booths built in gardens and on terraces.

taamim (pl. of *taam*): Masoretic signs added to the consonantal text of the Bible and complementary to those of the vowels. They are used to indicate accentuation, syntactic segmentation, and traditional intonation or psalmody.

takkanot (pl. of *takkana*): ordinances or statutes of an *aljama.*

tallith: shawllike garment with fringes and a *zizit* at each end worn for prayer in the synagogue.

Talmud: canonic collection of the oral law consisting of the Mishnah and other classical rabbinical sources developed by the Amoraim in the last two editions of the Gemara—that of Palestine (4th century) and Babylonia (6th century).

Talmud hakham ("disciple of the sage"): erudite and studious student or rabbi.

Tammuz: tenth month of the Jewish calendar; it lasts twenty-nine days and begins between June 10 and July 9.

Tannaim (Ar. *tanna*, "one who studies"): one of a group of Jewish sages of the oral law whose opinions and rulings are found in the Mishnah.

tappuhim (pl. of *tappuah*, "apple"): Sephardic name given to the pair of adornments with small bells affixed to the end of the Sefer Torah spindles; also called *rimmonim* (pl. of *rimmon*; "pomegranate").

targum: translation or paraphrase in Aramaic of a book of the Old Testament.

tefillin: phylacteries; small, black leather cubes with leather straps containing a piece of parchment inscribed by a sofer with four passages alluding to the Torah (Exodus 13:1-10 and 11-16, and Deuteronomy 6:4-9 and 11:13-21). The cubes are worn on the left arm and forehead. Tefillin are worn by Jewish males over the age of thirteen during the morning service and on days other than the Sabbath and holy days.

terefah: unsuitable, against the Jewish dietary law.

tevah: desk in front of the heikhal, often on a platform, before which the officiant stands (also called the *bimah*).

Tevet: fourth month of the Jewish calendar; it lasts twenty-nine days and begins between December 4 and January 2.

thkine (Yd.): private prayers of supplication, outside the liturgical canon.

Tishah be-Av ("Ninth of Av"): high holy day of fasting and mourning that commemorates the destruction of the temple and other sorrowful events of classical Jewish history.

Tishri: first month of the Jewish calendar; it lasts thirty days and begins between September 6 and October 5. Rosh Hoshana, Yom Kippur, and Sukkot all fall in this month.

Torah: literally, the Pentateuch and book, or scroll, where it is written; in general, the code and doctrine of Judaism that, according to tradition, was given to Moses on Mt. Sinai; the written law, as established in the Old Testament, and the oral law, passed down from master to disciple and established in various recensions.

tosafists: Ashkenazic commentators and followers of Rashi, authors of notes and additions to Rashi's commentaries on the Babylonian Talmud.

Tu Bi-Shevat ("Fifteenth of Shevat"): festival marking the appearance of the first new plants; also called the "New Year for Trees."

yad ("hand"): pointer used to follow the text in the Sefer Torah.

yeshiva (pl. *yeshivoth*): school or academy of rabbinic studies.

Yiddish: language consisting of Hebrew, Germanic, and Slavic elements that is spoken and written by Ashkenazic Jews.

Yom Kippur ("Day of Atonement"): the most solemn day of the Jewish year, dedicated to repentance and the expiation of sins. Falling on the tenth day of Tishri, it brings to an end the ten days of penitence that begin with Rosh Hoshana. It is observed with fasting and mortification, exclusive dedication to prayer and abstinence from materialistic activity.

zaddik (pl. *zaddikim*, "just, righteous"): in Hasidism the name given the spiritual leader or master who acts as intermediary between man and God and who is believed by his followers to possess supernatural powers.

zeroa: roasted shank bone served at the Passover seder.

Zionism: political and ideological movement originating in the 19th century that advocated the return of the Jewish people to the land of Israel and the creation of a national homeland.

zizit: fringes of the tallith.

Bibliography

Abrahams, Israel. *Jewish Life in the Middle Ages.* Reprint. New York: Antheneum, 1969.

Ainsztein, Reuben. *Jewish Resistance in Nazi-occupied Eastern Europe.* London: Paul Elek, 1974.

Alon, Gedalyahu. *Jews, Judaism and the Classical World: Studies in Jewish History in the Times of the Second Temple and Talmud.* Jerusalem: Magnes Press, Hebrew University, 1977.

Arendt, Hannah. *The Origins of Totalitarianism.* Revised edition. New York: Harcourt, Brace Jovanovich, 1973

Ashtor, Eliyahu. *The Jews of Moslem Spain.* 3 vols. Philadelphia: Jewish Publication Society, 1984.

Baeck, Leo. *Judaism and Christianity.* Philadelphia: Jewish Publication Society, 1958.

————. *This People Israel.* Philadelphia: Jewish Publication Society, 1965.

Baer, Yitzhak. *A History of the Jews in Christian Spain.* 2 vols. Philadelphia: Jewish Publication Society, 1966.

Barnavi, Eli, ed. *A Historical Atlas of the Jewish People.* New York: Alfred A. Knopf, 1992.

Baron, Salo W. *History and Jewish Historians.* Philadelphia: Jewish Publication Society, 1964.

————. *The Jewish Community.* Philadelphia: Jewish Publication Society, 1942.

————. *The Russian Jews under Tsars and Soviets.* New York, 1964.

————. *A Social and Religious History of the Jews.* 18 vols. New York: Columbia University, 1952-83.

Ben-Ami. *Between Hammer and Sickle.* Philadelphia: Jewish Publication Society, 1967.

Benjamin, Chaya. *The Stieglitz Collection: Masterpieces of Jewish Art.* Tel Aviv: Israel Museum, 1987.

Ben-Sasson, H. H., ed. *A History of the Jewish People.* Cambridge, Mass.: Harvard University Press, 1976.

Bialer, Yehuda L., and Fink, Estelle. *Jewish Life in Art and Tradition from the Collection of the Sir Isaac and Lady Edith Wolfson Museum, Hechal Shlomo, Jerusalem.* Jerusalem: Hechal Shlomo, 1980.

Bickerman, Elias J. *The Jews in the Greek Age.* Cambridge, Mass.: Harvard University, 1988.

Blatter, Janet, and Milton, Sybil. *Art of the Holocaust.* New York: Rutledge Press, 1981.

Buber, Martin. *Tales of the Hasidim: The Early Masters.* New York: Shocken Books, 1947.

Carmi, T., ed. and trans. *The Penguin Book of Hebrew Verse.* New York: Viking Press, 1981.

Chagall, Marc. *My Life.* Trans. by Elisabeth Abbott. New York: Orion Press, 1960.

Chaim, Raphael. *The Road from Babylon.* New York: Harper & Row, 1985.

Chazan, Robert. *European Jewry and the First Crusade.* Berkeley: University of California Press, 1987.

Cohen, Israel. *History of the Jews of Vilna.* Philadelphia: Jewish Publication Society, 1943.

Cohn-Sherbok, Dan. *The Blackwell Dictionary of Judaica.* Oxford: Blackwell, 1992.

Davidovitch, David. "Ceramic Seder Plates from Non-Jewish Workshops," in *Journal of Jewish Art* 2 (1975), pp. 50-61.

Davidowicz, Lucy S. *The War Against the Jews, 1933-1945.* New York: Holt, Rinehart & Winston, 1975.

Dinur, Ben Zion. *Israel and the Diaspora.* Philadelphia: Jewish Publication Society, 1969.

Dubnow, Simon. *History of the Jews.* Trans. by Moshe Spiegel. South Brunswick, N.J.: Thomas Yoseloff, 1967-73.

Elbogen, Ismar. *A Century of Jewish Life.* Philadelphia: Jewish Publications Society, 1944.

Encyclopaedia Judaica. Jerusalem: Keter Publishing House, 1971.

Feldman, Louis H. *Jew and Gentile in the Ancient World: Attitudes and Interactions from Alexander to Justinian.* Princeton: University Press, 1993.

Feuchtwanger, Lion. *The Jews of Rome.* New York: Viking Press, 1936.

————. *Josephus.* New York: Viking Press, 1932.

————. *Josephus and the Emperor.* New York: Viking Press, 1942.

Finkelstein, Louis, ed. *The Jews, Their History, Culture, and Religion.* 2 vols. New York: Harper Bros., 1960.

Friesel, Evyatar. *Atlas of Modern Jewish History.* New York: Oxford University Press, 1990.

Gay, Ruth. *The Jews of Germany: A Historical Portrait.* New Haven, London: Yale University, 1992.

Glatzer, Nahum N., ed. *Josephus: Jerusalem and Rome.* New York: Meridian Press, 1960.

Goitein, S. D. *Jews and Arabs.* New York: Schocken Books, 1955.

Goodblatt, Morris S. *Jewish Life in Turkey in the 16th Century.* New York: Jewish Theological Seminary, 1952.

Graetz, Heinrich. *History of the Jews.* 6 vols. Philadelphia: Jewish Publication Society, 1891-8.

Grayzel, Solomon. *A History of the Contemporary Jews: From 1900 to the Present.* Reprint. New York: Atheneum, 1969.

————. *A History of the Jews.* Reprint. New York: The New American Library, 1968.

Guttmann, Julius. *Philosophies of Judaism.* Trans. by D. W. Silverman. New York: Holt, Rinehart & Winston, 1964.

Hacohen, Joseph. *The Vale of Tears.* Trans. by Harry S. May. The Hague: Martinus Nijhoff, 1971.

Halevi, Judah. *The Kuzari.* Trans. by Hartwig Hirschfeld. New York: Schocken Books, 1964.

Hannover, Nathan. *Abyss of Despair.* Trans. by Abraham J. Mesch. New York: Bloch Publishing, 1950.

Heine, Heinrich. *Rabbi of Bacherach.* Trans. by E. B. Ashton. New York: Schocken Books, 1947.

Hertzberg, Arthur. *The French Enlightenment and the Jews.* Philadelphia: Jewish Publication Society, 1968.

————. *The Zionist Idea.* New York: Doubleday, 1959.

Hilberg, Raul. *The Destruction of the European Jews.* Chicago: Quadrangle, 1961.

Hill, Brad Sabin. *Incunabula, Hebraica & Judaica.* Exhibition catalog. Ottawa: National Library of Canada, 1981.

Idelsohn, Abraham Zevi. *Jewish Liturgy and Its Development.* New York: Holt, 1932.

————. *Jewish Music in Its Historical Development.* New York: Holt, 1929.

Johnson, Paul. *A History of the Jews.* New York: Harper & Row, 1988.

Juhasz, Esther, ed. *Sephardi Jews in the Ottoman Empire: Aspects of Material Culture.* Jerusalem: Israel Museum, 1990.

Kastein, Josef. *History and Destiny of the Jews.* New York: Viking Press, 1935.

Katz, Jacob. *Exclusiveness and Tolerance in Medieval and Modern Times.* New York: Schocken Books, 1959.

————. *Tradition and Crisis: Jewish Society at the End of the Middle Ages.* Glencoe, Ill.: The Free Press, 1961.

Katz, S. *The Jews in the Visigothic and Frankish Kingdoms of Spain and Gaul*. Reprint. New York: Kraus, 1970.

Kaufmann, Yehezkel. *The Religion of Israel*. Trans. by Moshe Greenberg. Chicago: University of Chicago Press, 1960.

Kedourie, Elie, ed. *The Jewish World*. New York: Harry N. Abrams, 1979.

Keen, Michael E. *Jewish Ritual Art in the Victoria & Albert Museum*. London: HMSO, 1991.

Kogon, Eugen. *The Theory and Practice of Hell: The German Concentration Camps and the System Behind Them*. Trans. by Heinz Norden. New York: Berkley Publishing Corp, 1950.

Kohansky, Mendel. *The Hebrew Theatre: Its First Fifty Years*. Jerusalem: Israel Universities, 1969.

Krinsky, Carol Herselle. *Synagogues of Europe: Architecture, History, Meaning*. New York: The Architectural History Foundation; Cambridge, Mass.: MIT, 1985.

Leon, H. J. *The Jews of Ancient Rome*. Philadelphia: Jewish Publication Society, 1960.

Levin, Nora. *The Holocaust*. New York: Schocken Books, 1973.

Mahler, Raphael. *A History of Modern Jewry, 1780-1815*. New York: Schocken Books, 1971.

Malino, Frances, and Sorkin, David, eds. *From East and West: Jews in a Changing Europe, 1750-1870*. Oxford: Basil Blackwell, 1990.

Mann, Vivian B., and Bilski, Emily D. *The Jewish Museum New York*. New York: Scala, 1993.

Marcus, Ivan G. *Piety and Society: The Jewish Pietists of Medieval Germany*. Leiden: 1981.

Marcus, Jacob R. *The Jew in the Medieval World: A Source Book, 315-1791*. Cincinnati: Union of American Hebrew Congregations, 1938.

Margolis, Max L. *The Story of Bible Translations*. Philadelphia: Jewish Publication Society, 1917.

Margolis, Max L., and Marx, Alexander. *A History of the Jewish People*. Jewish Publication Society, 1927.

Melker, Saskia R. de; Schrijver, Emile G. L.; Voolen, Edward van, eds. *The Image of the World: Jewish Tradition in Manuscripts and Printed Books*. Catalog. Amsterdam: University Library and Jewish Historical Museum; Leuven: Peeters, 1990.

Mendes-Flohr, Paul R., and Reinharz, Jehuda, eds. *The Jew in the Modern World: A Documentary History*. New York: Oxford University Press, 1980.

Meyer, Michael A. *Ideas of Jewish History*. Reprint. Detroit: Wayne State University Press, 1974.

————. *The Origins of the Modern Jew: Jewish Identity and European Culture in Germany, 1749-1824*. Detroit: Wayne State University Press, 1967.

Narkiss, Bezalel. *Hebrew Illuminated Manuscripts*. Jerusalem: Keter; Steimatzky, 1992.

————. *Hebrew Illuminated Manuscripts in the British Isles: The Spanish and Portuguese Manuscripts*. 2 vols. Jerusalem: Israel Academy of Sciences and Humanities; London: British Academy, 1982.

Neuman, Abraham A. *The Jews in Spain*. 2 vols. Philadelphia: Jewish Publication Society, 1942.

Parkes, James. *The Jew in the Medieval Community*. New York: Sepher-Hermon Press, 1976.

Reitlinger, Gerald. *The Final Solution: The Attempt to Exterminate the Jews of Europe, 1939-1945*. New York: A. S. Barnes, Perpetua Books, 1961.

Roback, A. A. *The Story of Yiddish Literature*. New York: Yiddish Scientific Institute, 1940.

Rotenstreich, Nathan. *Tradition and Reality: The Impact of History on Modern Jewish Thought*. New York: Random House, 1972.

Roth, Cecil. *A History of the Jews in England*. Oxford: Clarendon, 1964.

————. *The History of the Jews of Italy*. Philadelphia: Jewish Publication Society, 1946.

————. *The Jewish Contribution to Civilization*. Cincinnati: Union of American Hebrew Congregations, 1940.

————. *The Jews in the Renaissance*. Philadelphia: Jewish Publication Society, 1959.

Rudavsky, David. *Emancipation and Adjustment*. New York: Diplomatic Press, 1967.

Sachar, Howard Morley. *The Course of Modern Jewish History*. Revised edition. New York: Vintage Books, 1990.

————. *Diaspora*. New York: Harper & Row, 1985.

Salzman, Marcus. *The Chronicle of Ahimaaz*. New York: Columbia University Press, 1924.

Scholem, Gershom. *Sabbatai Sevi, the Mystical Messiah, 1626-1676*. Princeton: Unversity, 1973.

Schwartz, Leo W., ed. *Great Ages and Ideas of the Jewish People*. New York: Random House, 1956.

Schweitzer, Frederick M. *A History of the Jews*. New York: Macmillan, 1971.

Sed-Rajna, Gabrielle. *The Hebrew Bible in Medieval Illuminated Manuscripts*. New York: Rizzoli, 1987.

Shachar, Isaiah. *Jewish Tradition in Art: The Feuchtwanger Collection of Judaica*. Jerusalem: Israel Museum, 1981.

Stern, Menahem. *Greek and Latin Authors on Jews and Judaism*. 3 vols. Jerusalem: Israel Academy of Sciences and Humanities, 1974-84.

Stern, Selma. *The Court Jew*. Philadelphia: Jewish Publication Society, 1950.

Tcherikover, Victor. *Hellenistic Civilization and the Jews*. Philadelphia: Jewish Publication Society, 1959.

Thackeray, Henry St. John. *Josephus, the Man and the Historian*. New York: Ktav, 1968.

Toaff, Ariel, and Schwarzfuchs, Simon, eds. *The Mediterranean and the Jews: Banking, Finance and International Trade (16th-18th Centuries)*. Ramat Gan: Bar-Ilan University, 1989.

Trachtenberg, Joshua. *The Devil and the Jews*. New Haven: Yale University Press, 1943.

Vogelstein, Hermann. *History of the Jews in Rome*. Philadelphia: Jewish Publication Society, 1940.

Wallach, Luitpold. *Liberty and Letters: The Thoughts of Leopold Zunz*. London: East and West Library, 1959.

Waxman, Meyer. *A History of Jewish Literature*. 4 vols. New York: Bloch Publishing, 1938-41.

Wigoder, Geoffrey. *The Story of the Synagogue*. London: Weidenfeld and Nicholson, 1986.

Wigoder, Geoffrey, ed. *The New Standard Jewish Encyclopedia*. New York: Facts On File, 1992.

Zangwill, Israel. *Children of the Ghetto*. Philadelphia: Jewish Publication Society, 1892.

Zeitlin, Solomon. *Rise and Fall of the Judean State*. 2 vols. Philadelphia: Jewish Publication Society, 1967.

Index of Names

235

237

238

Credits